SUN OF DEVOTION, STREAM OF BLESSINGS

PREVIOUSLY PUBLISHED
BY THE LAMA YESHE WISDOM ARCHIVE

BY LAMA ZOPA RINPOCHE

Virtue and Reality

Teachings from the Vajrasattva Retreat

Daily Purification: A Short Vajrasattva Practice

Making Life Meaningful

Teachings from the Mani Retreat

The Direct and Unmistaken Method

The Yoga of Offering Food

The Joy of Compassion

How Things Exist

The Heart of the Path

Teachings from the Medicine Buddha Retreat

Kadampa Teachings

Bodhisattva Attitude

How to Practice Dharma

The Perfect Human Rebirth

A Teaching on Heruka (initiates only)

A Teaching on Yamantaka (initiates only)

BY LAMA YESHE

Becoming Your Own Therapist

Make Your Mind an Ocean

The Essence of Tibetan Buddhism

The Peaceful Stillness of the Silent Mind

Ego, Attachment and Liberation

Universal Love

Life, Death and After Death

BY LAMA YESHE &
LAMA ZOPA RINPOCHE

Advice for Monks and Nuns

Freedom Through Understanding

OTHER BOOKS

Teachings from Tibet by various great lamas

The Kindness of Others by Geshe Jampa Tegchok

IN ASSOCIATION WITH
TDL PUBLICATIONS

Mirror of Wisdom
by Geshe Tsultim Gyeltsen

Illuminating the Path to Enlightenment
by His Holiness the Dalai Lama

*May whoever sees, touches, reads, remembers, or talks or thinks about these books
never be reborn in unfortunate circumstances, receive only rebirths in situations
conducive to the perfect practice of Dharma, meet only perfectly qualified
spiritual guides, quickly develop bodhicitta and immediately
attain enlightenment for the sake of all sentient beings.*

• • • •
•

LAMA ZOPA RINPOCHE

Sun of Devotion, Stream of Blessings

Edited by Gordon McDougall

LAMA YESHE WISDOM ARCHIVE • BOSTON
www.LamaYeshe.com

A non-profit charitable organization for the benefit of all
sentient beings and an affiliate of the Foundation for
the Preservation of the Mahayana Tradition
www.fpmt.org

First published 2016

LAMA YESHE WISDOM ARCHIVE
PO BOX 636
LINCOLN
MA 01773, USA

© Lama Thubten Zopa Rinpoche 2016

Please do not reproduce any part of this book
by any means whatsoever without our permission

Library of Congress Cataloging-in-Publication Data

Names: Thubten Zopa, Rinpoche, 1945- author. | McDougall, Gordon,
1948- editor.
Title: Sun of devotion, stream of blessings / Lama Zopa Rinpoche ;
edited By Gordon McDougall.
Description: Boston : Lama Yeshe Wisdom Archive, 2016. | Includes
bibliographical references.
"In 2014 Lama Zopa Rinpoche gave extensive teachings in Leeds and
London, England. He covered such essential topics as guru devotion
and emptiness, talked about the dakini Khadro-la, told stories from his
life and explained the dangers of the spirit Dolgyal. This book is suitable for both beginners and advanced students of Tibetan Buddhism"
—Provided by publisher.
Identifiers: LCCN 2016024514 (print) | LCCN 2016025638 (ebook)
| ISBN 9781891868856 | ISBN 9781891868870 ()
Subjects: LCSH: Buddhism—Tibet Region.
Classification: LCC BQ7604 .T493 2016 (print) | LCC BQ7604
(ebook) | DDC 294.3/4—dc23

ISBN 978-1-891868-85-6

10 9 8 7 6 5 4 3 2 1

Cover photograph by Thubten Kunsang
Designed by Gopa&Ted2 Inc.

♻ Printed in the USA with environmental mindfulness on 30% PCW recycled paper. The
following resources have been saved: 24 trees, 760 lbs. of solid waste, 11,000 gallons of water,
2,175 lbs. of greenhouse gases and 11 million BTUs of energy. (papercalculator.org)

Please contact the LAMA YESHE WISDOM ARCHIVE
for more copies of this and our other free books.

Contents

Publisher's Acknowledgments

W E ARE EXTREMELY GRATEFUL to our friends and supporters who have made it possible for the Lama Yeshe Wisdom Archive to both exist and function: Lama Yeshe and Lama Zopa Rinpoche, whose kindness is impossible to repay; Peter and Nicole Kedge and Venerable Ailsa Cameron for their initial work on the Archive; Venerable Roger Kunsang, Rinpoche's tireless assistant, for his kindness and consideration; and our sustaining supporters—Christine Arlington, Roger and Claire Ash-Wheeler, Tom and Suzanne Castles, Nick and Gisela Dawson, Richard Gere, Goh Pik Pin, Annelies van der Heijden and Annette van Citters, Barry and Connie Hershey, Dr. S.T. Lee, Ho Sau Ling, Therese Miller, Janet Moore, Ven. Gyalten Palmo, Erick Rinner, Tham Poon King, Thubten Yeshe, Yeshe Khorlo Foundation, and several anonymous benefactors.

With respect to *Sun of Devotion, Stream of Blessings*, in late 2014 I received a call from Ven. Roger that Rinpoche would like his recent teachings in England published soon. So Gordon got to work and produced a manuscript not long after, and after Sandy Smith's final polish, here it is. Thank you Gordon and Sandy for your great work.

Thanks are also due to Rajiv Mehrotra of the Foundation for Universal Responsibility of His Holiness the Dalai Lama and Ashok Chopra of Hay House Publishers India for permission to use the line drawing of the wheel of life from *The End of Suffering and the Discovery of Happiness: The Path of Tibetan Buddhism*, by H.H. the Dalai Lama.

We are also deeply grateful to all those who have become members of the Archive over the past few years. Details of our membership program may be found at the back of this book, and if you are not a member, please do consider joining up. Due to the kindness of those who have, we now have several editors working on our vast collection of teachings for the benefit of all. We have posted our list of individual and corporate members on our website, LamaYeshe.com.

Furthermore, we would like to express our appreciation for the kindness and compassion of all those other generous benefactors who have contributed since we began publishing free books. Thankfully, you are too numerous to mention individually, but we value highly each and every donation made to spreading the Dharma for the sake of the kind mother sentient beings and greatly appreciate the support of those who partner with us in this amazing and beneficial work. Thank you so much.

Finally, I would like to thank the many other kind people who have asked that their donations be kept anonymous; my wife, Wendy Cook, for her support and editing skills; our dedicated office staff, Jennifer Barlow and Ven. Ani Tenzin Desal; our editors Ven. Ailsa Cameron, Ven. Sarah Thresher, Ven. Connie Miller, Gordon McDougall and Sandy Smith; Ven. Kunsang for recording Lama Zopa Rinpoche; our transcribers Ven. Thubten Munsel, Diana van Die, Mer Stafford, Su Hung and Pat Lee; our social media and e-publishing manager Megan Evart; Ven. Bob Alcorn for his work on our videos; David Zinn for his digital imaging expertise; FPMT Australia for help with our distribution in Australia, and Amitabha Buddhist Centre and Losang Dragpa Centre for their help with our distribution in Singapore and Malaysia respectively; and everybody else who helps us in so many ways. Thank you all.

If you, dear reader, would like to join this noble group of openhearted altruists by contributing to the production of more books by Lama Yeshe or Lama Zopa Rinpoche or to any other aspect of the Lama Yeshe Wisdom Archive's work, please contact us to find out how.

Dr. Nicholas Ribush

Through the merit of having contributed to the spread of the Buddha's
teachings for the sake of all sentient beings, may our benefactors
and their families and friends have long and healthy lives,
all happiness, and may all their Dharma
wishes be instantly fulfilled.

· · · · ·

Editor's Preface

THIS BOOK IS the record of a remarkable series of events. In July 2014, Lama Zopa Rinpoche, the spiritual director of the Foundation for the Preservation of the Mahayana Tradition (FPMT), visited the United Kingdom for the first time in thirteen years, teaching in Leeds and London. That Rinpoche taught was not remarkable—Rinpoche teaches with every breath—but the timing of the event and the power and clarity of his teachings after so long an absence were something none of us there at the time will forget.

The first event took place at Trinity University in Leeds on exactly the same day and within a few kilometers of the start of the Tour de France, the 3,600-kilometer cycle race that is the greatest sporting event in France (and for some reason started in the UK in 2014). The million people who came to witness the start made the logistics of getting to Rinpoche interesting. I remember arriving at Leeds station and seeing a sea of humanity filling every platform, making Delhi railway station at rush hour look deserted by comparison. Miraculously, just outside, empty taxis were waiting and there was a clear run to the university. A local said to me, "This is the most amazing day Leeds has ever seen." I had to agree with him, although which of the two events was the more amazing I will leave for you to decide.

I feel very fortunate to have been at those teachings (albeit flagging a bit by dawn of the second all-nighter in London) and so in editing them I wanted to retain the flavor of a great master giving precise instructions to the students in front of him.

Besides omitting the end-of-session dedications and event-specific aspects—the giving of an oral transmission and an initiation—I have tried to keep the subjects in the book as close to how Rinpoche taught them and in the order they were given. I have merged one or two sections, especially where in Leeds and London he said basically the same thing, and shifted the order of a few small sections to give the book greater overall cohesion, but this is still the record of an oral teaching. Therefore you will notice many interjections where, for example, Rinpoche explains a side issue (sometimes at length) within the context of the main subject. Bear with this. If you have ever had the good fortune of actually experiencing one of Rinpoche's teachings you will know that this is his style.

Furthermore, the way he kept coming back to certain ideas, as if to reinforce and expand on what he had said previously, felt incredibly powerful to me as I sat there in front of him. As I edit the transcripts it still feels that way. I hope the way I have edited the book has not lost too much of the power of Rinpoche's presentation.

His profound explanation of *sang-gyä* is one instance of this, which he reiterates many times. Rather than use the stock English translation of "buddha," Rinpoche dissects the Tibetan term and shows that *sang*, the complete elimination of all obscurations, and *gyä*, the complete attainment of all realizations, is what a buddha is, is what buddhahood—enlightenment—is. For most of us, the Buddha is a guy sitting under a tree glowing with light. Rinpoche explodes that very limited view. As he says, "Don't get hung up on the words."

The other two themes he kept returning to were the danger of following the worldly protector Shugden, or Dolgyal, as he has here more often referred to him, and the great qualities of Khadro-la, the incredible being who has become very important to Tibetan Buddhism, FPMT and the world. Having had the fortune of doing two retreats with her, I feel that what Rinpoche says of her importance is no exaggeration at all.

Usually with edits of Rinpoche's teachings I am unable to thank people individually because it has been a team effort often spanning decades. Although there have been many people involved in the production of this book, I would like to thank two in particular, Ven. Thubten Munsel, who transcribed the audio files, and Diana van Die, who checked the transcripts. They both did their work with such speed, accuracy and devotion that my job was made very easy indeed. Whatever mistakes and confusions there might be in the book are entirely of my doing.

May this book of Rinpoche's UK teachings inspire all who read it and bring them compassion, patience and wisdom. In particular, may it be the source of harmony and strength to the various UK centers and study groups, especially the brand new Land of Joy retreat community, which became physically manifest during Rinpoche's visit.

May whatever small merit gained from the creation of this book be dedicated to the long and healthy lives of His Holiness the Dalai Lama, Lama Zopa Rinpoche, Khadro-la and the other great teachers of the FPMT, of Tibetan Buddhism and of all Buddhist traditions. Through the sun of our devotion, may the stream of their blessings always pour down upon us.

Bath, UK
February 2015

Roger Kunsamg

We at LYWA dedicate this book to our dear friend and colleague, the late Ven. Thubten Kunsang (Henri Lopez), who worked with us for many years recording Rinpoche's teachings (including the ones that constitute this book) and taking photos and video. At Ösel Labrang, Sera-je Monastery, India, January 2016. This was his last meeting with Rinpoche.

1. Taking Care of the Mind

THANK YOU VERY MUCH, everybody I've met in this life and in past lives. The reason we are gathered here is because we have met in past lives or past times. So, to all of you, my brothers and sisters, thank you very much for coming and I offer you my best wishes.

What are we going to talk about? I think the most important thing in the world is to realize how all our happiness and problems come from our mind—all our hour-to-hour happiness and problems, minute-to-minute happiness and problems, second-to-second happiness and problems come from our mind.

Sometimes in certain situations in our life we are able to recognize that thinking one way brings peace to others and ourselves whereas thinking another way brings harm. The way we act with others in any situation determines the outcome. Understanding this shows us that we have total freedom in our hands—freedom to stop problems and freedom to bring peace and happiness to others and ourselves.

Even when great anger arises, we can be aware there is a choice. Our usually uncontrollable self-cherishing thought arises, bringing self-concern, anger, pride and so forth, but sometimes that can make us aware that there is a choice. We *can* choose. We always have the choice of bringing either happiness or suffering to another person, but because of our anger, the wish to hurt, we generally choose wrong. This clearly proves that our mind is the creator of all our day-to-day life's problems and happiness.

Seeing how this life's problems and happiness come from our mind, we can go beyond that and see that all the suffering we have experienced and will experience throughout all our lifetimes comes from the mind, including the heavier suffering of the animals, hungry ghosts and hell beings.

Everything we have experienced in the past and will experience in the future comes from the mind.

Samsara is Sanskrit for cyclic existence or circling, and *nirvana* is Sanskrit for the ultimate, blissful state of peace for ourselves, the total cessation of all the oceans of samsaric suffering. Both samsara and nirvana come from our mind. Enlightenment is the peerless happiness, the state of omniscient mind. The Tibetan term, *sang-gyä*, means exactly this, the total cessation of all obscurations and the completion of all realizations. Enlightenment also comes from our mind. It does not come from anywhere else, from temples or anywhere outside. It comes from our mind.

Every day, every minute, we have either happiness or problems. If we can learn to think in a better way our problems will disappear and we'll have peace and happiness in our life. But when we don't change the way we think, problems fill our entire life, day and night. Then we have to go to see psychologists and doctors. Seeing all these specialists makes our life very expensive! On top of the food and household expenses we generally incur there are all these extra expensive doctors' fees, probably thousands, hundreds of thousands, millions of dollars! Life is so expensive because we don't know how to take care of our mind, we don't know how to take care of our life.

Actually, Dharma practice, meditation—there are many different names—is the best psychology for the healthiest mind. And the healthiest mind allows us to have the healthiest body. This is impossible if we don't care for our mind, treating it like garbage, throwing it in the bin.

Failing to take care of our mind always brings unpleasant results, creating many worries, many problems, one after the other. No sooner have we solved one problem than another arises, on and on, our whole life getting worse and worse. Out of control, we receive more and more bills, incur more and more debt, over and over again. Like that, our whole life passes.

The key to happiness is the mind. With the mind, we can switch our life to suffering or we can switch it to happiness, just as we change television channels, choosing to watch programs about fighting and war, or peaceful things, like the nature programs people seem to enjoy. Experiencing happiness or suffering depends entirely on what we do with our mind.

Taking care of the mind, taking care of life, means meditating. Practicing meditation should be just that—taking care of our mind, taking care of our life, taking care of ourselves. This is what I'd like to talk about. I don't know Buddhism well but I can say a few words about what I'm a little bit familiar with.

THE METHOD TO TRANSFORM THE MIND

Leaving aside the various higher levels of happiness we can obtain in this life and the happiness beyond this life, most people don't know that even this life's mundane happiness comes entirely from the mind. All they consider is this life, which might seem long now but is, in reality, very, very short.

This becomes very apparent at the moment of death. After having had this human body with all its comforts and pleasures—car, house, family and so forth—when the moment of death arrives everything is gone. One minute we have it and the next it's gone. This is what we will experience as we die because during our life we never meditated; we failed to make use of this most important psychology to make our mind positive and healthy. This is what the Buddha taught in his fundamental teaching on the four noble truths, the main focus of the Hinayana: true suffering, true cause of suffering, true cessation of suffering and its cause and the true path that leads to the cessation of suffering and its cause.

Within this fundamental teaching of the Buddha are the teachings on impermanence and death. As long as we remain unaware of impermanence—not so much gross impermanence but mainly subtle impermanence—we will experience problems with our life, relationships and so forth.

In the same way that most people do not understand the mind, they also do not understand death. Yet it is vital to understand what happens at death so that when we are actually in the death process we can be happy. Although we are still not free from death, by knowing about it we can make it most beneficial for ourselves and all the other living beings, who also have to experience the suffering of death.

We still have to experience death because we have yet to eliminate its cause, karma and delusion. Without a direct perception of emptiness, we cannot do this. So, this is what we need to do. Destroying the cause makes it impossible to experience the result: the suffering of death, the suffering of rebirth, the suffering of sicknesses, the suffering of old age and—again—the suffering of death, over and over, again and again.

People spend a lot of money to stop looking old—hundreds, thousands or even millions of dollars. However, if we were to stop painting our body to beautify it but just let it remain natural, aging would show; we would notice it more and more with each passing year.

It also depends on how a person has lived life. Even within a year, someone experiencing great unhappiness can become externally old, her[1] skin wrinkled, her hair quite gray. On the other hand, another person whose life is very stable and peaceful and without much suffering—especially if her mind is very happy—changes very little physically, even though the aging process is there in the same way.

We are getting old all the time—not only day by day but also hour by hour and minute by minute. We cannot remain the same because we are changing, even second by second. Geshe Lamrimpa, a Tibetan meditator, mentioned that even within a second, very subtle imprints causing changes occur. This is evolution; this is what happens. This is impermanence, the fact we are constantly aging, getting older. Here, of course, we are generally referring to external things, such as the body.

The happiest person is the one who always thinks positively, who practices Dharma, particularly *bodhicitta,* the most positive mind. With such a mind we can use whatever problem arises to make it most beneficial and transform it into happiness, using it to free ourselves from the oceans of samsaric suffering. Not only that, but we can use it to achieve peerless happiness, the state of omniscient mind, *sang-gyä,* the total elimination of obscurations and the completion of all realizations. We can use it not just for ourselves but for others, to free numberless sentient beings from the oceans of samsaric suffering and also bring them into peerless happiness, the state of omniscient mind.

With such a mind, we can use whatever problem we experience in our life in this way, even death or cancer. That is truly unbelievable. We use problems to collect skies of merit; more than skies of merit. If such merit were to manifest in form it would be bigger than the sky. The Buddha explained this in a sutra and Lama Atisha said the same thing:

> If the bodhicitta you actualized
> Were to take form,
> What you collected
> Would be bigger than the sky.

This is the best purification. Bodhicitta purifies the obscurations collected from beginningless rebirths that bring suffering in this and future lives and

---

[1] Or his. Rather than use "they" or "their" for non-gender specific examples like this, we shall just alternate the genders.

cause us to be reborn in the lower realms. The minute we practice, the second we practice, this is what happens. This is the best way to practice.

In America it sometimes happens that small schoolchildren kill many people. Not only small children but adults as well. This happened last year and, from time to time, it has happened before; suddenly, surprisingly. I'm sure it's not only in America but in the rest of the world as well.

For example, in America they have talked for years without ever deciding about the right to have guns. At present, everybody can have a gun, so if your enemy or somebody shoots at you, you can shoot back. That seems to be the ordinary mind in America. And so it has happened many times that even young children have killed many people.

After such a shooting incident, people talk about it on TV and elsewhere for weeks and weeks and weeks. They wonder how a small child could kill so many people. They talk and talk and talk but there is no solution. Once, after a man had killed many people, they checked for insanity but found he was a normal person, or what they call a "normal" person. He was just doing a normal job and living a normal life, like those who are regarded as sane by the government and other organizations. On that particular day, however, his way of thinking suddenly changed, he got a gun and killed many people. This happened.

Everybody was very surprised. On CNN, Anderson Cooper demanded to know how this could happen, but at the same time said he knew people wouldn't have an answer. To his mind there was no answer as to how to stop this kind of killing. I'm sorry to say this but he was wrong, there is a way. If the killer had met the Dharma and listened to the teachings of the Omniscient One, he would know there is a method to transform his mind so that such things wouldn't happen. The method is to purify past negative karma, the obscurations, not just from this life but also from all the beginningless rebirths; to confess and purify. If he could have purified the obscurations that caused him to change his mind and kill all those people, that negative thought would not have arisen and the shooting would not have happened. People might be shocked at what I'm saying but this is the solution.

Similarly, if the victims of the shooting had known the practice of purification then the result of being killed would not have happened. This is possible. In that way, both victim and perpetrator need purification.

There is a method, there is something we can do, and that is to work with the mind, not simply to try to effect change from outside but to transform the mind. It's a purely mental action. Just working with the mind can do that. But unfortunately, because these people have not met the Dharma, they don't know the method, the solution.

That is the reason I want to talk about the mind, about how to transform the mind, to stop thinking in unhealthy, nonvirtuous ways that brings problems to others and ourselves and to transform the mind into a positive way of thinking, to be able to live the happiest, most positive life.

IN A WELL-CULTIVATED FIELD, WHATEVER IS PLANTED WILL GROW

In *Heart Instructions of the Book of Kadam*, Lama Atisha is quoted as saying these lines:

> If the field is well cultivated, whatever you plant will grow.
> With a good heart all your higher wishes will succeed,
> And so whatever you do must come from the awakening mind.
> Lama Atisha said this to the spiritual mentor Dromtönpa.
>
> With perseverance and stability there will be no obstacles.
> If you are learned in what to practice and what to abandon,
> You will go to liberation abiding in the sphere of wisdom.
> Lama Atisha said learning, discipline and kindness must
>   complement each other.[2]

He starts with the example of the field. If it is well plowed and well cultivated, then whatever we plant there will grow well. In the same way, if we have a good heart, we will attain all our wishes. Everything we wish for will happen. When we have perseverance we will have no obstacles, which means obstacles to any happiness, most importantly, ultimate happiness—freedom from the oceans of samsaric suffering, and especially peerless happiness, the state of the omniscient mind. For example, I myself am lazy, so nothing is happening. But those who have perseverance have no obstacles. They will achieve whatever they want to achieve.

There's a Tibetan saying that a turtle goes very, very slowly but reaches its goal, whereas a flea jumps all over the place and never gets anywhere.

---

[2] By Yongzin Yeshe Gyaltsen, section 8, vv. 18–19. Cf. Thupten Jinpa's translation in *The Book of Kadam*, p. 555.

Somebody who has a little perseverance and is active for a short time but does not persevere continuously will not succeed. I think this Tibetan saying is very useful.

Even though we do a tiny amount of practice, it is very important that we continue it. We shouldn't just practice for a short time but then, due to lack of perseverance, allow our mind to become weaker until we no longer feel we can practice. Then maybe, after having stopped practicing for a long time, we meet somebody or hear a talk and become inspired, causing us to try again for a few days or a few months. It should not be like that. Even though the Dharma practice we do might be very small, it is most important that we persevere with it.

As well as perseverance, we also need to know what should be practiced and what should be abandoned. Whether we want to practice the Dharma or not is up to us, but if we do, investigation and learning, or knowledge, are so important. If we know the Dharma, the Omniscient One's teachings, we develop the wisdom to discriminate right from wrong in our life. Then we can abandon what is wrong and practice what is right and because of that achieve liberation, ultimate happiness, the blissful state of peace. This is the advice from *Heart Instructions of the Book of Kadam*.

I haven't yet seen a commentary on this, but my view is that this is achieved by realizing the "skillful means of appearances," the Prasangika view of very subtle dependent arising. The Madhyamaka school is subdivided into Svatantrika and Prasangika, and this is the view of the latter, the Prasangika—very subtle dependent arising.

The Buddha realized ultimate wisdom and then revealed it to us sentient beings. Because of that, numberless sentient beings have already been liberated from oceans of samsaric suffering and brought to peerless happiness, full enlightenment. "Abiding in the sphere of the wisdom" means gaining a direct perception of emptiness through equipoise meditation.

We can then lead the other transmigratory beings to liberation. In Tibetan, the word for transmigratory beings is *dro-wa*, meaning they are not free from the cause of suffering, karma and delusion, but have perpetually been circling in samsara. Hell beings, hungry ghosts, animals, gods, demigods and human beings have been circling in the suffering realms from beginningless rebirths. If they don't meet the Dharma, if they don't know the Dharma, they will have to suffer like this endlessly, so they are called *dro-wa*, transmigratory beings. However, by the skillful means of appearances, we are able to liberate those transmigratory beings from the oceans of samsaric suffering and bring them to ultimate happiness, the state of omniscient mind.

Just reading a little bit about Buddhism without really meditating is like a child playing at meditating. We must do more than that.

Happiness is a dependent arising

What we want is happiness and what we do not want is suffering. This is what everybody wants. Even ants running about busily, day and night, are doing so because of this. When I'm in Nepal, if I spill some sweet tea on my table, almost immediately there are ants crawling all over it. They come in the daytime but at night they are not there. Maybe they are sleeping, I don't know. Maybe they have a good sleep at night. It seems that some ants do and others don't, but generally ants are very busy, climbing up trees, climbing down them, so incredibly busy. Just like human beings and everybody else.

In that we are all the same. Just like the insects, like every being, we are all looking to have happiness and avoid suffering. For that reason we are all constantly moving about, looking for food, looking for comfort, looking for everything.

Every single fish in the ocean is like this. I don't know who guides all those billions and billions of tiny fish, but they are always looking for food while at the same time trying to escape their enemies. There are millions of them, not just the small ones, going everywhere for food and at the same time trying to escape their enemies. That's just one example, but everyone is like that.

When we look down at the sea from an airplane it is so blue. It looks so peaceful, so calm, with a kind of happiness, without any sense of violence at all. But were we to go just below the surface of the water, the story is very different. There are whales and sharks and other big fish, all eating one another. Sea lions, those great fat creatures, come out of the ocean and laze on the rocks, then go back in and eat the penguins swimming there. The sea lions eat the penguins and then they are eaten by whales or other big animals. One eats another, another eats another and on and on and on.

This is what we would see if we were to go just below the surface of the water, the whole ocean full of numberless sentient beings being eaten by each other. They are always either trying to escape or trying to find food. Most of us humans, fortunately, don't have that problem.

What a pleasant life we human beings have, what comfort, what freedom. We should use this great opportunity to benefit all living sentient beings, particularly those in this country and this world.

All beings want happiness and do not want suffering. We humans are the same, whatever we are doing, whether we are going by airplane, by boat, by car or by bicycle. The bike race has just finished in Leeds.[3] I wasn't there but I saw it on TV. Everyone everywhere—in the shops, in the restaurants, in the offices, on bicycles—everyone wants happiness and does not want suffering, including the tiny insects that we can only see through a microscope. We all have the same motivation.

What should we do to succeed in our wish to only have happiness? This is an important question, especially after the collapse of the world economy and the destruction of the Twin Towers in New York. I even heard that many airlines went bankrupt in both America and other countries, impoverishing many people, making them unable to look after their children. So many people in many countries lost their jobs and were reduced to poverty when those two buildings were destroyed and the economy of the whole world suffered.

Success and happiness are what everybody wants, both believers and nonbelievers—people who are practicing Dharma and people who are not practicing Dharma.

I have just a tiny bit of understanding from hearing about Buddhism and from reading some texts, but what I would like to say is that whether we are believers or nonbelievers, practicing Dharma or not, since we are looking for happiness, since we want success, first we need to create the cause. The success that we want is not independent; it is a dependent arising. Because it depends on causes and conditions, we need to create those causes and conditions. Of course, there is no way animals can understand this. Ants and those small jumping ones, grasshoppers, cannot understand our language.

Not only from reading the Omniscient One's teachings but maybe a little from my own experience, I can suggest that the first thing we need to do is to fulfill other sentient beings' wishes, whether they are animals or people. In everyday life, whether we are believers or nonbelievers, whether we meditate or not, it doesn't matter. If we want happiness and don't want suffering, this is what we must do. We must serve others and fulfill their wishes for

---

[3] The day Rinpoche started this series of teachings, the Tour de France, the most important cycle race in the world, was starting in Leeds city centre a few miles away, with an estimated million people in the streets watching.

happiness. If we do that, by depending on that cause, the result of happiness will come to us. First we create the cause by bringing happiness to others and then we ourselves achieve the result, happiness.

Perhaps we wish for something and without effort it just happens. Perhaps it happens in the same month, the same day or even after just a few hours. And then it happens more and more, seemingly without effort. Logically, it seems impossible, but because we have created the cause it just happens without any effort. That is really amazing.

I'll tell you this from my own tiny experience. Over the years I have made some small offerings to the Buddha, Dharma and Sangha. Now, as a result, I'm able to offer more than I could in the past, when I was stingy, miserly, thinking, "If I offer this, what will happen to me in the future? I will lose everything; I will become sick." Trying to keep everything for ourselves is the wrong way.

If we want success and happiness, first we need to cause others to have success and happiness. From that comes the result, achieving all our wishes—not only temporary happiness but even liberation from samsara and the ultimate happiness of enlightenment, *sang-gyä*, the total elimination of all obscurations and the completion of all realizations.

Of course, I'm not talking about that from my own experience, but to give a small example, I once offered a pearl *mala*; I got some pearls and offered them to the Twenty-one Taras. After that I got a dependent arising. From that cause, I received a pearl mala where the pearls were not just fake ones but real, and then more and more came and I was able to offer to the Twenty-one Taras in different places, not just at FPMT centers but at other centers as well, offering more and more. I'm just giving this small example to show how success comes as a dependent arising.

Then there are the general offerings to the Sangha. At Sera Je there are about three thousand monks and we have been offering food to them for about twenty-five years. First they were served a portion of their lunch; then we could offer them a real lunch, and then dinner and breakfast as well. Before that, many monks who came from Tibet had to share their teachers' food and they never got enough. Their stomachs were never filled and many of them had to return to Tibet, so there was no continual study. However, after we started offering them meals, they were able to stay and continue their studies.

I offer food to Sera Je, but of course, if I could, I would also offer to all of Sera, Ganden and Drepung. Altogether there are six main Gelug monasteries: Sera Me, Sera Je, Ganden Shartse, Ganden Jangtse, Drepung Loseling and Drepung Gomang, but Sera Je is the largest monastery in the Lama Tsongkhapa tradition and the monks who study there are able to continually study Buddhist philosophy, which is as vast and profound as the Pacific Ocean is wide and deep.

This is not just faith; this is also logical. If the monks complete their studies there they become *geshes* and we can invite them to teach Buddhadharma in the rest of the world. In that way, many sentient beings all over the world get the opportunity to learn and to awaken their minds and to eventually achieve enlightenment.

If conditions in the monasteries deteriorate, however, we won't be able to get qualified teachers to teach in the rest of the world, like Geshe Tashi Tsering[4] here in London, who has been enlightening beings in the United Kingdom for so many years, always teaching the lam-rim and helping the Westerners and Tibetans. If the monasteries become weak, sending great geshes like Geshe Tashi to other countries won't be possible and sentient beings will no longer get any opportunity to awaken their minds and attain enlightenment.

Even just in the FPMT we have forty-five teachers teaching the Dharma and awakening the minds of students. And this is without considering the other great traditions: Nyingma, Kagyü and Sakya as well as the other organizations within Lama Tsongkhapa's tradition.

I was using myself, my little tiny bit of experience, as one example but there are many others. From the offerings I normally make to my gurus they build monasteries and *khangtsens* in different places. There are so many other things like this. Collecting more merit, I am able to benefit the teachings of the Buddha and sentient beings more and more. That's what I do. That is just to show logically what you need to do if you want success.

Karma is definite. This is the first of the four outlines of karma. If we create virtue, engaging in positive, healthy karma, or action, we will definitely experience happiness in this life and future lives. If we create nonvirtue, engaging in unhealthy, disturbing karma, or action, then the result is suffering in this life and other lives.

The second outline is that karma is expandable. If we help somebody—if we give food to an ant or a person, if we fulfill the wishes of one sentient

---

[4] The resident teacher at Jamyang Buddhist Centre, London, since 1994; author of the *Foundation of Buddhist Thought* series of books.

being—the result is that we will have happiness for many lifetimes, for ten, five hundred, even a thousand lifetimes from just that one action of helping somebody, from fulfilling their happiness just one time.

Cherishing even one sentient being brings us to buddhahood, the state of omniscient mind, the cessation of all obscurations and attainment of all realizations. Even cherishing just one sentient being. It helps to keep this in mind. Killing one insect means we will be killed by others for five hundred lifetimes. Cheating one sentient being means we will be cheated for a thousand lifetimes. This is mentioned in the commentary of Aryadeva's *Four Hundred Verses*. Therefore, any negativity, any harm we do will bring us suffering from life to life to life to life. All this has come from our mind; it has not come from others. The reason others are forced to harm us, to cause us suffering, is because of our past mind. It has come from us, from our mind.

The last two outlines of karma are that if the karma has not been created, the result of happiness or suffering cannot happen, and that if the karma has been created, the result of happiness or suffering will never get lost—even after a billion, zillion, trillion eons we will experience it. It never gets lost. We can purify negative karma, but if we don't purify it, then this is what happens. Similarly, if we don't destroy the cause of happiness, then we will definitely experience it.

Success, all the way up to enlightenment, has to come from our mind. Therefore, the real, real meditation, the real Dharma practice, is to serve others, to cherish others.

If we help one sentient being, one insect, one person, that is the best offering to the numberless bodhisattvas and the numberless buddhas because that is what they cherish the most. This sentient being—even this one insect, even this one mosquito, even this one ant, even this one person—is most cherished by numberless bodhisattvas and buddhas.

2. Our Happiness Is in Our Hands

Transforming suffering into happiness

To our hallucinated mind it looks like all our day-to-day happiness and problems—every hour's, every minute's, even every second's happiness and problems—come from the outside. But in reality, they come from our mind, from our concepts. They are the results of actions, karma, done in the past. Of the two components of our being, body and mind, they come from the mind.

There are six principal consciousnesses and fifty-one secondary minds, thoughts or mental factors. With respect to any particular object, the mental factors that accompany the principal consciousness are similar to it in five ways: object, aspect, time, entity and basis.[5]

Among those fifty-one secondary minds are the five omnipresent mental factors that always accompany the principal consciousness: feeling, cognition, contact, intention and attention.[6] Intention—*sem-pa* in Tibetan, what we usually call *karma*, which literally means *action*—is one of the omnipresent mental factors. Because intention is always there, we label things as positive or negative every minute, every second; our mind merely labels things as positive or negative all the time.

---

[5] The five similarities are: they are produced in dependence on the same *basis* (Skt: *ashraya*; Tib: *ten*); they observe the same *object* (Skt: *alambana*; Tib: *mig-pa*); they are generated in the same *aspect* (Skt: *akara*; Tib: *nam-pa*); they occur at the same *time* (Skt: *kala*; Tib: *dü*) and they are the same substantial *entity* (Skt: *dravya*; Tib: *dzä*). See *Mind in Tibetan Buddhism*, pp. 35–36. Also *The Mind and Its Functions*, pp. 105–6, where they are listed as basis, duration, aspect, referent and substance.

[6] See *Mind in Tibetan Buddhism*, p. 36, where the five omnipresent factors (Tib: *kün-dro nga*) are listed as feeling, discrimination, intention, mental engagement and contact.

Whatever we perceive—another person's body, speech or mind or some material object—we label it positive or negative. In this way we label the world. All the time, every hour, every minute, every second we are labeling, and not just labeling but *merely* labeling, *merely* imputing things. In that way we create the I, we create the action, we create the object, we create the whole world as positive or negative. So positive and negative are merely designations of our own mind.

Because the results of happiness or suffering are ripening results of imprints in our own mind and not other people's imprints, we have control of our life. There is a practice called *lo-jong*, thought transformation, where we utilize our problems, turning them into happiness, making them worthwhile. Any problem we have—a relationship problem, a disease such as cancer, being in debt—is all to do with the mind; it is a concept of the mind. It depends on how we look at it. Therefore we can reinterpret it, putting a positive label on it instead of a negative one. In that way we are able to utilize the problem, transforming it not just into temporary happiness but ultimate happiness. This is what we really need to be able to do.

In all our beginningless lives, there is no temporary happiness that we have never achieved. We think a temporary happiness we experience is new because we have not encountered it before in this life, but there is nothing new for us. Whatever happiness or problem we experience, we have experienced it numberless times before.

Just recently I went to Land of Medicine Buddha, one of the FPMT centers in California, to greet a high lama, the second highest lama in the Gelug tradition after the Ganden Tripa, who had come to give teachings. There was a group of people there with cancer, meditating and having discussions. I met them outside and I told them my view. I said this is nothing new. This is something they have already had numberless times in the past, even though it might seem new for them. I said the most important thing is to use the cancer they have and make it useful, worthwhile—make it beneficial for all living beings.

There are numberless hell beings, numberless hungry ghosts, numberless animals, numberless human beings, numberless gods and numberless demigods. There are numberless human beings, not only in this world, this southern continent, but also in the numberless universes. That there are numberless universes is not something asserted by only Buddha, the Omniscient One, but by modern science as well.

The important thing is to make our cancer beneficial for everybody. If we find we have cancer we should make it beneficial for all living beings who are suffering but don't want suffering and who need happiness. We experience it for them to let them be free from the oceans of samsaric suffering. Actually, even though people have no idea what it means, everybody wants not just ordinary happiness but ultimate happiness, which means attaining the dharmakaya, the truth body of a buddha.

There are also many other sentient beings who even now have cancer. We can make our own cancer worthwhile by experiencing it for them and letting them be free from all suffering, not only cancer. In that way we make our own experience of cancer most happy, most useful. This is what I suggested to that group at Land of Medicine Buddha.

Because everything is created by the mind, because problems are projected, merely labeled by the mind, we have the ability to transform them into happiness. We can make cancer most useful. We can even transform death into the happiest possible death, making it most beneficial for other sentient beings. We do this by experiencing it with compassion for other sentient beings, who are numberless, who are like our family. We can see the different sentient beings, not only in this world but also in the numberless realms, as our family. We humans, insects and even ants are all just one family. We can experience the suffering for them; we can let the numberless beings have happiness.

We have the opportunity to transform suffering into happiness in daily life because it's up to our mind. It's up to our own mind whether any situation becomes a suffering or a happy one. It depends on how much knowledge we have, on whether we know the Dharma or not, whether we know inner science. Knowing Dharma and knowing inner science is the same thing.

We can choose whether a situation is a problem or not. We say, "I have a problem! When can I be happy? When can I be happy?" Then we make ourselves sick. Nobody else makes us sick, we make ourselves sick; our own mind makes us sick. That's how we do it. Unless we transform our way of thinking, this is how it will stay, our old mind, our old concepts will create the same problems for us over and over again.

With the same old mind we remain the same old person—old in terms of having to endure the same kinds of suffering rather than old in age. Rather than using our short life to become a happy person we continue to create the same causes of suffering. Because our life is created by our mind, however, we also have the chance to have a healthy, awakened life. We have the ability to choose happiness or suffering.

Even though cancer or some other sickness—even death—happens as the result of some previous action we have done, if we have a wise mind we can utilize the best psychology, the best meditation, and transform that situation into happiness. By looking at the situation in a different light we are able to change from disliking it to liking it.

And we do this not just for ourselves. Doing this becomes beneficial for numberless living beings: numberless hell beings, numberless hungry ghosts, numberless animals, numberless human beings, numberless gods and numberless demigods. Even though we can't comprehend all that, we can at least see that it benefits numberless human beings.

The ultimate mind is sang-gyä

The goal of Mahayana Buddhism is to use whatever problem we have to free numberless living beings from the oceans of samsaric suffering and bring them to peerless happiness—the total cessation of all obscurations and the completion of all realizations. That is the actual meaning of the Tibetan word *sang-gyä*, which is generally translated as "buddha." *Sang* means the cessation of all the gross and subtle obscurations of the mind, and *gyä* means the complete attainment of all realizations and all levels of happiness. There is nothing more to be eliminated and there is nothing more to be developed. There is no other happiness that still needs to be achieved. Everything has been completed.

Don't get hung up on words. Don't get hung up on the Sanskrit terms or whether *sang-gyä* refers to a buddha or the state of buddhahood. *Sang* is the cessation of all the gross and subtle obscurations of the mind. Because the mind is not oneness with the obscurations but just temporarily obscured, it can be cleansed of them just as a dirty cloth can be cleansed from dirt. Dirt cannot be separated from dirt but a cloth that is dirty can be washed so that the dirt is completely removed. With soap or whatever other cleansing agent, it can become completely clean, without a trace of dirt. It's the same thing with the mind. The mind can also become completely, totally cleansed of the dirt of the obscurations. Totally ceasing gross and subtle obscurations, we can then fully develop the power, the potential of the mind and complete all realizations. That is peerless happiness; that is "buddha" or "buddhahood." That is *sang-gyä*.

This is just a simple description of our mind. Everybody's mind is similar. Even a mosquito's mind, an ant's mind, a bee's mind is the same. We all have buddha nature. We all have that capacity to be *sang-gyä*, to be totally free from all obscurations and to complete all realizations. After we have freed ourselves from the gross obscurations we attain nirvana, ultimate happiness, liberation from the oceans of samsaric suffering, the blissful state of happiness for ourselves. Then, after even the subtle obscurations have been removed by actualizing the path, the remedy, we attain peerless happiness, actualizing all realizations, *sang-gyä*.

Even insects like mosquitoes or ants have the potential to attain *sang-gyä*. They have buddha nature. They have the nature, or potential, of *sang-gyä*. Even tiny insects only visible through a microscope have a mind whose ultimate nature, like ours, is buddha nature. Their mind can become a buddha's holy mind, the dharmakaya, the truth body, which has two aspects: the transcendental wisdom truth body and the natural truth body, the self-nature of the omniscient mind. Even the tiniest insect can become that.

Because every sentient being, including us, has buddha nature, the nature of *sang-gyä*, no matter how much suffering we have, it is only temporary. We can become free from it. Like the example I have just given, just as a cloth can be cleansed of dirt because it is not one with the dirt, our mind can be freed from suffering because it is not one with suffering but is only temporarily obscured. Because the mind has buddha nature, it is possible to eliminate not just suffering but the very cause of suffering.

EDUCATION IS MORE THAN LEARNING

During its lifetime, a tiny insect like a mosquito has no chance to develop its buddha nature. On the other hand, because we can think in a more subtle way, we human beings have not only the potential but also the incredible opportunity to develop our buddha nature in this lifetime. Our ability is so much vaster than that of nonhuman beings like insects. In their present form, animals and insects do not have the ability to learn and practice meditation, to understand the inner science of the Dharma. Only if they can become like us, humans, will they have that ability.

Our thinking is so much more complex and profound than that of nonhumans, whether we use it for positive or negative things. His Holiness the Dalai Lama has given the example of Bin Laden, how he must have had an incredible brain to mastermind those planes flying into the World Trade Center. His intelligence was truly amazing but he used it to harm others. We can use the incredible potential we have to bring happiness or suffering to the world. Therefore, while we are so fortunate to now be human, our education is very important. People think that education is just learning but it's much more than that.

What about this? There is a person with a degree from a top university, so learned, so knowledgeable—knowledgeable about external things, I mean, not about the mind—but his individual life is always suffering, always confused; there is no happiness. He has so many problems such as jealousy, pride, anger, attachment and so forth. His life is always up and down. Only ever thinking of this one life, not knowing what else to do, he is so overwhelmed with problems that suicide might even seem the easy way to end it all.

Then there is another person who doesn't have a high degree or much formal education at all but her life is so happy. Poorly educated, how can her life be happy? The answer is that the person with the high degree, whose life nonetheless is filled with much suffering, pride, jealousy, fear and worry, is ruled by the self-cherishing thought, whereas the poorly-educated person has a good heart. Of course, she still has self-cherishing but it is not very strong. Because of her good heart, her life has much happiness.

Education doesn't only happen at school, there is education at home with the parents as well. Parents set a strong example for their children. I'm not only referring to specific family relationships but also, in general, we are all children compared to our parents, just as they are children compared to their parents. Children spend much more time at home than at school and their main education is there. How their parents raise them is vital.

Real education is not just gaining knowledge of the subjects taught at school. The very essence of education is compassion. Parents' main aim should be showing their children how to develop compassion at home. They should be an example of that to their children, knowing how to skillfully guide them.

Of course, it's not easy. It's also not easy guiding children at school, because to really guide others without making any mistakes, we need to have an omniscient mind. Parents need omniscient minds; teachers in school need omniscient minds. Only then can they guide children perfectly without the slightest mistake. Only then can they be perfect guides.

At least parents and teachers should have ordinary clairvoyance[7] to know the present and see the future; otherwise they are totally ignorant. How can

[7] Rinpoche differentiates ordinary clairvoyance, also called common siddhis, such as reading minds, seeing into the future and so forth, from the supreme siddhi, which is enlightenment.

they help children to live in this world? How can they even guide themselves? Not only skillful speech, not only a knowledge of Dharma, they need ordinary clairvoyance. Guiding children is not easy!

Padmasambhava's ways of diagnosing illness

In the past, doctors could diagnose a disease exactly by following the texts, such as those of the Medicine Buddha. These texts, which clearly showed holy beings the route to enlightenment, gave detailed explanations of the diseases that existed and the medicines needed to cure them, as well as how to make those medicines, so doctors would know simply by reading these texts. But in these degenerate times it is no longer possible to gain a clear diagnosis of a person's illness just from a text. I'm not saying for every person, but many illnesses are no longer normal ones that can be diagnosed in that way.

What can be done when the texts no longer give a clear diagnosis? The powerful yogi, the enlightened being Padmasambhava, explained one of the ways to Yeshe Tsogyal,[8] who asked him about this very point. Padmasambhava explained that the method was to do a Medicine Buddha retreat, using the Medicine Buddha retreat text. After the retreat, you are able to diagnose the person's disease. After I read this text, I mentioned it to a Western doctor I met in Dharamsala who had learned Tibetan medicine, but I somehow doubt that he followed the text's advice and did a retreat.

However, the best way to be able to diagnose disease is to have clairvoyance. Whatever disease the person has just comes into your mind, without mistake. Such knowledge does not come through study but through retreat.

Another way of telling is by consulting *dakinis*, female sky-goers. There are different levels of dakinis, those who are unenlightened beings and those who are enlightened. There are dakinis who have generated realizations of the tantric path, of the gross and subtle generation stages and of the graduated completion stage. There are dakinis who have actualized clear light and dakinis who have actualized the unification of clear light and illusory body. It is possible in trying to find a diagnosis for a disease to consult dakinis who can tell clearly what the illness is.

Another way is through dreams. Whatever patient you are going to meet the next day, that night you dream of the patient and see what disease that

---

[8] The principal consort of Padmasambhava.

person has and what medicine should be taken. Even though you have not done years of study on diseases and diagnoses, even though you haven't learned anything normal, this is one method to help sick people. This is what Padmasambhava mentioned.

Otherwise you are unable to make a proper diagnosis and, thinking the person has such-and-such a disease, you give the wrong medicine. This is how it has become nowadays. Because the time has become greatly degenerated, there are more and more diseases that are outside the range of what is found in the normal texts.

WHAT IS SAMSARA?[9]

We are so lucky to be human at this time. As His Holiness explained, we can use our mind in a positive way to not just benefit ourselves but to benefit the world. We really can do that. And we can benefit others, not just in this world but in all worlds, bringing them as much happiness as possible. That is the reason for and purpose of our life, and it is as deep as the Pacific Ocean and as vast as the sky.

Whatever we call the heaviest possible suffering, "hell" or whatever, where does it come from? It all comes from the mind. And where does the greatest possible happiness come from? Peerless happiness, the total cessation of all obscurations and completion of all realizations—*sang-gyä*—also comes from the mind. Nirvana comes from our mind and samsara comes from our mind.

Samsara is divided into three realms: the desire realm, which depends on the five senses, which in turn are dependent on external objects, the form realm and the formless realm. The form realm is achieved through calm abiding meditation, which has nine stages, the last stage being firm contemplation.[10] When you experience this, you are in the form realm.

Then you become bored with even this inner experience and, due to that, you are reborn in the formless realm, which has four levels: infinite sky, infinite consciousness, infinite nothingness and the tip of samsara. In the formless realm there is only consciousness; there is no body.[11] At the moment we have five aggregates—form, feeling, cognition, compounding aggregates

---

[9] For a more detailed discussion of samsara, see Rinpoche's *Bodhisattva Attitude*, pp. 75–90.
[10] See *Meditative States in Tibetan Buddhism*, pp. 42–45.
[11] See *Meditative States in Tibetan Buddhism*, pp. 45–47.

and consciousness—but there are not necessarily always five. In the formless realm, without form, there are only four.

We have been born in the desire, form and formless realms numberless times. And after the formless realm we have been reborn in the lower realms as hell beings, hungry ghosts or animals, or we have been reborn as human beings or in the form realm. This has happened to us numberless times in the past, from beginningless rebirths, because we have never been able to generate complete renunciation for the whole of samsara.

Samsara is the continuity of the cycle of rebirth of these aggregates we have. This continuity of rebirths is due to the contaminated aggregates caused by karma, which is motivated by delusion, by wrong concepts. That is why our aggregates are in nature of suffering—they are pervaded by suffering.

This continuity of the circling of rebirths of the contaminated aggregates caused by karma and delusion is the real samsara, not the aggregates themselves. This was mentioned by the Seventh Dalai Lama, Kelsang Gyatso, as well as by Lama Tsongkhapa in the *Lamrim Chenmo*, where he described samsara as "the part of the continuity of the contaminated aggregates caused by karma and delusion."

He emphasized that samsara is the *part* of the continuity of the aggregates because there are five paths to liberation—the paths of merit, preparation, right-seeing, meditation and no more learning—and a meditator who has achieved the path of meditation already has the wisdom directly perceiving emptiness. As he is no longer under the power of karma and delusion, the cause of samsara ceases and he does not have to reincarnate. The meditator who has achieved the path of meditation is excluded. That is the reason for adding the word "part" here.

Because, I suspect, none of us have achieved the exalted path of meditation and directly perceived emptiness, we will all have to reincarnate again, so this does not apply to us. If we were to achieve the path of meditation before we die, however, we would be free from that "part" that Lama Tsongkhapa mentioned, the part of the continuity of the circling of the contaminated aggregates caused by karma and delusion. We would no longer be in samsara.

Practicing Dharma is subduing our mind

This samsara we are trapped in comes from our mind, but so does nirvana. The problems we have to face, the happiness we can experience, every day, every hour, every minute, all come from the mind. Therefore, meditation, Dharma practice, the inner science, is so important to help our mind. That is what the Buddha said:

> Do not commit any nonvirtuous actions,
> Perform only perfect virtuous actions,
> Subdue your mind thoroughly—
> This is the teaching of the Buddha.

That is why the practice of Buddhadharma is taking care of our own mind, subduing our own mind. Unless we eliminate the confusion within the mind that is the source of all suffering we will forever remain in the prison of samsara, the prison of suffering. We have been there for beginningless lifetimes and if we don't do something about it we will never get out.

Therefore, practicing Buddhadharma *is* subduing our mind. Taking care of our mind leads to every possible happiness: all the happiness of our day-to-day life, all our future lives' happiness, the ultimate happiness of liberation from samsara and, finally, peerless happiness, *sang-gyä*, the omniscient mind.

Practicing Dharma means developing a positive mind, a healthy mind, which leads to a healthy body and a healthy life. Nowadays even psychologists and doctors commonly agree that a healthy body and a healthy lifestyle depend on a healthy mind. Taking care of our mind means not letting ourselves suffer. From beginningless rebirths until now we have suffered, but we no longer let ourselves suffer. Instead, freeing ourselves from confusion, we allow ourselves to have every kind of happiness, right up to enlightenment, the state of the omniscient mind. Meditating means that. Practicing Dharma means that. To have a positive, healthy mind we have to understand how it all depends on taking care of the mind.

Even when we tell a friend "Take care of yourself" we should have that meaning in mind. We have great freedom. Everything is in our hands. Our enlightenment, the state of omniscient mind, *sang-gyä*, is in our hands. Ultimate happiness, liberation from samsara, is in our hands. And our day-to-day life's happiness is in our hands.

Whether we want problems or not is up to how we think. If we think in a positive way, we'll have happiness; if we think in a negative way, we'll have problems. It's like that. It's all in our hands. What we do with our life is in our hands.

We have incredible freedom. Please recognize and enjoy this. Enjoying our life in this way, having a healthy mind and a healthy life, is practicing Dharma.

THE INNER EDUCATION OF PATIENCE AND COMPASSION

I mentioned how the very essence of education is compassion. Education is not just learning new things. I saw a story on TV about a couple who for the last six or seven years have been been studying a small pod of whales. They are still studying them. All day long they take their boat out into the ocean to look for and study the whales. There is also somebody who has been studying spiders, maybe in fireplaces, for years. There are probably organizations that pay people to study things like that.

Scientific knowledge is good, but education is not just learning new things. The essence of education is developing compassion for living beings—compassion not only for our family and friends but for all living beings. That especially includes our enemy, the one who dislikes us, who gets angry with us, who harms us. If we can generate compassion for that person, it's an unbelievable thing. If we can bring peace to that person, then it is easy to bring peace to anybody. This is how we learn to bring peace to the world. Starting with one or two people, we can slowly bring peace to the world.

That's an unbelievable accomplishment, more incredible that climbing Mount Everest a hundred times or...what else? Going to the moon or the sun a hundred times, or a *billion* times. It's a much greater accomplishment than any of that. It is really so special if we can generate patience and compassion toward our enemy, not to mention generating compassion toward the numberless other beings.

From time to time in the world it happens that there is a person who doesn't practice patience or compassion toward others. If that person has power and influence he can kill many millions of people. There are different stories about this kind of thing happening, where millions of people, including children, have been killed, burned or gassed by this one powerful person.

That person had power and influence but he didn't have the education that taught him how to practice patience and compassion. Without those qualities, patience and compassion, what happened? It's like Bin Laden. He was able to think big, but in a negative way, to harm others. He knew how to harm and cheat others in such an unbelievably vast way.

Patience and compassion are the two very fundamental qualities of our inner education. Without them, powerful people have brought so much harm to the world, killing millions of people and gaining the worst reputation because of it. If they *had* practiced patience and compassion, none of that harm—killing and torturing those millions and millions of people— would have happened. Incredible happiness would have come to those millions of people from that harm being stopped. This is the influence that one powerful person can have on the world.

There are great holy beings in all the different religions, like Saint Francis or the Buddha in his past lives as a bodhisattva, who have brought many millions of people happiness and peace. Through practicing patience and compassion, the most fundamental, important education, even one person has the power to bring great happiness to the people of the world.

Even if we are not able to become like that now, despite the fact that our body will not continue, there is the continuation of our consciousness, constantly moving from life to life. For that reason, the most important practice, the most important education, is developing patience and compassion so that we can become like those holy beings in future lives. Then, from life to life, we will be able to give happiness to billions and billions of beings— not only to people, but even to animals—to all other living beings.

News programs on TV usually only mention people, rarely animals. When bombs destroy a place can you imagine how many animals are killed? There must be countless animals and insects in the ground, fields and forests that are killed, but they're not mentioned. It's as if they don't count.

We must train in this important, innermost education, the education of mind, now, in this life while we have all the possibilities to transform our mind.

Our family is our mind training

Even people with no belief in any religion or philosophy need harmony in their relationships with others, with their family, spouse and children. Maintaining a long-lasting relationship relies on harmony and that comes from practicing patience and compassion. No relationship can last without patience. If we follow anger rather than patience, our relationship with our spouse, family or friends will inevitably deteriorate and finally perish. At first the other person might try to be tolerant of us but that won't last and soon she will no longer be bothered. She might try to physically stay with us but her mind will drift away and there will no longer be any harmony. Soon, even physically, she will be gone.

We all need help, so to maintain comfortable relationships even non-believers need to practice patience and compassion—with their husbands, wives, parents and children. That's the way to make relationships harmonious and long lasting.

Even if only one person within a relationship practices patience and compassion, it helps greatly to maintain harmony and keep the relationship together long-term. Practicing patience, not getting angry, not harming the other person with our body, speech and mind, that is peace; that is the peace we're giving to the other person.

Our family is our mind training. We train our mind with our wife or husband, with our children, with our parents. The most important thing in following any spiritual path is mental development and in one way our family is there for our mental development. The question is whether we recognize this or not. Our family is there to help us develop our patience and compassion; they are there to train us in this. When we have trained with them we can then move on to our neighbors and the people around us. In that way we are able to generate more and more patience and have less and less anger. Then, after some years, even if anger arises it is weak and doesn't last long, just remaining for a short while before evaporating. We slowly train our mind to have less anger and more patience toward more and more people and then toward all sentient beings. That absence of harm means peace for everybody. That's how mental development works. That's how we can develop our mind.

Besides being the foundation of a harmonious relationship, generating a good heart and patience brings additional benefits to our family members and all other sentient beings. Refraining from harm, we lead not only those around us into peace and happiness but all the beings of this world.

We have that responsibility. The world's peace and happiness is on our shoulders. Practicing patience and compassion, refraining from harming others, we bring great happiness to numberless living beings: to the numberless hell beings, hungry ghosts, animals, human beings, gods, demigods and intermediate state beings. In that way, we are responsible for the peace and happiness of all beings of the six realms.

Then, with the compassion we have developed toward all living beings, we develop wisdom. In that way, we are able to bring them not only the temporary happiness of this life but also that of future lives. Then, by understanding the mind they understand karma, cause and effect, what specific results come from the actions of body, speech and mind—what brings suffering and what brings happiness. By having the wisdom understanding karma, they are able to gain ultimate happiness, liberation from the oceans of samsaric suffering. In that way, we are able to bring them to the blissful state of peace, individual liberation from the oceans of samsaric suffering forever. They no longer have to experience any suffering: the suffering of pain, the suffering of change and the cause of those two sufferings, pervasive compounding suffering.

Not only that, by developing compassion and wisdom, we are able to bring all the numberless living beings to peerless happiness, *sang-gyä*, the state of the total cessation of all obscurations and the complete development of all realizations.

There can be no happiness following the self-cherishing thought

Developing compassion and wisdom is amazing. What our mind can do, what our heart can do, is just amazing. However, if you are like me, your heart at the moment is full of self-cherishing. We think, "*My* happiness is more important than anybody else's. *My* happiness is more important than that of the numberless buddhas, the numberless bodhisattvas, the numberless sentient beings. It is the most important thing of all, more important than the happiness of the numberless hell beings, the numberless hungry ghosts, the numberless animals, the numberless human beings, the numberless gods and demigods and the numberless intermediate state beings. *I'm* the most important one! *My* happiness is more important than anybody else's!"

At the moment our mind is in that condition, but the mind itself is not oneness with the self-cherishing thought. Not at all. It is just temporarily obscured by delusions. Holding the self-cherishing thought has no logical reason. Cherishing the I is just an ego trip!

The self-cherishing thought is nothing but a dictatorship and there is no logical reason for that dictatorship. It cannot posit one valid reason why this I is more important than anybody else, whereas there are infinite valid reasons to cherish the numberless others who only want happiness and who do not want suffering. There are numberless buddhas and bodhisattvas and there are numberless sentient beings who do not have bodhicitta, so there are numberless beings to cherish. Using valid reasoning we can transform our mind.

In *A Guide to the Bodhisattva's Way of Life* the great bodhisattva Shantideva said,

> Thus whoever wishes to quickly afford protection
> To both the self and other beings
> Should practice that holy secret:
> The exchanging of self for others.[12]

If we want to quickly help and protect ourselves and others, the ultimate method is transforming our mind from one that cherishes the I and renounces others to one that renounces the I and cherishes others.

Shantideva says we practice this secretly. Here he's referring to us and the lower bodhisattvas. Exchanging oneself for others, renouncing the I and cherishing all other beings more than the I instead, is beyond us at this stage. Even lower bodhisattvas are not yet brave enough to physically do that, therefore it is done as a secret practice, which might mean it is only a mental practice. At this stage the mind is being transformed even though physically there is no change, so it's secret in that way also.

We have to remember that. This is the best way to help others and ourselves. Shantideva continued,

> Whatever joy there is in this world
> All comes from desiring others to be happy,
> And whatever suffering there is in this world
> All comes from desiring myself to be happy.
>
> What need is there to say much more?
> The childish work for their own benefit,
> The Buddhas [Mighty Ones] work for the benefit of others.
> Just look at the difference between them![13]

---

[12] Ch. 8, v. 120.
[13] Ch. 8, vv. 129 & 130. The cited text has "Buddhas"; when Rinpoche was translating this verse during the teachings he used "Mighty Ones," an epithet of the buddhas.

"Mighty Ones" means the buddhas. They are "mighty" because they have destroyed all the obscurations and completed all the realizations and so they have finished their work for self and now work only for others. Shantideva asks us to look at the difference between the buddhas and the childish ones—us—who only work for ourselves.

In Dharma texts, "child" does not mean a physical child but somebody who is mentally childish. We could live to be a hundred years old—or a thousand or a billion—but if our mind remains under the control of the self-cherishing thought then we are childish. We are just like small children who, when they play, do so only for their own happiness. Therefore this is used as an example.

A child plays in the sand, piling it over her feet and thinking that this is her house or some such thing. Then another child comes along and destroys it and she cries out, "You destroyed my house!" This is the example. If somebody harms us, because of the self-cherishing thought, the emotional thought arises, "Somebody has harmed me! He doesn't love me, he doesn't love me, blah, blah, blah...." Many negative emotions arise and this creates suffering.

We have been following the self-cherishing thought from beginningless rebirths until now and because of that we have been suffering. We have lived our life with the self-cherishing thought; we have followed the self-cherishing thought. The self-cherishing thought has been like our parents, like our guru. And because we have followed it we have been suffering in samsara for countless lifetimes. That is what has been happening and will continue to happen if we don't transform our mind. The suffering of samsara will be endless. Therefore, while we have this life where we have all the opportunities to learn and practice, we *must* practice the Dharma and generate the ultimate good heart, bodhicitta.

The Buddha transformed his mind. He was the same as us, beset with all the same problems, the same relationship problems, selfish thoughts, negative emotions and so forth. Just like us, he suffered in samsara from beginningless rebirths. But the Buddha managed to change his mind from cherishing the self to cherishing others. He achieved ultimate happiness, enlightenment, *sang-gyä*, the cessation of all obscurations and completion of all realizations.

This is something we have not yet done. By following the self-cherishing thought, the suffering of samsara has not ended. If we don't do something in this life to change that by developing a good heart, the ultimate good heart, bodhicitta, then the suffering of samsara will probably become endless.

That is what Shantideva means when he asks us to compare ourselves to the buddhas. Look at the difference. From having so many problems, like us, Guru Shakyamuni Buddha became the "Mighty One," the Buddha, whereas we are still suffering sentient beings. Shantideva also mentioned,

> If I do not actually exchange my happiness
> For the sufferings of others,
> I shall not attain the state of Buddhahood
> And even in cyclic existence shall have no joy.[14]

Unless we give others our happiness and take their suffering upon ourselves we will be unable to completely transform our mind and so will not be able to eliminate all the obscurations and complete all the realizations. In other words, we won't be able to achieve the highest goal. Furthermore, while we are trapped in samsara there is no real happiness. Leaving aside happiness in future lives, by following the self-cherishing thought even our work for this life will fail.

Because of the self-cherishing thought we have to experience so many obstacles, such as not succeeding in what we do, being unable to find a job and so forth. That is the result of our karma, from past lives or this life, of being jealous of others' success or not letting them have success. The motivation was the self-cherishing thought, thus creating jealousy and causing us to harm others in order to steal their success. Even if we are able to find a job, no matter how hard we work we are unable to succeed. In that way, cherishing the I ensures we will fail in whatever we do.

If we renounce self-cherishing and cherish others instead, if we practice patience and compassion for others, then the numberless sentient beings receive no harm from us. That is peace and happiness. That is what every one of them receives from us. And, as I have just said, that allows them to develop inner wisdom, to understand karma and so forth and that leads to their future lives' happiness. In that way, they are brought to complete happiness.

What we are able to do when we generate patience and compassion is unbelievable. We are responsible for the happiness and peace of every

---

[14] Ch. 8, v. 131.

sentient being: for everyone in our family, in our society, in our country, in this world and in all worlds—and finally for ourselves. We can offer all this happiness to every sentient being.

The practice of patience and compassion should really be the main education in the family and in schools. Only with that can there be peace in the world and an end to suffering.

3. The Hallucination of the Real I

IF MODERN TECHNOLOGY is used in a positive way it has the potential to benefit billions of people and animals in the world. But used in the wrong way it can bring unbelievably disastrous harm to billions of beings. This is especially true of digital technology, the Internet and so forth, which has the power to benefit immediately, sending images and words all over the world in a second, but at the same time it also has the power to do great damage, harming billions of people, polluting their minds, destroying their lives. It all depends on how such things are used.

In a positive way the benefits from life to life are unbelievable. Watching His Holiness online, for instance, allows the mind to develop like a lotus opening, bringing greater happiness, more success from life to life, for hundreds of lives, thousands of lives, millions and billions of lives. It leads to the total liberation from the oceans of samsaric suffering and ultimately to the total elimination of all obscurations and the completion of all realizations, to that peerless happiness, where there is no trace of ignorance, no obscurations. Therefore, we must be very careful how we use modern technology.

BUDDHISM COMES TO TIBET

In Tibetan Buddhism there are four traditions: Nyingma, Kagyü, Sakya and Gelug. When the Nalanda Monastery abbot Shantarakshita went to Tibet to purify the land, he built the first monastery in Tibet in Samye. However, each night, after the human beings had erected the monastery walls during the day, the spirits would tear them down so that the next day the people would have to rebuild them. This happened again and again.

So King Trisong Detsen invited the powerful yogi Padmasambhava from

India to visit Tibet. There is a whole book—probably several books—on the life story of Padmasambhava. When he got to Tibet, he arose in the aspect of an enlightened wrathful deity and hooked the spirits. Three ran away according to the karma of the Tibetans, but he subdued the other twelve and made them pledge to protect and not harm the Buddhadharma in Tibet and to protect its practitioners as well. Having been subdued, those twelve spirits became Dharma protectors. Since then, Tibetans have been making offerings and doing prayers to those protectors and asking them for help. From that, Buddhism became firmly established in Tibet.

Thus the Buddhadharma came to Tibet from India, from Nalanda Monastery—not Nalanda in France but Nalanda in India. And speaking about Nalanda in France, that is now a real monastery, not a diluted one, because they now do the three main practices of a monastery there: the twice-monthly confession ceremonies, the yearly abiding in summer retreat and following Vinaya.[15] It also fulfills the description of a monastery in that it is isolated from villages and crowds. In Nalanda in India there were three hundred pandits. After the Buddha achieved enlightenment and revealed the teachings, great pandits like Asanga and Nagarjuna, who was like a second Buddha, came. These great pandits were holy beings who actualized the path. They were not just scholars, not just experts in words whose minds remained ordinary—these three hundred holy beings all actualized the path.

The Buddha's teachings are contained in the Kangyur, a collection of more than a hundred volumes, and the commentaries to the Buddha's teachings by those great Indian pandits are contained in the Tengyur, a collection of more than two hundred volumes. This is what came from India to Tibet. In that way, there is a vast and pure lineage within Tibetan Buddhism that can be referenced back to the Buddha himself. It's not like some black magic made up by Tibetan lamas.

Before Buddhism came to Tibet there was the Bön religion. There were the black Bönpos, which I think was a form of shamanism, and the white Bönpos, whose teachings seem similar in subject to *dzog-chen* but using different language. The founder of the Bönpo was Yungdrung Tonpa. I don't

---

[15] These are customs the Buddha established for monasteries. *So-jong* (Tib.) is a confession ceremony where Sangha members admit any wrongdoings; abiding in summer retreat (Tib: *yar-ne*) occurred every summer in India during the rainy season; and following Vinaya means following the rules of discipline that the Buddha laid down.

know if the white Bönpos take refuge in him but he is not a buddha. It's like in Hinduism there are Shiva and Maheshwara and other deities who are not buddhas.[16]

The teachings of most of the lineage lamas of the four Tibetan traditions can be traced back to Nalanda, so we can say that Buddhadharma in Tibet, both sutra and tantra, came from Nalanda and, therefore, the Buddha.

After Padmasambhava subdued all the spirits in the different important places of Tibet and they became Dharma protectors, Buddhadharma spread, mainly in the monasteries, where there was extensive study, as deep and wide as the Pacific Ocean. From the commentaries by the Nalanda pandits, the great Tibetan teachers wrote their own commentaries. The many enlightened beings from all of the four traditions, such as Lama Tsongkhapa, all studied extensively, listening, reflecting, meditating and then actualizing the path. After that, they wrote commentaries based on their own experiences and taught others the path that they themselves had practiced and actualized.

At that time there were a great many lay practitioners and ordained Sangha living in caves. There were so many caves that the mountains were like ants' nests. Now so much has been destroyed or has become old and ruined. I didn't see the whole of Tibet when I went there, only that which was on the way to Lhasa, but in the early times it must have been amazing.

These great lamas actualized the whole path to enlightenment, the extensive study, the middle study and the heart study. The Kadampa geshes started with Lama Atisha, the great pandit who in the eleventh century was invited from India to Tibet to make Buddhism pure again when its practice in Tibet had degenerated and there was much misunderstanding of tantra. People felt that if they practiced sutra they could not practice tantra and vice versa. There was much confusion.

Seeing this, the Dharma king of Tibet, Lha Lama Yeshe Ö, collected gold to offer to Lama Atisha in order to invite him to Tibet. He first sent the

---

[16] Bön is the religion in Tibet that is often said to have preceded Buddhism. His Holiness the Dalai Lama has recognized Bön as the fifth tradition along with the four major traditions of Nyingma, Sakya, Kagyü and Gelug. Practitioners of Bön are called Bönpos. The founder's full name was Tonpa Shenrab Miwoche. Yungdrung is the name of one of the Bön traditions, they do consider Tonpa a buddha and the Yungdrung school is essentially Buddhism. Some scholars assert that Bön arose only in the eleventh century and was therefore not a pre-Buddhist religion in Tibet and that the religion that did precede Buddhism was probably not called Bön.

translator Gyatsoen Senge to India but he could not meet Lama Atisha and was therefore unable to invite him.

The second time, while Lha Lama Yeshe Ö was looking for more gold to offer Atisha, he was captured by an irreligious king and put into prison. In order to free his uncle, his nephew, Jangchub Ö, offered the gold meant for Lama Atisha but the irreligious king said that there wasn't enough, that gold the size of the king's head was still missing and that to free the king he had to be offered gold the size of the king's body plus his head.

When Jangchub Ö reported this to his uncle, the Dharma king said, "I will die in prison for the sentient beings in Tibet and to spread pure Buddhism, so don't give him even a handful of gold. Take all the gold to India, offer it to Lama Atisha and invite him here." The king sent Atisha a message that he would meet him in his next life. Then the translator Nagtso Lotsawa went to India carrying the gold. He offered it to Lama Atisha and explained all the problems and misunderstandings prevalent in Tibet.

So Lama Atisha asked Tara, the female embodiment of all the numberless buddhas' holy actions, whether he should go to Tibet to spread the pure Buddhadharma. He often prayed with great devotion to Tara for success, as did many great yogis, lamas, pandits, Sangha and lay practitioners, because Tara had manifested specifically in order to fulfill the hopes and wishes of sentient beings. Tara said, "Your time in Tibet will be highly beneficial but your life will be shortened by seven years." Lama Atisha replied, "I don't mind if my life becomes shorter, as long as it's beneficial for Tibet."

He then pretended he was going to Nepal on pilgrimage, not telling the monastery or the Indian people that he was going to Tibet, because they would not have let him undertake such a long journey. In that way he went to Tibet via Nepal.

When Lama Atisha arrived in Tibet, Jangchub Ö explained the situation fully to him, telling him, "We Tibetans are very ignorant, so please explain refuge to us." Jangchub Ö didn't request initiations or teachings on *shunyata* or other high teachings. This is what he requested of Lama Atisha. Lama Atisha was extremely pleased, so he wrote a short text, the *Lamp for the Path to Enlightenment*, in which he integrated all the teachings of Buddha into what has become known as the graduated path to enlightenment.[17]

He was able to condense the essence of the 84,000 teachings of the Buddha—all the Hinayana teachings, the Mahayana sutra teachings and

---

[17] (Tib: *lam-rim*). See *Teachings from Tibet*, appendix 2, for a translation of Atisha's text.

the Mahayana tantra teachings, the three levels the Buddha taught—into a few pages. He made how to practice very clear, without any contradiction between sutra and tantra practice, so people could practice both. Those who practiced tantra could also practice sutra and those who practiced sutra could also practice tantra. That helped so much.

In those days, before newly written works could be published they had to be checked by a group of pandits. If a text was found to be correct it would be approved for publication but if it had mistakes it would be tied to the tail of a dog, which would then be chased around the city by people proclaiming the name of the disgraced author. So before making his text available Atisha sent it to his monastery for review. The pandits there were extremely surprised by the quality of Lama Atisha's writing and praised him highly for writing it.[18]

After that, many other great meditator lamas wrote commentaries on that first lam-rim teaching according to the experiences they had had by reading, reflecting and meditating on it. Lama Tsongkhapa, who was one of these, wrote the most elaborate commentary (the *Lamrim Chenmo*, *The Great Treatise on the Stages of the Path to Enlightenment*), the *Middle Length Lam-rim*, a short one called *Songs of Spiritual Experience* and, finally, the very short *Three Principal Aspects of the Path to Enlightenment*. The term "lam-rim" comes from Lama Atisha's *Lamp for the Path to Enlightenment*.

Thus the misconceptions about Buddhism that prevailed in Tibet were completely eliminated, the Dharma was made pure and much sutra and tantra was practiced and actualized.

Attaining enlightenment comes from the base, the two truths: the truth for the all-obscuring mind and the truth for absolute mind. These two truths are the base, the path is practicing method and wisdom—putting the essence of method and wisdom into the path—and the goal to be achieved is the buddha's holy body and holy mind. This is the entire Buddhadharma, and both sutra and tantra are what the monks studied in the monasteries in Tibet for their whole lives. Through that, numberless meditators became bodhisattvas and were able to achieve buddhahood, becoming enlightened beings.

In many other holy places in Tibet practitioners also achieved realizations; not only Milarepa but many others attained enlightenment there as

---

[18] See *Liberation in the Palm of Your Hand*, pp. 49–50. The book contains a complete biography of Lama Atisha.

well. Because of that, there are many, many places in Tibet that are unbelievably blessed.

Just as the pandits did in Tibet, you Western students also need to study
what is written in the texts and, through intensive contemplation, meditate
on and actualize the path. You must try to hold in your heart the teachings that the Buddha and those other great holy beings in India and Tibet
explained. If you can do that then the West too can become an extremely
blessed place, like India, Nepal and Tibet.

Otherwise it is just studying words, as people do at universities. Of course,
you have to start with words, but without actualizing the path in your mind,
without transforming your life, then it is merely study. It is still unbelievably
fortunate that you can do it, but it's not Buddhadharma as found in India,
Nepal and Tibet. When *tsampa* is thrown into a river it doesn't sink, it stays
on the surface. Likewise, if the Buddhadharma you study does not enter
your heart but just stays on the surface, all you're doing is studying words.
It's kind of empty. However, I think there are many people who are learning
and trying to meditate and practice, and gradually this is having a beneficial
effect on their mind. That is very good.

THE BUDDHA MANIFESTS IN AN ORDINARY
FORM TO GUIDE US

His Holiness the Dalai Lama is the sole object of refuge for the numberless
sentient beings of the six realms: for the beings of the hell realm, the hungry
ghost realm, the animal realm, the human realm, the god realm, the demigod realm and the intermediate state. He is the sole object of refuge for all
sentient beings including us. He is the embodiment of the compassion of
all the numberless past buddhas, present buddhas and future buddhas, the
definitive meaning of Avalokiteshvara, the Compassion Buddha.

The buddhas manifest in human form in order to show us how to be free
from the lower realms, from samsara and even from the peace of lower nirvana. Through their guidance we can become free from all subtle obscurations and actualize all realizations and so attain buddhahood, the peerless
state of the omniscient mind. In order to guide us, to explain the teachings in a way that we can understand, the buddhas manifest in an ordinary
aspect, in a human form.

"Ordinary" means this. Although for them there is no suffering of
rebirth, they show the suffering of rebirth; although they have no suffering

of old age, they show the suffering of old age; although they have no suffering of illness, they show the suffering of illness; although they have no suffering of death, they show the suffering of death.

Arhats are free from only the disturbing-thought obscurations, not the subtle obscurations to knowledge, yet they are free from these four sufferings. So how can enlightened beings, who are free from even the subtle obscurations, have old age, sickness, death and rebirth? Since there is no cause for these sufferings, it's impossible. The buddhas don't have these sufferings but they show the aspect of having them for our sake.

Take Guru Shakyamuni Buddha, for example. According to the Mahayana teachings, in reality the Buddha achieved enlightenment numberless eons ago. He did not become enlightened two thousand six hundred years ago in Bodhgaya. All the twelve deeds were to show us what to do. Taking birth in Lumbini, achieving enlightenment in Bodhgaya, teaching the Dharma and passing away in Kushinagar—performing all these holy deeds was purely to show us the path.

In many universes at different times the Buddha simultaneously shows different aspects of the twelve deeds. While the Buddha was taking birth here in this world all those centuries ago, in another universe he was showing the aspect of becoming enlightened. Even now, in one universe he is showing the aspect of passing away while in another he is showing the aspect of sitting under the bodhi tree, and in yet another he is showing the aspect of turning the Dharma wheel. He manifests in numberless aspects without effort and gives various teachings in numberless different universes to numberless sentient beings. This is beyond our imagination.

According to the Hinayana teachings, the teachings for that level of mind, his enlightenment in Bodhgaya was the first time, but according to the Mahayana, the Buddha was enlightened eons ago and he performed the twelve deeds just to show us suffering sentient beings that although there is suffering that none of us want, there is both a cause for that suffering and a path that leads to its cessation.

Rather than complaining that we are suffering and never doing anything about it, we see that there is an evolution; that suffering is a dependent arising. Since any suffering we are experiencing depends on causes and conditions, if we apply the correct method, the cause of suffering—karma and delusion—can definitely be eliminated and we can become free from it.

The Buddha showed us that our mind has this possibility, this potential. Because there is a path we can actualize we can definitely achieve ultimate happiness, the blissful state of peace for ourselves, liberation forever from the oceans of samsaric suffering. We can learn, we can reflect, we can meditate on the path and we can actualize it.

EMPTINESS ONLY, TONG-PA-NYI

In particular, we can actualize the direct perception of emptiness, emptiness *only*. That *only*—*nyi*—makes it a specific emptiness, not just any emptiness. The *nyi* cuts ordinary emptiness.

Not understanding this specific emptiness is the root of our suffering, the root of the oceans of samsaric suffering, the sufferings of rebirth, old age, sickness, death and so forth. And that is only the suffering of pain, which is not the only suffering in samsara. There is also the suffering of change and pervasive compounding suffering, which is the cause of the other two.

We are afraid of cancer and many people die from it, but they don't know that the root cause of cancer is not understanding this particular emptiness. It is also the root cause of AIDS and all the other diseases that medicine has no cure for, not to mention all the other sufferings of samsara, not just sickness. It is where all our relationship problems and depression come from. It is the cause of anorexia, bulimia, obesity and all other eating disorders. This ignorance is the very root of the problems experienced by every individual, by every family, by every society, by every country, by the entire globe. Whatever suffering there is, this ignorance is the root.

All problems come from this root, which is a wrong concept, therefore this wrong concept is what we need to eliminate. By studying, reflecting and meditating, by realizing the ultimate truth, we can come to realize that this concept is totally wrong.

I don't understand emptiness well so I can only explain it in a simple way. There is a base—the five aggregates—that exists and, depending on that, the thought of the I arises. For instance, if the base, the aggregates (in this case the body), is sitting, then the thought of the I arises, the merely labeled, "I am sitting." We label this on the sitting aggregates.

When the aggregates stand up, again there is the thought of the I. The aggregates are the base upon which the I is labeled. There is the subject that labels the I and the aggregates that are the object. When the aggregates are standing, the thought of the I *merely* imputes, "I am standing." When the form aggregate is standing, the thought of the I doesn't label, "I am sitting." No. The thought of the I is dependent on what we do. When walking, the thought of the I merely imputes, "I am walking." Whatever action we are doing—eating, standing, sitting, sleeping, lying down—the aggregates are doing the action and then, on top of that, the thought of the I is merely imputed and we believe it.

When the aggregates are jogging to become skinny—maybe that's not correct, maybe it's to become fit—then the thought of the I merely imputes "I am jogging." When the aggregates are talking, depending on that action, the thought of the I merely imputes, "I am talking." We put the I on the action of talking, or "I am in silence" or whatever it is.

When we are meditating, in dependence upon the mind meditating the thought of the I, the subject, applies the label, "I am meditating." We call the merely-imputed I and the merely-imputed action of the I "meditating."

So, depending on what the aggregates—our body and mind—are doing, depending on the action, the labeling thought merely imputes the I and merely imputes the action of the I.

From the moment we wake up in the morning until we go to sleep in the evening, all day long, depending on what our body and mind does, the labeling thought merely imputes the I and the merely labeled action of the I, whatever the I does. The I and the action of the I—whatever we have believed from morning until night—has *all* come from our mind, has *all* been labeled by our mind.

This meditation is incredibly powerful, like an atomic bomb, destroying our enemy. An atomic bomb is considered the most powerful weapon to destroy an external enemy. Ordinary people in the ordinary world believe that the true enemy is the external enemy. According to Dharma this is not so at all, and this mindfulness meditation is really the best way to destroy the one true enemy, the inner enemy.

What we do to protect this nonexistent real I

If we do some profound scientific analysis, some *inner* scientific analysis, we can see how much we believe in this totally real I that actually does not exist. It appears to be real from its own side, we believe it to be one hundred percent real, but it is not there. By doing this inner scientific analysis, this meditation, we can come to see this very subtle point, the nonexistence of this "real" I.

Otherwise, without checking, because of our belief in its reality we have all these worries, all these fears. Because of this wrong projection, when somebody passes us with her nose in the air, looking down at us disdainfully, it hurts so much. Or when we do a good deed for somebody, such as giving a thirsty person a glass of water, and don't even get a simple thank you, that really hurts. Being shouted at, being complained about, hearing disrespectful words—all these things hurt us.

Especially nowadays, with the world economy in recession, people are trying to find ways to make money, so they complain about any small thing that somebody else does. I don't know about England, but I've heard that in America you are supposed keep the front of your house clear of snow and if you don't clear it away well enough and somebody falls over you will be sued, which in America means a *huge* expense.

There is a good example from the FPMT center in Sicily, Centro Muni Gyana. Once, while I was giving a talk there a student explained how she had been sued. Her job was assisting in the births of babies, delivering them from their mothers' wombs, and one day a baby had died. I'm not sure whether the baby was dead in the womb or it died during delivery, but the mother blamed this girl, telling her she had killed the baby, that the baby died because she had made a mistake. The girl talked with all her friends and they confirmed what she did was right, that it wasn't her fault, but the mother blamed her and wanted money from her. She was trying to make money out of the situation. This is just one example.

Nowadays, with the downturn in the world economy, many people are trying to make money in this way, trying to prove that somebody else has made a mistake, whether they have or not. The girl asked me what to do and I did my own Mickey Mouse divination and told her to recite the *Vajra Cutter Sutra* eight times. She did this immediately and later she told me that she had won the court case.

Just reading the *Vajra Cutter Sutra* is unbelievably powerful but, of course, the main thing is to realize emptiness, to eradicate the very root of samsara. That is what reading the *Vajra Cutter Sutra* eventually does. Then we become free from oceans of samsaric suffering, achieving ultimate happiness. Without talking about enlightenment, just that is unbelievable.

Our whole life is spent being afraid of something happening to this I, to this *real I* that appears to us from *there*. We totally, one hundred percent believe it is real and do everything we possibly can to protect this real I, which is *not* there. We see all the possibilities of being hurt. "This will make me sick. This will kill me. This will hurt me." We take every possible precaution to prevent this real I that doesn't exist from being hurt.

Determined to keep fit, we do hours of exercise every day, jogging or working out on machines. There is a big industry making new types of machines for our real I to keep fit on. After a machine has been on the market for a few months a new one comes out and our real I has to have it. Each machine makes us exercise differently—from lying upside down to putting our head between our legs—and we are forced to buy new ones because the experts in advertisements convince us that these new ones are better.

All this is done for our real I, for the I that appears real and we believe one hundred percent is truly there. Even exercising the body, doing many hundreds of pushups, is for this real I. Everybody jogging, running and exercising is doing it so that this I does not get sick. They are protecting this I. They have injections to prevent diseases before they happen. They take every single precaution they can to protect this real I.

If we were to meditate for just one day, analyzing, checking, going to a subtler level, we would see that this real I is not there. What appears as the real I, what we believe one hundred percent to be real, is not there. However, we don't check and this labeling process goes on continuously. It has been going on since we were born and will continue up to death.

Because the aggregates—the body and mind—are there, because they exist, they are the valid base on which the labeling mind merely imputes the I. Then, depending on what that base does, the labeling mind merely labels the action.

The labeling thought merely labels I on the subject and the merely labeled action on whatever the aggregates do. It has been and will be like that, from the time our consciousness entered the fertilized egg in our mother's womb until our death, when the extremely subtle mind, what we call the subtle mind of death,[19] leaves from the heart, the place where it entered the fertilized egg at the very beginning. This happens after the person is clinically dead: after the breathing has stopped, the heart has stopped beating and there is no more brain function.

When we analyze, we can understand very clearly the great difference between the reality of the I and actions and how we believe they exist when we don't think about it. The way we normally think is a total hallucination, a total illusion; it is like a dream.

From beginningless rebirths up to now there has always been the continuity of existence of the aggregates, although not necessarily always of the physical body—a formless realm rebirth doesn't have a physical body. And

---

[19] Tib: *sem shin-tu tra-mo.*

just as there has always been the valid base, the aggregates, their continuity, there has always been the labeling thought that merely imputes the I and merely imputes the action of the I, depending on what the aggregates do. When we analyze dependent arising—not the gross one but the Prasangika view of subtle dependent arising—we see that it has always been like this from beginningless rebirths up to now.

How everything appears to us as truly existing

As long as there is the continuity of the valid base, the aggregates, there is always the mere I existing and there is always the mere action of the I existing. While we are circling in samsara it will be like that. This will not change, even after we become enlightened, when our mind is totally free from subtle obscurations and completes all the realizations. It is like that forever.

The I exists and the action of the I exists because the valid base exists. They exist in mere name, not from their own side. Even the valid base exists in mere name.

Saying the I exists "in mere name" does not mean that it does not actually exist. It *exists*, but the *way* of existing is unbelievably subtle. This is incredibly interesting. The way of existing is so subtle that, for our hallucinating mind, it is *like* it does not exist. In fact, for our hallucinating mind, what *exists*—the merely labeled I—seems to be nonexistent and what *doesn't exist*—the real I—we totally, totally believe in. When we check, when we search, when we meditate, using our inner science, we find that what really exists seems to be nonexistent to the hallucinated mind.

Our normal life is totally like a dream, like a hallucination, like an illusion, like a mirage. By thinking about what really exists, we can understand the hallucination. By considering what is the truth in life we can understand what is false in life. Otherwise we can know neither the full truth nor what is false.

To summarize, the valid base, the aggregates, is there. Because of that, the thought of I arises, the merely labeled I and the merely labeled action arise, depending on what the valid base does.

In the first moment the labeling thought merely imputes the I and the action. For instance, if the I is sitting—if sitting is the merely labeled action of the I—there is firstly the merely labeled I and then secondly the merely labeled action, "sitting."

Therefore, it is *so* subtle. How the I exists is extremely subtle; it is never the way we normally believe it to be from birth; from beginningless rebirths in fact. It is *never* the way that our mind projects it to be—truly existent. The I that exists is extremely subtle. It's *like* it doesn't exist compared to how it appears to our normal hallucinated mind.

That happens in the first moment. In the second moment, when it appears back it should appear back as merely labeled. It has just been merely labeled by our mind a moment ago so it should appear back to us like that. But for us that is not what happens. It only appears back to the buddhas as merely labeled, only to those beings who have no disturbing-thought obscurations, for whom there is no trace of negative imprints at all. Only the enlightened beings, the buddhas, apprehend it as merely labeled. Until that time, for us sentient beings, we have this hallucination of the truly existing appearance because the negative imprints of the disturbing-thought obscurations have not yet ceased.

There are sentient beings who are *arya* beings, who have the direct realization of emptiness only, shunyata. When their mind is in equipoise meditation they don't have the dualistic mind, the appearance of true existence. However, in the post-meditation break time, they have the hallucination. Even with bodhicitta and compassion, they still all have the appearance of true existence. For us, however, the moment after the mind merely imputes the I, it appears back as a real I, not as a merely imputed I. This is a *huge* hallucination. How does that hallucination happen?

Take color, for instance. We see light appearing from an object, such as black letters on white paper or a bunch of roses appearing as white and red. Or when we are driving and see a traffic light appearing as red, we stop. The red color appears to exist from there but actually it is our mind that has imputed that red. We don't see that this is so. Just as with the I, everything that appears to our senses appears in this way. There is this hallucination. This is exactly what the *Heart Sutra* refutes.

To understand how all phenomena appear like this, the I is a good example. The reason the merely labeled I appears as a real I is because of past ignorance holding the I as truly existent, while it is not, while it is totally empty of existing from its own side. That particular ignorance has left a negative imprint on the mind and that negative imprint projects. Firstly, depending on the base, the mind merely imputes the I, then in the next moment the negative imprint left by the past ignorance projects the real I. It projects it just as a film put into a movie projector is projected onto a screen. The real I has never existed in that way and it will never exist in that way.

And then, in the third moment, we believe that this I really exists as it appears. In Tibetan it is called *ti-mug ten-dzin ma-rig-pa*, the ignorance holding the I as truly existent. That concept, that this is real, is the root of samsara, the root of all the sufferings of samsara. It is where all the suffering of rebirth comes from, where all the suffering of sickness comes from, where all the suffering of old age comes from, where all the suffering of death comes from, where *all* the suffering of pain comes from.

If, for example, we don't want cancer, we have to realize emptiness and eliminate this gross wrong concept of the self-existent I. By eliminating it, none of the three poisonous minds of attachment, anger or ignorance or any of the other delusions can happen and we therefore cannot experience the oceans of the suffering of samsara.

Similarly, what is the root of all our depression? Some people get depressed when the sun sets, some at night, some in the morning, but always at a fixed time. For some it is dependent on the situation. Some people spend years and years suffering from depression. Where does it come from? It comes from this root, this wrong concept from where all the suffering of pain originates.

With respect to the suffering of change, all temporary samsaric pleasures—pleasures that neither last nor increase—arise because they are in the nature of suffering. This also comes from the same wrong concept.

These two types of suffering, of pain and of change, come from the third type of suffering, pervasive compounding suffering, the root of all these sufferings. For Buddhists, this is what we should be free from. This is what we should understand. This is the suffering we should generate the wish to be free from. The way we free ourselves is by actualizing the path, thereby achieving ultimate liberation.

The root of even that basic suffering is this wrong concept. All problems come from this: global problems, countries' problems, family problems, society's problems, the problems of individuals who live in a city or who live in the wild—even insects' problems and those of dinosaurs as well.

When we consider this belief in the real I, this thing that is the root of all our problems, it is very interesting. It is colorless and shapeless, without physical form. It is just a concept, just a way of thinking. This concept is the total opposite of the reality of how the I exists. It is the total opposite of how the aggregates exist. We have this wrong concept and then we believe in it. This is so subtle but *this* is where the whole of our suffering comes from.

How do we eliminate this? The essence of Buddhism is renunciation, bodhicitta and right view. So it is very important to study, understand and reflect and meditate on the right view in order to develop the ultimate wisdom realizing emptiness. By developing a direct perception of emptiness we are able to eliminate this disturbing thought-obscuration, this wrong concept, the seed of these wrong concepts and achieve nirvana, the sorrowless state, the blissful state of peace.

The Prasangika view of emptiness

What eliminates the root of ignorance is the right view according to the Prasangika, the most subtle of the four Buddhist philosophical schools: Sautrantika, Vaibhashika, Cittamatra and Madhyamaka, which has two sub-schools, Svatantrika and Prasangika.

Even though each school has an idea of ultimate reality, it is the Prasangika view that really cuts the root of the oceans of samsaric suffering: the suffering of pain, the suffering of change and pervasive compounding suffering. The only thing that can completely eliminate that ignorance is the Prasangika view of emptiness, emptiness-only, shunyata. To bring us to that understanding, the Buddha gave us the teachings on dependent arising, which have the power to lead us to the end of samsara.

Padmasambhava, Nagarjuna and Asanga as well as Lama Tsongkhapa— all of them—actualized the Prasangika view and were therefore able to give teachings from their experience and to guide us, helping us to be free from the oceans of samsaric suffering and bring us to full enlightenment. Whatever it is called by different people, whether it is called emptiness or not, it is this specific emptiness, the Prasangika view.

Our understanding of emptiness can only be considered correct if it helps us understand subtle dependent arising and does not contradict it. If it contradicts dependent arising—if, instead of supporting dependent arising, it leads us to the conclusion that there is no dependent arising, there is no existence—that means there is a mistake in our understanding.

Lama Tsongkhapa uses the example of a vase (vases and pillars are common examples in debating texts). He says when we check and see that there is no vase—that the top is not the vase, the neck is not the vase, the belly is not the vase, the bottom is not the vase—if we conclude that there is no vase at all, this view of emptiness does not help us see how the vase *does* exist. Unless our conclusion is an understanding of dependent arising—the truth for the all-obscuring mind, conventional truth—we are led into a sense that there is no vase, and that is nihilism.

That meditation leads to nihilism when we begin with the big mistake and leave out the object to be refuted. When we look for the vase that exists, from the very beginning we fail to touch the object of refutation, that which does not exist. What we are looking for is the general vase and in the end we conclude that there is no vase.

Many people believe that is the correct way of meditating on emptiness. There are debaters in the monastery—geshes even—who debate well but still think that this is the correct meditation to do, without touching the thing we have to realize as empty, without touching the *gag-cha* at all. This is what we are looking for.

Lama Tsongkhapa very clearly mentioned this in both the *Lamrim Chenmo* and the *Middle Length Lam-rim*. There are many pages emphasizing *gag-cha*, the object to be refuted, explaining it and clearly showing what we need to understand in order to realize emptiness.

If the previous meditation were correct, then why would we need to understand the four-point analysis?[20] The other meditation does not touch that at all, it does not even question it, and so what the meditator is looking for is incorrect. It might help some people initially, but finally it will prove to be incorrect. That is why the four-point analysis must come first.

Only if the meditation on emptiness supports the understanding of dependent arising and does not contradict it in any way can we say it is a correct meditation on emptiness. So, you can see, these two things are not separate. Dependent arising and emptiness are not two separate phenomena. In Tibetan, dependent arising is *ten-ching drel-war jung-wa* or *ten-jung*. *Ten*, "dependent," eliminates nihilism and *jung*, "arising," eliminates eternalism. That is the middle way, neither nihilism nor eternalism.

What is a dependent arising is empty of existing from its own side, being merely labeled by the mind. Nothing exists from its own side. And emptiness is a dependent arising. In that way dependent arising and emptiness are unified.

---

[20] Also known as the four vital points of analysis, this is one of the main techniques for meditating on emptiness.

4. The Need for Ethics and Refuge

WE HAVE MET THESE EIGHT FREEDOMS AND TEN RICHNESSES[21]

LAMA TSONGKHAPA MENTIONED,

> Because at this time we have received the eight freedoms and ten richnesses and are free from being hell beings, hungry ghosts, animals and so forth, we have the freedom to practice the Dharma.

At this time we have attained the perfect human rebirth with the eight freedoms and ten richnesses. The eight freedoms are:

1. The freedom of not being born as a hell being
2. The freedom of not being born as a hungry ghost
3. The freedom of not being born as an animal
4. The freedom of not being born as a long-life god
5. The freedom of not being born where no buddha has descended
6. The freedom of not being born as a barbarian
7. The freedom of not being born as a fool
8. The freedom of not being born as a heretic

The ten richnesses are:

1. Being born as a human being
2. Being born in a religious country
3. Being born with perfect organs

---

[21] See Rinpoche's *The Perfect Human Rebirth* for extensive teachings on this topic.

4. Being free of the five immediate negativities
5. Having devotion to the teachings
6. Being born when a buddha has descended
7. Being born when the teachings have been revealed
8. Being born when the complete teachings exist
9. Being born when the teachings are being followed
10. Having the necessary conditions to practice Dharma

Because we have been born as human beings rather than in the lower realms, as hell beings, hungry ghosts or animals, we have the freedom to practice Dharma.

We have not been born as long-life gods. They have awareness at the beginning and the end of their life but for its entire duration—which can last thousands or millions of human years—it's as if they're in a deep sleep. Because of that, these gods have no freedom to practice Dharma. We, however, have not been born as long-life gods and so we have that freedom.

We have not been born in a place where the buddha has not descended, where there's no chance to meet the Dharma. Since we have not been born in such a place, we have the freedom to practice Dharma.

We have also not been born as barbarians, living in an irreligious country, where there is no chance to practice the Dharma.

We are neither mutes nor fools. If we were, we would be unable to learn and practice the Dharma, but we are free from being born in that state, so we have freedom to practice Dharma.

Finally, we have not been born as heretics. Heretics have very closed minds. Without an open mind, there is no freedom to understand the inner science—knowing what is beneficial and what is harmful—no freedom to attain even temporal happiness, let alone ultimate happiness. Heretics believe there is no Buddha, Dharma or Sangha, no four noble truths. We are not heretics, nonbelievers, so we should feel happy that we have the freedom to practice Dharma.

It is unbelievable that we have all these eight freedoms, which are so precious. We should feel incredible happiness just thinking about it.

We also have the ten richnesses, the first of which is being human. In Tibetan, the normal definition of a human being is one who is able to communicate and understand. Having this richness means we have an incredible opportunity to practice Dharma. As I have already explained, nonhuman beings such as spirits or gods and demigods, as well as other lower realm beings whose suffering is unbelievable, have no freedom to practice Dharma. Even in the god realms, their lives are full of unbelievable distractions caused by attachment. Always chasing pleasure, they have no interest in the Dharma. Our life is not like that. Being born human, we have the richness to practice Dharma, and that is unbelievably precious.

We have the richness of being born in a religious country. That has two meanings. One is by place, which means in a religious center, such as where the Buddha achieved enlightenment. But I think the main thing is where there is the lineage of the vows of fully ordained monks and nuns. There are also the novice monk and nun lineages of thirty-six vows. Even if the *gelongma* lineage no longer exists, the other three lineages do.[22]

If we live where the lineage of the vows exists we can consider ourselves to be in the center of a religious country because those vow holders help us achieve liberation from samsaric suffering and achieve the blissful state of peace ourselves. It also means that there are the right conditions and freedom from obstacles that make it easier to attain enlightenment.

The next richness is having perfect organs, which also makes it much easier to practice Dharma. Then there is the richness of not falling into any of the five extreme actions: killing one's father, mother or an arhat, causing disunity among the Sangha or maliciously causing blood to flow from a buddha. We have not engaged in these heavy negative karmas, which result in having to experience rebirth in the hottest hell right after death. If we had done any of these actions we'd be disqualified from taking vows, but not having done them gives us the opportunity to practice Dharma.

We live in a place where there are the teachings. Traditional texts say Vinaya teachings, but it is more than that. In particular, it means where there are lam-rim teachings, the graduated path to enlightenment. The way that Lama Atisha presented the lam-rim is that all the teachings are set up to subdue the mind because, as I often mention, all our happiness and suffer-

---

[22] The Sangha consists of different levels of ordination: entering, *rabjung* (*pravrajya*) or *rabjungma* (*pravrajyi*), with eight vows; novice, *getsul* (*sramanera*) or *getsulma* (*sramaneri*), with thirty-six vows; and fully ordained, with 253 vows for monks and 364 vows for nuns. The tradition of fully ordained nuns has been lost in Tibet, where the only nuns' vows are the *rabjungma* and *getsulma*. At present, Western nuns in the Tibetan tradition wishing to take full ordination do so in other traditions, such as the Chinese or Vietnamese, but the International Congress on Buddhist Women's Role in the Sangha, supported by His Holiness the Dalai Lama, is investigating how full ordination in Tibetan Buddhism can be reinstated. See also *Mandala*, April 1988, "Focus on Full Ordination for Buddhist Women," at fpmt.org.

ing come from our mind. Therefore, to attain happiness we have to subdue the negative mind, our disturbing thoughts. That is what the lam-rim helps us do, leading us from the wrong thinking that causes suffering to the right thinking that causes happiness—every happiness up to enlightenment.

The next richness is having devotion to the lam-rim. This gives us an incredible opportunity to practice Dharma. The next is being alive at a time the Buddha has descended on earth. Because the Buddha descended we now have the teachings, the Dharma, that he left for us. Once, the Buddha was an ordinary person like us, with just as many problems, but then he was able to transform his mind, generating bodhicitta, letting go of the I and cherishing others. In that way he attained the complete Mahayana path and achieved enlightenment.

We have this opportunity because the Buddha generated great compassion for all sentient beings including us. For three countless great eons he collected the merits of wisdom—the cause of the dharmakaya, the holy mind of a buddha—and the merits of virtue—the cause of the rupakaya, the holy body of a buddha. He gave his cherished limbs and his life to sentient beings, not only to the tiger mother in Nepal,[23] but to numberless other sentient beings, practicing charity, morality, patience, enthusiastic perseverance, concentration and wisdom—the six perfections and the ten perfections. Then he achieved the purification of all obscurations and completion all realizations and became a buddha. He did this for us.

And then, for us, the Buddha revealed the 84,000 teachings, the Hinayana and the Mahayana, and, of the Mahayana, the Mahayana sutra and the Mahayana tantra, the different levels of teachings that are needed as our mind develops more and more. He left the teachings for all sentient beings, and that includes us.

That means we must learn and practice as much as we possibly can in order to not harm others and ourselves but to benefit ourselves and others, other sentient beings who are numberless, who want happiness and who do not want suffering, like ourselves.

The way to do that is not by following the ways of the worldly beings but through following what the Omniscient One taught. He has shown us the path, what is right and what is wrong in life. That is the real education, the

---

[23] Rinpoche is referring to the famous Jataka tale of the Buddha, who, in a life when he was a bodhisattva prince, came across a starving tigress and her dying cubs and sacrificed his body so that she and her cubs could live.

whole thing condensed into compassion and wisdom. The way the lam-rim is set up serves the mind in this way, so we definitely need to study and practice the lam-rim.

The next richness is that, not only has the Buddha descended and revealed the teachings, but that the complete teachings still exist. We don't live in a time after the teachings have finished. We are here now, just before the end of the teachings, like the sun just before it sets. Because of that, we have this incredible opportunity to learn and practice Dharma and to actualize realizations.

Finally, from our side, we follow the teachings with an open mind; gurus such as His Holiness the Dalai Lama, having great compassion, reveal the Dharma to us; and we have benefactors who support our study and practice. This gives us such an unbelievable, incredible opportunity to enjoy the Dharma, to learn and practice the Dharma.

The perfect human rebirth is so rare and so fragile

These eight freedoms and ten richnesses we have give us the opportunity to develop our mind from where we are now, taking us step by step on the path all the way to enlightenment. The first step is to develop guru devotion, the root of the whole path to enlightenment, which leads to the other practices that comprise the *graduated path of the lower capable being*.

By not creating negative karma and by purifying that which has already been created, we purify the causes of the lower realms. Then, by practicing morality on the basis of taking refuge and protecting our karma, we are reborn in the upper realms as a human or god.

Then we can meet the Dharma again, practice it and actualize the path. By actualizing the practice of the *graduated path of the middle capable being* we are able to be free from the oceans of samsaric suffering and achieve nirvana, the blissful state of peace for ourselves.

We can even practice the Mahayana, where we can become free from even lower nirvana, peace, and achieve the full state of the omniscient mind for sentient beings. This is the *graduated path of the higher capable being*, where the focus is actualizing bodhicitta, the mind that wishes to attain enlightenment in order to free the numberless sentient beings from the oceans of samsaric suffering and bring them to peerless happiness, the full state of the omniscient mind. We can then free numberless hell beings, numberless hungry ghosts, numberless animals, numberless human beings, numberless gods, numberless demigods and numberless intermediate state beings.

Therefore, this perfect human body we have achieved is so precious, more precious than a wish-granting jewel. It requires an incredible amount of merit to be able to find a wish-granting jewel, which is much more precious than diamonds, sapphires or gold. If we ever found one, whatever we wished for in this life—material needs, comfort, all the helicopters, Rolls Royces, elephants or diamond palaces we could ever want—would be effortlessly obtained.

However, with a wish-granting jewel alone we cannot purify past negative karma and we cannot be assured of a higher rebirth as a god or human being, because a human rebirth comes only from pure morality—not just morality but morality kept purely. Even the most miserable human existence, such as a porter on an Indian train, doesn't come from broken morality but from pure morality. Therefore, a human body is extremely rare and a perfect human rebirth is even more rare. It's like a dream, like some impossible thing has somehow happened. It's inexpressible.

With a wish-granting jewel we cannot get a higher rebirth but, by taking refuge and practicing morality using this perfect human body we now have, we can. Then, by practicing the higher training of morality, the higher training of concentration and the higher training of wisdom, we can free ourselves from the oceans of samsaric suffering and attain nirvana, the blissful state of peace.

We have already received this perfect human rebirth, so we can generate compassion for all sentient beings, attain bodhicitta and go on to achieve full enlightenment. Therefore this precious human body is much, much more precious than a wish-granting jewel or a whole sky filled with wish-granting jewels. Even if we owned that amount, its value would be nothing by comparison; it could meet only the material needs of this life. All those wish-granting jewels could not bring us all the different levels of happiness up to enlightenment, but this perfect human rebirth can.

For example, Milarepa didn't have even one rupee, even one dollar. He ate nothing but nettles. One day, when a thief came to rob him, Milarepa invited him to eat but there were only nettles. The thief asked for some chili to spice up the nettles, so Milarepa put in some more nettles and said, "This is the chili." Then the thief wanted some salt, so Milarepa added more nettles and said, "And this is the salt." He had nothing else. Before he met his guru Marpa he had practiced black magic and killed many people and animals by making a house collapse on them. However, because he had received a perfect human rebirth he was able to transform his mind and attain enlightenment in that very lifetime.

If Milarepa could do that after killing so many living beings, we too should be able to achieve lam-rim realizations. In his *Hymns of Experience*, Lama Tsongkhapa said,

> This life of leisure is even more precious than a wish-granting
> jewel.
> Only this once have I found such an existence,
> Which is so hard to find and yet, like a flash of lightning, can so
> easily vanish.[24]

This precious human life is not only much more precious than skies of wish-granting jewels but it can also end at any moment. Therefore we must not waste it by using it to create negative karma, thus ensuring ourselves of rebirth in the lower realms.

Whatever we do must be a Dharma action. That does not mean we should simply close our eyes and sit cross-legged all the time, never eating or sleeping. It means whatever we do, whether it is Dharma practice or any other action—eating, walking, sitting, sleeping or working at our job—we must make everything as virtuous as possible. In that way everything we do becomes a Dharma action.

So far we have not died. We have been most fortunate to be able to stay alive each day, each hour, each minute, each second. We are extremely fortunate to have obtained a perfect human rebirth, to have met the Buddha's teachings, the Dharma, and to be learning and trying to understand them. These teachings lead us to free ourselves from the oceans of samsaric suffering. They show us the path and prepare our mind so that even if we don't have realizations in this life, by learning and meditating, in future lives we will quickly gain a good understanding of the Dharma and attain realizations and then, sooner or later, achieve enlightenment.

This incredibly precious human body we have does not last. It can end at any time. We can't say we are assured of this body lasting for a hundred years, that during that period death won't happen. We can't even say that

---

[24] V. 13. (In the bibliography as *Songs of Spiritual Experience*.)

we are assured of having this body for fifty years or that we will still have it in another year. We can't say, "Tomorrow I won't die." We can't even sign a guarantee that we won't die today.

We normally don't think like this. We think that we will always be alive; we have a kind of belief in permanence. We really believe that we will live for a long time. Five minutes before somebody dies in a car crash or has a heart attack he has the concept that he is going to live for a long time. We all live with this concept of permanence.

At this moment there are numberless people dying, even while they are still in their mother's womb. There are those who have just been born who are dying and those dying in their early childhood, as well as people of all ages—teenagers, adults, old people—who are dying at this very moment. There are people dying in so many ways: in accidents, in natural disasters, through disease and so forth.

There are many people who have already died today even without having cancer. Usually it's only when somebody has cancer that we think that because of the disease that that person is dying. We consider those without terminal diseases to not be dying, but, in reality, we are the same, those of us with cancer and those of us without. There are many healthy people who will die before those who have cancer.

I heard that the parents of one of the older FPMT students, Tubten Pende, a former Nalanda monk, were talking in their kitchen and, while they were talking, Pende's father turned his head a little to look somewhere and just then, while he was looking away, still talking, his wife suddenly died, collapsed on the floor.

I heard about another student who was walking along a road one day, talking, talking, talking, talking, talking, when she suddenly collapsed and died.

We cannot guarantee we will live much longer at all. Death can happen at any time. Even now, being born in the upper realms as human beings, it is as if we are prisoners who have been allowed outside for a short time— an hour or something—and very soon we will have to return home to the lower realms. An hour's respite and then we have to go back inside again to live in the prison we came from. Our permanent residence is the lower realms. That is where we came from.

Our life is getting shorter, day by day, hour by hour, minute by minute, second by second. We have a certain number of breaths from now until death, so the number of remaining breaths is constantly decreasing. With every in-breath we take, every out-breath we make, our life becomes that much shorter. In reality, we are constantly dying.

When we die, our body stops but our mind continues. There is always the continuation of consciousness, migrating between the various realms. There are only two ways our consciousness can go at death: with nonvirtue, to the lower realms, or with virtue, to the upper realms.

Taking refuge and protecting our karma is what saves us from rebirth in the lower realms. This is the foundation of all realizations, the basis of all happiness up to enlightenment. For that reason we take refuge in the Buddha, Dharma and Sangha.

Believer or nonbeliever, we must still lead an ethical life

The very essence is that we all want happiness and we don't want suffering. Therefore, whatever we do, whether or not we believe in karma, reincarnation and so forth, we must still practice an ethical life. No matter what feelings we have about karma, not thinking there is a need for ethics will naturally lead to unethical conduct and that will lead to suffering and could even end up with us in prison. This has nothing to do with our philosophies about karma or future lives but with our conduct in this life. Of course, if we really like being in prison—if that's what we enjoy the most—then that's OK!

As I have mentioned, even nonbelievers need to practice patience and compassion. Similarly, nonbelievers also need to practice ethics, not harming others. That is the very basic practice. Even in this life, without considering the results that will happen in future lives, if we harm others we will have to face terrible consequences, such as getting a bad name, being treated badly by others, being prosecuted and jailed and many other negative things. We see this all the time with people who have so much wealth— billionaires and zillionaires whose lies are exposed and end up in prison, despite their great wealth.

All of us, believers or nonbelievers, need to practice an ethical life, not harming others: not killing, not lying, not stealing and so forth. That is the basis. In that way, we don't suffer and others don't suffer. Not being harmed by others, we have happiness and then, in turn, we can benefit others more and more. As a result, we become happier and happier and so too do others. We can bring great happiness to those around us, to our family, our country and the world.

We will be able to do all that, even without believing in karma and reincarnation. People who do not necessarily have such beliefs but have a very good heart bring much happiness to others and, because of that, gain everybody's respect. In that way they can benefit others more and bring more happiness to themselves, their families and the world.

If ethics is important for the happiness of just this life, it becomes a much more important issue when we consider more than one life. The conclusion is this. The suffering we experience in this life might look like it comes from others, from external sources, but it does not; it comes from our own mind. It is the result of our own past karma, the intention to harm others, which left a negative imprint on the continuity of our consciousness. We then experience the result in this life.

Similarly, all the good things we experience in this life are due to our past good intentions, our good karma, the help we have given others, which left a positive imprint on the continuity of our consciousness, resulting in our experience of happiness, joy and success in our wishes.

Others are not the main cause, they are just a condition; therefore there is nothing to blame others for. It has all come from our mind, from our past lives. Because we want to be successful in this life, we can see that what we need to do is not harm others. Whether or not we believe in karma and reincarnation, we need to not harm others and to bring them happiness, to use our life to fulfill their wishes. We must bring happiness to everyone—people, animals, even insects, whatever size they are. Because it is a dependent arising, if we do that, it will become the cause of our own success and happiness—using our life to bring happiness to others, to making others' wishes succeed, is the best cause.

Karma is definite. If we create the cause we will definitely experience the result, happiness. The result of nonvirtue is suffering; the result of virtue is happiness. And karma is expandable. One karmic action results in many lifetimes of results. From one act of good karma we can experience many lifetimes' happiness. To be able to fulfill somebody's wishes of happiness, which is *one time*, we can then experience five hundred or a thousand lifetimes of happiness and success for ourselves—from just one good karmic act. You should understand that and keep it in mind.

Conversely, if we harm somebody once, cheating or harming them, we experience the suffering results for five hundred or a thousand lifetimes, depending on how harmful the action is. In his *Four Hundred Verses*, the Nalanda pandit Aryadeva said that if we cheat one sentient being we will be cheated by others for a thousand lifetimes. If we kill an insect with a negative mind then, because karma is expandable, the result will be to be killed for five hundred lifetimes. Keeping this in the mind, we should dare not give even a small harm, even once, to anybody.

This is the way to make our wishes, our life, successful. Without understanding Dharma, without understanding karma, the rest of the world believes something else. They think the cause is totally something else, but that doesn't work because what they think of as a main cause is only a condition. Dharma practice is the main cause.

I mentioned before how in America it is common to have a gun and how even small children sometimes kill many people. If the gun victims had met the Buddhadharma, if they had purified—especially with the four opponent powers—if they had accepted karma and reincarnation and because of that purified the negative karma beforehand, they wouldn't have had to experience being killed like that. Similarly, if the killer could have purified his past lives' negative karma of killing, he wouldn't have had to kill those people. But neither the victims nor the killer had met the Dharma and purified their negative karma. The karma for all of them becomes very powerful to have this experience at this time and so it happens, where one person kills and others are killed.

Therefore, in our life, whether we believe in karma, reincarnation and so forth, we need to help others as much as possible. As my guru, Kyabje Serkong Tsenshab Rinpoche, says, we need to try to help even an insect that is suffering from having fallen into water by taking it out and freeing it. And if two insects are fighting, killing each other, we need to separate them. Even if we just offer to carry an older person's heavy luggage or offer somebody a seat on the bus or train, even if it is just a small benefit in our everyday life, we should do whatever we can to help free others from suffering, to benefit them.

Once we have an understanding of the Dharma, especially the lam-rim, we will have many skillful ways to help those with psychological problems. If we see somebody with suicidal thoughts, we will have the tools to talk to her and bring her around from killing herself and thus cause her to have a long life. Normally, we liberate lots of animals that are going to be killed and, saving them in that way we cause them to have a long life. But there are many human beings who want to kill themselves, so by giving them advice and guiding them, doing whatever we can do, we give them a long life. That creates the karma for us to live long ourselves, in this and future lives, and for all our wishes to succeed. That happens, and we are able to help others more and more.

To practice Dharma, the *real* thing is to serve others, to benefit others. Sentient beings are the objects most cherished by the buddhas. Not only Guru Shakyamuni Buddha, but the numberless buddhas and bodhisattvas also cherish them. This tiny ant, this mosquito, this human—whether a rich man or a beggar—is the object most cherished by the numberless buddhas and bodhisattvas.

In whatever way we can care for them, through our education, our wealth or whatever, that is the best offering to the numberless bodhisattvas and the numberless buddhas. That is really the best service we can offer to the bodhisattvas and buddhas. That is the best Dharma.

What is life? However many years, months, days and hours we have left, we must make the most of it. We must do the best. For whom? For others. And then the best for us just naturally happens.

THE NEED FOR REFUGE IN OUR LIFE

Pervasive compounding suffering, the third kind of suffering, gives rise to the other two kinds of suffering: the suffering of pain and the suffering of change. Because our aggregates are under the control of karma and delusion, they are pervaded by suffering, which is why this type of suffering is called pervasive.

When we pinch our skin, it hurts. We feel pain because our aggregates are pervaded by suffering. That itself is an explanation about reincarnation, about the continuity of the consciousness from life to life. That is why it is suffering. If this life were the first one, why should there be suffering? What is the cause of that first moment of suffering? It doesn't make any sense.

However, our aggregates are contaminated by the seed of disturbing thoughts, and because of that they are pervaded by suffering. And that is *compounding* suffering because there is the continuation of consciousness from life to life. Our consciousness carries negative imprints from past lives. That compounds this life's and future lives' suffering.

From the fundamental ignorance of reality arises the ignorance of not knowing karma, not knowing Dharma, what is right and wrong. And then, from that, attachment and anger arise toward desirable and dislikeable objects respectively. That itself is suffering but, motivated by that, we create karma. Then that karma leaves negative imprints on our mind and they produce future lives' rebirth and suffering. Therefore, these aggregates not only compound this life's suffering but future lives' suffering as well. This is how pervasive compounding suffering is the foundation of the two other sufferings.

That is why taking refuge in the Buddha, Dharma and Sangha is vital. The purpose of taking refuge is to be free from the third level of suffering, pervasive compounding suffering. If we can be free from this we will never ever have to experience the other two sufferings again. We are totally liberated, forever—not just for a few days, a few months, a few years, then we have to come back again. It's not like we have a brief holiday from suffering and then have to return to it again.

If we have refuge in our heart, that is the basis for the various sets of vows we can take: the *pratimoksha* vows, the bodhisattva vows and the tantric vows. These are the means that can lead us to not just attaining liberation but attaining enlightenment for sentient beings, to free them from the oceans of samsaric suffering and to bring them to enlightenment. Becoming a bodhisattva and achieving enlightenment are based on the three sets of vows.

With refuge in our mind we are no longer outer beings but inner beings. With refuge in our mind, all the negative karma we have collected in the past from beginningless rebirths becomes purified and we immediately collect skies of extensive merit any time we want. Every time we have the opportunity, every day, we can do this.

By taking refuge in Buddha, Dharma and Sangha we do not receive harm from either human beings or nonhuman beings—spirits and so forth. All our wishes are successful no matter what they are: our own freedom from samsara or enlightenment for the sake of all sentient beings. We will not be reborn in the lower realms and we will quickly become enlightened, achieving the omniscient mind.

We need all three objects of refuge: Buddha, Dharma and Sangha. To be free from the lower realms we need just one object of refuge, for example, we can take refuge in the Buddha alone or simply chant mantras, recite holy names or remember Dharma texts such as the *Heart Sutra*. If we have devotion for even one monk or nun and remember that person when we're dying or if we take refuge in the Buddha at the time of death, we will be saved from rebirth in the lower realms. But to be free from pervasive compounding suffering, to be free from samsara completely, we need all three.

The Dharma is the actual refuge, the medicine that cures our samsaric suffering. The Buddha, the founder of the refuge, is like the doctor who gives the medicine and the Sangha, who help us actualize the Dharma, are like the nurses who help us take what the doctor has prescribed, giving us the medicine and helping in all those things. The Sangha lead us by example, showing us how to practice Dharma.

Relying on all three, Buddha, Dharma and Sangha, is a hundred thousand times more effectual than relying on external doctors, medicines and nurses. They might be able to cure physical illness, but, without eliminating karma and delusion, that can only be temporary. That is why taking refuge in Buddha, Dharma and Sangha is vital.

We take refuge in the Buddha by remembering the meaning of "buddha," one who has totally ceased all obscurations and completed all realizations. The qualities of a buddha are unbelievable. A buddha can see all past, present and future phenomena directly at the same time. By taking refuge in the historical Buddha we are taking refuge in all the buddhas, and they all know we have taken refuge in them. Every one of the numberless buddhas has that quality—*sang-gyä*—so we can be assured that we will receive guidance from them. That is a reason for great joy.

Taking refuge in the Dharma means taking refuge in both the absolute Dharma and the conventional Dharma. The absolute Dharma is both the cessation of all obscurations—the cessation of all suffering—and the true path that leads to that cessation, the absolute wisdom directly perceiving emptiness. That is the medicine that eliminates the cause of suffering, karma and delusion, and allows us to achieve nirvana and enlightenment. Conventional Dharma is the Tripitaka—the three divisions of the Buddha's teachings: the Vinaya, the Sutra, and the philosophical texts, the Abhidharma. These are condensed into the lam-rim texts.

Again, when we take refuge in the Sangha we do so in the absolute Sangha and the conventional Sangha. The absolute Sangha is anybody, lay or ordained, male or female, who has the wisdom directly perceiving emptiness, realization of the absolute Dharma. The conventional Sangha refers to four fully ordained monks or nuns who are living purely in the vows.

Very often when a lama gives refuge, the disciples can also choose to take lay vows. If you can, it is very good to do this. There are five lay vows:

- abstaining from killing
- abstaining from sexual misconduct

- ▸ abstaining from stealing
- ▸ abstaining from telling lies
- ▸ abstaining from taking alcohol

Generally, you are given the choice of taking all five or some or none when you take refuge. The Buddha is so kind, so compassionate, giving us incredible freedom like this.

You can think of sexual misconduct as having sex with a person who doesn't belong to you, who is committed to somebody else. However, Lama Atisha is stricter than that. He said that even having sex with your own wife or husband in the daytime is also regarded as sexual misconduct.

From a long time ago in Kopan, we also included taking recreational drugs in the vow of abstaining from alcohol, because they make you kind of hallucinated, crazy, and cause you to harm yourself and others. But the texts mainly refer to alcohol. Abstaining from alcohol is important. It creates so many problems within the family, causing whole families to break up and forcing the drinkers onto the streets, turning them into beggars. This seems to happen at lot in the West, and with alcohol there are many other dangers as well. It is easy to see how drinking alcohol interferes with Dharma development, but abstaining from it is important for normal life as well.

When we take these five lay vows we do so for more than our own temporary happiness. The main purpose is to be free from the oceans of samsaric suffering and, not only that, to achieve enlightenment for sentient beings, to free them from the oceans of samsaric suffering. We take the vows to free all sentient beings from cancer, from AIDS, from all sickness, and from all the sufferings of rebirth, old age and death. We take the vows so that all sentient beings can be free from the suffering of change and from pervasive compounding suffering. We take vows to bring every sentient being to full enlightenment by becoming enlightened ourselves. Taking the five lay vows is not just a small thing.

The importance of the Namgyälma mantra

When I give refuge and lay vows, I often give the students a Namgyälma mantra amulet to wear, as well as a blessing string and a picture of the bodhisattva Ksitigarbha. These things are incredible because just having them constantly purifies negative karma.

Putting the Namgyälma mantra up somewhere in your house or flat brings protection and makes it a holy place. Then, whatever sentient beings are inside—dogs, cats, mosquitoes etc.—always have their negative karma and defilements purified and they obtain a higher rebirth. If even the shadow of the house touches any being, like insects or people, their negative karma is purified and they get a higher rebirth. If the Namgyälma mantra is on top of a mountain, the whole mountain become holy and the negative karma of any being who climbs or touches the mountain is purified and they obtain a higher rebirth.

I often tell people in the West that having a Namgyälma mantra card in the car is vital, because not only the sentient beings inside but also all beings who touch the car have their negative karma purified and they obtain a higher rebirth. When you drive, many insects and ants are killed, especially at nighttime when so many insects fly into your windscreen or are crushed under the wheels of the car. With a Namgyälma mantra inside [or a decal on the window], the negative karma of all those small insects is purified. Of course, that doesn't mean you should drive over rabbits or dogs or children! As a policeman drags you to prison you can't really tell him you did it because you have a mantra in the car! I suspect that would be inadmissible in a court case.

One of the most important things to do when a person or animal dies is to put the Namgyälma mantra on the body for little while. Then, definitely, a hundred percent, their consciousness will not go to the lower realms but will have a higher rebirth instead. This is very important to keep in mind when a person or animal dies. Even when you yourself die, you can ask your friends to do that. That is very beneficial.

At the Aptos house in America[25] we have a big, well-decorated board with different size mantras carved on it that we place in the ocean. We put a tent on the beach and have lunch or tea while the board is in the water. In that way we bless the Pacific Ocean. When we place it in the ocean and recite OM MANI PADME HUM it not only blesses the water but it purifies all the numberless sentient beings living in the water, the ones as large as a mountain, like the whales, and the ones so small that you can only see them through a microscope. Likewise, all the people playing in the waves, riding surfboards, get the same benefit. All their negative karma and defilements are purified and they get a higher rebirth and the possibility to meet the Dharma again and, because of that, to develop their minds and achieve

---

[25] Lama Zopa's residence in California, near Santa Cruz.

enlightenment. Before we only did this occasionally but now we try to do it at least once a week.

We also liberate fish that are caught for supermarkets. The people at the Aptos house and in Washington[26] do that quite often. They have probably liberated over a thousand already. We also buy worms that are sold live as bait for fishermen and liberate them. There are several hundred in one container, waiting for a hook to be pushed through them and to be then thrown in the water to catch the fish. So in Washington and Aptos every two weeks we buy several containers and take them around the stupa. We don't have a large stupa in Washington yet so we take them around the small stupas and relics and statues. There are many pictures of deities, statues and *tsa-tsas*. In Aptos we have a stupa behind the house, so we take them around that and recite mantras, as I have advised.

After I saw two ants' nests near the house in Washington we made charity to them using a text I have, and we also did *sur* practice for them every night. I recited the Namgyälma and many other mantras and sprinkled a little bit of almost-dry tsampa powder over the ants' nests and they came to eat it. In that way we made charity to the ants.

We found only two nests while I was there, but after I left, Venerable Tharchin from Nalanda Monastery in France found seven besides mine. He was studying philosophy but had a lot of *lung*, wind disease, so he went to Washington to make many water, light and flower offerings. I told him to recite mantras and bless the tsampa and put it on the nests. He does this every week. Even in such small ways we try to help sentient beings as much as we can. This is not only to fill their stomachs but also to purify their minds. That is the whole point, and it gives them the possibility of meeting the Dharma in future lives.

It's very interesting about ants. I have found that if we put honey or sugar down especially for them, which they would normally eat, if the karma is not there, they don't come. Otherwise they come into the kitchen and get involved in taking honey and many other things. But if we actually give it to them, they don't come. I think that is because we don't have the fortune, the good karma, for them to take it.

As I mentioned, besides the Namgyälma mantra, I often give students a blessing string. This is not just a Tibetan custom. Many mantras and prayers

---

[26] This is Buddha Amitabha Pure Land in Washington State, where Rinpoche has a retreat house.

have been recited and blown on it to purify the wearers' obscurations and for them not to be reborn in the lower realms. The mantra used is unbelievably powerful. Touching the body, the string purifies our negative karma and obscurations, decreasing problems we might otherwise have to face, so in that way it becomes a great protection. But it is also there to remind us to have a good heart, to benefit other sentient beings.

Finally, there is the picture of the bodhisattva Ksitigarbha. Ksitigarbha is in the *Guru Puja* merit field but he is not as popular in Tibet as in China, where he is considered very important for success in business and for healing. There is a one-volume text where the Buddha explained the unbelievable qualities of Ksitigarbha. Praying to him whenever you make offerings is a hundred million times more powerful for success than praying to other bodhisattvas.

5. The Room Before It Is Named

THINGS APPEAR AS truly existent when we fail to analyze them, but when we do analyze them we can see that everything is created by our mind. There is nobody else who has come and created our problems for us—"I'm creating your problems"—they are all created by our mind. We are the creator. That is why in his teachings the Buddha said,

> You are your own enemy
> And you are your own guide.
> You are the creator of your own suffering
> And you are the creator of your own happiness.

As I have mentioned, we are the creator of our day-to-day life's problems, hour by hour, minute by minute, second by second, and we are also the creator of our day-to-day life's happiness, hour by hour, minute by minute, second by second.

We need to go beyond this life, however, to past and future lives. We have been born as a human being this time but we are also the creator of all our past and future states, whether as a hell being or a god or whatever. Just as we are the creator of our own samsara, we are also the creator of our own nirvana—the blissful state of peace for ourselves, freedom from the oceans of samsaric suffering—and our own ultimate happiness, the total elimination of all obscurations and the completion of all realizations, the peerless happiness of enlightenment.

Everything depends on our mind. Everything, whatever we want, is in our hands. If we don't want nirvana, if we want samsara, it's in our hands.

If we don't want enlightenment, if we want hell, it's in our hands. If we want happiness instead of problems, it's in our hands; it's all up to us. It depends on how we use our mind. With our body and speech we do actions that lead to happiness or problems, but it all depends on the creator, our own mind.

Thinking in the correct way brings happiness; thinking in the incorrect way brings suffering. Thinking in a healthy, virtuous way brings a healthy life. We want others' help; we do not want harm from them. Similarly, numberless others want our help and do not want to be harmed by us. We are one; others are numberless. Whether we help or harm them is up to us, so we are responsible for their happiness or suffering.

Every day, every hour, every minute, we have total responsibility for all living beings. Not only human beings but also nonhuman beings: hell beings, hungry ghosts, animals, insects, gods, demigods—all living beings, all sentient beings, are our responsibility. It is like that in reality. We are not only responsible for the happiness of our family, our parents, our spouse and our children, we are responsible for *all* living beings.

In that way, our life is not meaningless, not at all. It is not at all hopeless. That is totally wrong. If we think like that, intellectually we may know the Dharma but we are not practicing, we are not thinking, we are not using the Dharma for our mind. Were we to understand the Dharma and practice it we would know that life is neither hopeless nor meaningless.

Our life is so important, so precious. We have the responsibility of freeing the numberless beings from the oceans of samsaric suffering: not only the suffering of pain but also the suffering of change.

Dharma happiness lasts, it increases. It is something we can complete when we achieve enlightenment. That is the big difference; that is why it is worthwhile dedicating our life to it. We have already experienced every samsaric pleasure numberless times. What other people are experiencing now, including the worldly gods and other humans, we have experienced numberless times from beginningless rebirths. This includes all the suffering experienced by other beings. There is no new samsaric happiness left to experience and no new suffering. As long as we are in samsara, it is always like that. It is only because you and I have neither an omniscient mind nor even ordinary clairvoyance and are unable to remember past lives that we cannot see this.

THE ROOM BEFORE IT IS NAMED

In the *Vajra Cutter Sutra* the Buddha explained we should look at causative phenomena as like a star or a visual aberration.[27] The example often given is that of hairs appearing to float in front of the eyes or dropping into our food where there are no hairs. It can also happen that we seem to see an animal running where there is no animal, or we see worms that aren't there. These are temporary defects in our vision. Sometimes it seems to happen more to me, sometimes less. I can't say why.

The Buddha explained we should look at all causative phenomena in this way, like a hallucination, but especially any object of our attachment or aversion, such as our own body, our friends, our possessions and other desirable and undesirable objects.

Defective view means we ordinary people see things that don't exist and don't see things that do exist. There is ultimate reality, emptiness. It exists—there *is* such a thing—but for ordinary people like me, it is like it does not exist. On the other hand, while what is true seems not to exist to us, the hallucination, what is false, seems to exist. Here "false" means the projection of our hallucinated mind, our ignorance that holds the I, the aggregates and so forth as truly existing from their own side or existing by themselves.

It is not like that at all. It has never been like that at all from the beginning, even for one second. It has never been as it appears to us, as we believe. Reality means how things exist. They exist because they are empty; because they are emptiness only, *tong-pa-nyi* in Tibetan or *shunyata* in Sanskrit. The *nyi*, the "only" of the term, makes it clear, not just "*tong-pa*" but *tong-pa-nyi*.

Because things are *tong-pa-nyi*, because their nature is emptiness, they exist. That is *why* they exist. That is why they exist, why you exist, why we exist, why everything exists. That is why there is birth, existence, cessation, why all actions happen. The objects exist in mere name, the actions exist in mere name and the effects exist in mere name.

It is this ignorance, this projection of our hallucinated mind, that fails to see this but creates the real I, the real action and the real object. All the six senses' objects—forms, sounds, smells, tastes, tangibles and mental objects—are projected as real; they have the appearance of being real to our hallucinated mind.

This is how they appear to us one hundred percent and we totally accept

---

[27] Tib: *rab-rib*. Visual aberration or defective view. See page 77.

this. We don't doubt it at all. We believe that all these things are one hundred percent real.

This is the foundation of our suffering. This concept, this ignorance, is the biggest problem in our life. All other problems are built on that foundation. Attachment arises for the real desirable object, because it not only appears to us as real but after appearing that way we believe it to be real, that this is the truth. Anger arises toward the real undesirable object. It appears to us as a real undesirable object, a real dislikeable object, then on the basis of that appearance we believe it to be real. And ignorance arises toward real indifferent objects. In that way, all our problems build from that foundation.

For ordinary people like us, everything that is false in life appears true. Whether something exists or is a fantasy, we believe it to be one hundred percent true. On the other hand, for our mind, for us, ultimate reality, emptiness only, shunyata, does not exist at all.

It is like stars in the daytime. Because the sun is too bright, even though the stars are there, we cannot see them. In reality, nothing has real, true existence from its own side. The I, action, object—nothing is real from its own side. It has never been real. Right from the beginning, from beginningless rebirths, it has never happened that anything has ever come into existence from its own side, for even a second.

Maybe I should give a few examples. Say, we want to rent a house. When a house is built there are many empty rooms. As we are shown about the house by the owner he names the rooms, "This is the bedroom. This is the kitchen. This is the office." Like that, we learn the names of the different rooms.

Before the name was given, we have the appearance of an empty room but after the owner has given it a name, such as "office," we then have the appearance of an office. Then later we move stuff in, like a desk and a computer, whatever we need to make that room into an office. That doesn't mean we can call any place we have our computer, such as outside or in an airplane, our office. But it is like that with this room we call the office and it is the same with the kitchen, the bathroom and so forth.

First the name is given and then, immediately after that, we have the appearance of the office or the kitchen. Being introduced to each room by the house's owner, we are "taught" the names of the rooms and the rooms appear to us as just that and we believe in that appearance.

It should appear to us as merely labeled by the mind, which is exactly what has just happened—the empty room was labeled by the mind. Now the big question is this: why doesn't the room appear like that? We don't remember, or we don't know, that it was merely labeled by the other person's mind and then our mind accepted the way it was labeled.

When it appears it should appear as merely labeled by our mind. That is the correct view, but that is not how it appears to our mind. It appears to be *not* merely labeled by our mind; it appears as a real one, existing from its own side, as a real office, a real bedroom, a real kitchen, a real toilet— each room existing from its own side, not merely labeled by our mind. Even though our mind, or the other person's mind, merely labeled that empty room right now, we do not remember.

That is totally, completely the wrong view; it is the opposite of reality. Appearing as merely labeled by mind, *that* is correct. That is according to reality. But, what appears to us is totally the opposite of reality, of how things actually exist. It is totally false. In our life there is what is true and what is false, and that is false.

That wrong view is the basis for all the other delusions: for ignorance, attachment and anger, for the six root delusions and the twenty secondary delusions[28] and then all the 84,000 delusions that are branches of ignorance, attachment and anger. Those wrong concepts are the basis for all the karmic actions we create and they in turn create samsaric suffering. That is how it works. We continuously create the oceans of samsaric suffering through this wrong way of thinking, this wrong belief.

Illusioned by the magician, ignorance

What appears to a buddha? A buddha has totally ceased all obscurations, both the disturbing-thought obscurations and the seeds of those, the subtle obscurations to knowledge. Even the trace of ignorance, the negative imprint left by ignorance, has been totally abandoned, totally ceased. So what appears to a buddha? A buddha has no projections of the hallucination of true existence at all but still sees what we, the six realm sentient beings, see. A buddha sees mere existence, merely labeled by mind.

When arya Sangha—arhats or arya bodhisattvas—are not in equipoise meditation directly perceiving emptiness only, when they are in post-

---

[28] Buddhist philosophy lists three main causes of suffering: the three poisons of ignorance, attachment and anger. The six root delusions consist of those three plus pride, doubt and deluded views, and, from these six, the twenty secondary delusions, such as envy, laziness, dullness and so forth, arise. See *The Mind and Its Functions*, pp. 137–62.

meditation break-time, they have the hallucination of truly existent appearance. Their bodhicitta has this hallucination; their compassion has this hallucination, *but*, unlike us, they do not believe it. Unlike us, they do not have the belief that the hallucination is real.

It is like having crossed a hot, sunny desert and looking back to see a mirage—the appearance of water. Because we have just come from there we know that, although the rays of the sun reflect off the sand to give the appearance of water, there is no water there at all.

Or it is like when we are dreaming and we are able to recognize the dream as a dream while it is happening. There is the appearance but no belief that the dream is real. There might be a sharp object in our dream but we are not afraid because we know it cannot hurt us and so we touch it. Of course it doesn't hurt; it's just a dream.

Usually we don't have that sort of dream and while we are dreaming we think that whatever we are dreaming about is real from its own side. This is not how arhats and arya bodhisattvas, who are much more advanced than us, see things. When they are not in equipoise meditation they have the hallucination of true existence but no belief in its being real. They see true appearance as like a mirage.

When we awaken from a dream we understand that what we thought was real was just a dream and not real at all. Unfortunately, in the daytime when we are no longer dreaming, we still believe that which is not real to be real. Can you imagine that?

Our whole life is like a mirage. We have a vision of water where there is none. It is like a dream, an illusion; it's as if a magician has used some mantras or some substances and illusioned the audience. I'm not sure of the English, but the audience is illusioned. What the audience sees appears as real and they believe it to be real.

For us it is like that all day and all night. Past ignorance has left a negative imprint on our mind. After the mere imputation, ignorance immediately projects the appearance of a real object, which makes things appear to us as real. This has come from our mind, just as a film put into a projector is projected onto the screen. Past ignorance has left negative imprints, and right after the mere imputation, the next second, our mind projects the hallucination of a real object existing from its own side. Then, if we fail to analyze it, we don't know that it has just come from our mind; we believe it to be real, to be true. We hold it as true. Among the delusions, that is the king of the delusions.

As those who have studied Madhyamaka philosophy know, there are many lines of logical reasoning to prove emptiness, but because dependent arising states that things are empty of inherent existence because they are dependent, it is considered the king of logical reasoning. Conversely, among all the delusions, the wrong concept that things exist from their own side is the king of the delusions.

UNDERSTANDING THE REAL I

From time-to-time in the world, great wars like the First and Second World Wars happen. With so much destruction and the deaths of millions of people with millions more being burned and injured, this is the most intense kind of suffering we can experience. As I have mentioned, such wars can be due to one person with power and influence. Because of that person's ignorance, he totally believes in the wrong concept and totally fails to comprehend that the I is merely labeled by the mind. He wants this I, this real I, to be happy, to have power. He takes what he likes and destroys what he dislikes in order to attain happiness for that real I, which is not there, which has never been there at all, from beginningless rebirths.

The I is merely imputed by our mind right now. Then follows the projection, the hallucination by our mind, by past ignorance that has left a negative imprint on our mind. The real I is a total projection, a hallucination. But we completely, one hundred percent, believe it to be true, real. First the imputation; then the appearance; then, in the third moment, complete belief in that appearance.

Believing in the real I is like believing we have a billion dollars in our hand. Like that dictator, we take what we like and destroy what we dislike for the happiness of our real I, which does not exist at all.

This wrong concept cheats us. It has been cheating us completely from beginningless rebirths up until now. If we don't study, meditate and realize ultimate reality—emptiness, *tong-pa-nyi*, shunyata—we're completely cheating ourselves. Right now in this life we have all the chances, all the opportunities. We have great teachers who are always teaching emptiness, particularly the emptiness taught by the Omniscient One, the kind, compassionate Shakyamuni Buddha, and the many pandits, Nagarjuna, Lama Tsongkhapa and so forth. If we are totally distracted by mundane pleasures, which are only suffering, and fail to take this opportunity, we have completely cheated ourselves.

We will realize this as we are about to die, but at that time it will be too late; there will be no time to do anything about it. No matter how sad we are, realizing we have wasted our life, that's it, it's time for death.

We have met the correct teachings

People who have the opportunity to take teachings, study and meditate are extremely lucky. Both correct teachings and a perfect, qualified teacher are needed. There are many, many teachings and just because the subject of a particular teaching is meditation does not necessarily mean it is correct. Actually, it all depends on an individual person's karma. If we have good karma, then we will meet the correct teacher, receive correct teachings and everything will happen correctly. If we do not have good karma, then we will meet the wrong teacher, receive wrong teachings and everything will go wrong. It is very rare to meet the right teacher and receive correct teachings.

We need to not only listen to the teaching but also reflect on everything we hear, analyzing the base, the path and the goal. As we have seen, the base is the two truths: ultimate truth and the truth for the all-obscuring mind. The path is wisdom and compassion. The goal is the dharmakaya, a buddha's wisdom body, and the rupakaya, a buddha's form body. We reach this goal by analyzing the base and developing through the path of study and debate. We do not attain the goal through belief but by studying with learned teachers and investigating their teachings for the whole of our life.

Kyabje Dudjom Rinpoche, the head lama of the Nyingma tradition, wrote a religious history about the different traditions within Tibetan Buddhism. In it he said that Lama Tsongkhapa was the teacher who wrote the clearest commentaries on the Buddha's teachings, both sutra and tantra. We are so fortunate to be following his tradition.

In the end, it all comes down to how much positive karma we, the students, have created. Having studied meditation and received teachings does not necessarily mean that what we have received is correct, but if we diligently follow Lama Tsongkhapa's teachings we will surely develop on the path. Therefore, we are so fortunate. We should feel great happiness, rejoicing all the time, day and night. There is no time for depression. Not even for an hour, a minute.

As I have mentioned, whether we practice Dharma is up to us, but the more Dharma we learn, the more wisdom we get and the more we are able to discriminate right from wrong. Then we have the wisdom eye to see what to abandon—that which harms ourselves and others—and what to practice—that which benefits ourselves and others.

The king of delusions

I'll give you another example. You have a child and you have to think of a name. You decide to call him "George." Whoever decides the name, you both agree and so the thinking is that this is "George."

When you first saw the baby there was no appearance of George. You didn't see George. After that, you decided on George. You are the main person to decide this name. Your mind not only labeled the aggregates of the baby "George" but *merely* labeled them. If your mind hadn't labeled those aggregates "George," George would not have existed.

Before the baby was conceived, before the aggregates came into existence, even though you might have already decided on the name for the baby, that name has no valid base. George does not exist, even if there is a mind that has given the name.

Therefore George only comes into existence by depending on the aggregates, the valid base, being there, and depending on the labeling valid mind that merely labels "George" onto those aggregates. Only then does George come into existence. So George exists in mere name.

In that first moment it is just the merely imputed George, but you do not know that, you do not realize that. Then, the next moment, the real George appears from there. A merely labeled George should appear—that is the reality—but that does not happen. What happens in the next moment is that George appears to exist from its own side. This George that didn't come from the mind, is not merely labeled by the mind, has never been labeled by the mind and totally exists from its own side is totally false.

So, the first moment there is the merely labeled George and then, the next moment, the negative imprint left by ignorance projects a real George. That is the hallucination. Then, in the third moment, you believe that real appearance. It appears real and you believe it to be real. You believe this is real George, but there is no real George. There is no real George existing from its own side at all. That never happened. That is the king of delusions, the basic problem. That is the root of all the delusions. All other delusions such as attachment arise on the basis of that wrong object.

Attachment arises on the basis of believing a real George to be there, but the object of attachment is not there.

In the *Lamrim Chenmo* there is a very good explanation of how delusions are all built on the basis of the wrong concept. There is no object of attachment or anger. It does not exist. The mind has projected it; the mind has created it. We have totally made it up and we have created the suffering ourselves.

The real George is a good example of this. It is totally false but on the basis of it there is *so* much attachment. We think, "*My* child," then when something disturbs our attachment, we get angry. Like that, all the other delusions arise. In that way, we live our whole life completely in the hallucination.

There is no real Lama Zopa. There is no real Jamyang Centre appearing from its own side. There is no real teaching appearing from there. All this is totally empty. There is no real home appearing from there. There is no real car that you drive, existing from its own side. There is no real shop, no real shopkeeper, no real money, no real coming and going. There is no real university, no real degree, no real job. There is no real cancer. Maybe that example is better. There is no real cancer, no real AIDS.

The emptiness of the Z

I want to end by mentioning this example for you to get a better idea. You might have heard it before because it is a common example I give, but I think using it again here will make this clearer.

Go back to your childhood before you knew your ABCs. Your teacher draws three lines on the blackboard, a Z. Before she teaches you what those lines mean, you see them but you have no appearance that this is a Z. You do not see those lines as a Z. Then the teacher introduces you to the name for that: "Z." Before that, you didn't have the appearance that this is a Z, there were just three lines. That is clear.

Once the teacher has introduced you to the label "Z" you believe in that. Following what the teacher says, your mind merely imputes Z and then, the next moment, you have the appearance of the Z. But the big question is this. It should appear as merely labeled by the mind if that is how you apprehended it the moment before, but you do not see that at all. Why is that?

The next moment, for you, there is this wrong projection, a real Z from there, a Z that never came from your mind, that was not merely labeled by your mind. That is so totally wrong; that is a hallucination.

In that second moment there is the appearance of a real Z and then, in the third moment, you totally believe this to be true, to be real. As it appears real, you believe it to be real. This is the fundamental wrong concept that gives rise to all other delusions. Seeing the merely labeled Z, seeing it as truly existing and then believing in that not merely labeled, truly-existing Z, those are the steps. I hope that makes it a little clearer. Thinking back to when you were a child, the first time you saw these three lines, helps to clarify this.

Another thing is to look for the real Z. Where is the real Z? Is it on the top horizontal line? Or the diagonal line? Or is it the bottom horizontal line? Or even all three lines? There is no real Z there, even on all three lines.

It is exactly the same as the valid base, the five aggregates of form, feeling, cognition, compounding aggregates and consciousness that we have. These are the basis to be labeled, the basis on which the mind merely imputes the I. Thus the I exists in mere name.

That is the reality. None of the aggregates separately is the real I nor are all the aggregates as a whole. These five aggregates are the possession and the I is the possessor of those aggregates, so how can the possession also be the possessor? They are not separate but different. For example, if we own a car we are the possessor and the car is our possession. How can it be possible for the possessor, we ourselves, to also be the possession, our car? It is not possible for possessor and possession to be one.

The aggregates are the possession and the I is the possessor, therefore they are not one. There are other logical arguments that prove the aggregates are not the real I; for example, because the real I is one, singular, then all the aggregates would have to be one, singular. That dangerous mistake can arise.

And if the aggregates are the real I, then what is the purpose of calling this thing "I"? If there is already a real I why place the name "I" on the already existing I? If the label "I" is needed for the already existing real I, then that I would also need to be labeled in the same way. We would need yet another label and so it would go in an infinite regression, creating numberless I's. That is pointless.

So, with the Z, none of the lines separately nor all three lines as a whole are the real Z. Thinking they are, mistakes like that occur.

Time to stop the tyranny of the real I

In our life, we have this ignorance, this wrong concept, believing in the real I and the real aggregates, which are in fact totally empty, which have never existed in the past, from beginningless rebirths. With this false concept we are always so worried and afraid. When can this real I that our ignorance believes in, which has never existed, ever be happy? When can it be happy? All the time, day and night, we worry about the happiness of this real I.

All through our life we worry about this—through kindergarten, primary school, high school, college, university, getting a degree and then a job. We try to earn a good salary, then we marry and have children. We feel that once we have accomplished all this, with a job, a partner and children, we'll be so happy! Yesterday, when I asked a student what he really wanted in his life, he said he wanted to see grandchildren. I asked if he wanted to see his grandchildren enlightened. I put it that way.

Because of believing in this real I, when somebody cheats us, lies to us, steals from us or blames us, we get angry. We get angry for this real I. We sue that person, bringing a court case against him, spending thousands of pounds or dollars—hundreds of thousands, or millions, I don't know—all for this real I to be happy, to harm and defeat its enemy. For the happiness of the real I we want to put that person into prison.

Perhaps we have to kill that person to make the real I happy. But then his friends get angry at us and so we have more enemies and have to kill them too. Because of this real I that doesn't exist we give much harm to others. This real I creates great confusion, so many problems in life. We see examples of this in newspapers and on TV all the time. But there *is* no real I there at all. It's all a joke—in reality, it's not there. We create all this negative karma for something that is not there at all, a total hallucination.

This ties in with what I said earlier about the tyrant with power and influence who can start wars and cause the deaths of millions of people. He does this because he has been completely cheated by this wrong concept. In the same way, we ourselves are completely cheated too.

It is very important to end this tyranny now. For beginningless rebirths we have been experiencing the sufferings of the hell beings, the hungry ghosts, the animals, the human beings, the gods, the demigods and the intermediate stage beings. As human beings we have the sufferings of rebirth, old age, sickness, death, meeting undesirable objects, not meeting desirable objects and losing desirable objects that we've found. Even if we manage to get what we want, we are still unable to find satisfaction. Never being able to find satisfaction is the greatest problem that affluent humans and gods face. No matter how many desirable objects we are able to acquire, we can never find satisfaction, but we try and try and try.

This is not the first time we have been like this, with all these sufferings. This has been our experience for countless lifetimes and if we fail to do something about it now, while we have the opportunity to realize emptiness, we will suffer in samsara endlessly.

All phenomena are empty; they do not exist from their own side, especially the I, the body, aggregates and possessions—the objects of our attachment and anger.

To remind ourselves of the vital subjects of impermanence, emptiness and dependent arising, it is most worthwhile to reflect on this four-line verse from the *Praise to Shakyamuni Buddha:*

> A star, a visual aberration, a flame of a lamp,
> An illusion, a drop of dew or a bubble,
> A dream, a flash of lightning, a cloud—
> See conditioned things as such![29]

I explained defective view before, how everything—I, action, object, everything—appears to be truly existent. The way that things appear, as truly existent, *rab-rib*, relates to that. Causes and conditions exist and therefore I, action, object and all other phenomena exist.

This is totally the opposite of what most people in the world believe. What most people in the world believe is not according to reality, that is why they suffer so much, why they have so much emotional suffering, depression and so forth.

If we can meditate on this every day, even though we might be far from attaining realizations, having a degree of familiarity will help very much; it will bring a lot of peace and happiness into our life, our mind. Then we will be able to practice Dharma more and more, and gain more and more freedom for ourselves. We will be able to attain the blissful state of peace, liberation from samsara, and enlightenment. Practicing Dharma every day means giving ourselves happiness every day. Especially by practicing *lo-jong*, thought transformation, any problem that we experience can bring us the best happiness.

---

[29] From *Praise to Shakyamuni Buddha*. Some translations say "defective view," some "mirage" for *rab-rib*. Taken from *Essential Buddhist Prayers, Volume 1*, p. 76.

Roger Kunsang

6. The Guru Is the Most Powerful Object

THE SUN OF DEVOTION, THE STREAM OF BLESSINGS

IF THE PURPOSE of our life is to achieve *sang-gyä*—the total elimination of all obscurations and the completion of all realizations—we need to find a guru and then correctly devote to and follow that virtuous friend. There is a distinction between devoting and following and we need to do both. Devoting is just to do with the mind but correctly following the virtuous friend is to do with thoughts and actions. We need to not only develop the mind of devotion toward the virtuous friend but also to correctly follow the advice of the virtuous friend, which is the root of the path to enlightenment. Much depends on our goal. Khedrub Sangye Yeshe said,

> Without a helmsman, a boat cannot take you across the ocean.
> Like that, without a guru, you cannot be liberated from samsara,
> even if you have complete knowledge of Dharma.[30]

Without a guru, we cannot be free from samsara even if we complete all the qualities and have all the education. That is very important to know. Even if we know by heart and can explain the entire Kangyur and Tengyur, if we do not have a guru we cannot be free from samsara.

Padmasambhava, who is like the second Buddha, also explained,

> If you don't recognize the guru as a buddha,
> Your mind cannot be liberated by the blessings.

---

[30] Khedrub Sangye Yeshe (1525–91) was Gyalwa Ensapa's closest disciple. Quoted in *Heart of the Path*, p. 7.

> Therefore, reflect on the qualities of the guru
> And then make requests to him.[31]

I'm not advertising myself as a buddha to you! You must know that. This quotation is what Padmasambhava has said; this is his instruction. So here, Padmasambhava is also teaching me as well as you.

Unless we realize that the guru is buddha, the guru's blessings cannot liberate our mind, which refers to freeing ourselves from the bondage of delusion and superstition. That relates to the ignorance holding the I, aggregates and phenomena as truly existent, and to the self-cherishing thought and attachment to samsara as well. We cannot be liberated from those as well as from impure appearance and impure thought, the dualistic mind and the dualistic view, the ordinary mind-wind and the subtle mind-wind. When Padmasambhava talks of liberating the mind this is what he is referring to.

Our practice should be to think of our guru not from the side of his apparent mistakes but from the side of his qualities. We should think of the guru as having a buddha's qualities and pray to him like that. This is the instruction of Padmasambhava.

Without a guru, there is no object of meditation to realize the buddha. Without that, we cannot receive the blessings of the guru. If we do not receive the blessings of the guru, our mind cannot actualize the path to enlightenment. Then we cannot liberate our mind from those delusions, from the disturbing-thought obscurations and the subtle obscurations, the obscurations to knowledge. For that reason, we have to think of the guru as having a buddha's qualities and pray to him on that basis.

The fourth Panchen Lama, Panchen Lobsang Chökyi Gyaltsen, who composed the *Guru Puja*, texts on mahamudra and many other collections of teachings on sutra and tantra, also explained,

> If you cherish yourself, don't follow just anyone you happen to meet, like a dog seeking food in the street. Examine well the lama who reveals the holy Dharma, then follow him with respect.[32]

We should not be like an old dog who runs toward anybody offering food without checking, gobbling it down as quickly as possible. We need to care-

---

[31] Quoted in *Heart of the Path*, p. 8.
[32] Quoted in *Heart of the Path*, p. 26.

fully examine the guru who is revealing the Dharma and then follow his advice and practice well.

There was also a great Kagyü lama called Kyobpa Jigten Gonpo.[33] From his holy mouth came these words,

> If on the guru, snow mountain of the four kayas,
> The sun of devotion fails to shine,
> The stream of blessings will not arise.
> Attend, therefore, to this mind of devotion.[34]

This means that we cannot receive realizations without the guru's blessings. Therefore, we must pay very careful attention to developing the minds of respect and devotion to the guru.

For example, while we are doing something that pleases the guru, a retreat or something, we have a dream. Maybe we have not even informed our guru, but we have a dream in which he is very happy and gives us a present. He is so pleased, so joyful; he has such a happy face. This happens.

I think one thing is that all the buddhas are happy with us because of our karma with that guru, so all the buddhas communicate with us through the guru. Receiving a present or something like that is an indication of this. Because we have a connection with that guru, they use the aspect of the guru to communicate with us, to give us a blessing. This is definitely there. Conversely, if the guru is displeased, that means all the buddhas are displeased.

Pleasing the buddhas through correctly devoting to and following the advice of the guru is not easy to understand but we have to think about it because it is an incredibly important consideration for our life. And not just this life but all our lives until enlightenment. Whether we can achieve enlightenment or not, that's the highest success. It means completing purification of all obscurations and attaining all realizations. There's no higher success. Only then can we do perfect work for sentient beings without the slightest mistake and free them from the oceans of samsaric suffering and bring them to enlightenment, the state of the omniscient mind.

---

[33] Drigung Kyobpa Jigten Rinpoche (1143–1217), better known as Jigten Sumgön, was the founder of the Drikung Kagyü lineage.
[34] From *Song of the Fivefold Profound Path of Mahamudra*, quoted in Khenchen Konchog Gyaltshen, *Opening the Treasure of the Profound: Teachings on the Songs of Jigten Sumgön and Milarepa*, p. 79.

What higher success can there be? And that depends on this alone, developing and maintaining a proper relationship with our guru. So it's not easy. We have to be incredibly careful. We have to think and understand well. It's not just playing a game. It's not like having a boyfriend or a girlfriend where we decide to stay with that person if we like them or leave them if we don't. I want to make that clear. This is a very deep thing, a really important matter.

To disrespect the guru is to disrespect all the buddhas

As I mentioned, after we have done something that pleases the guru, even if we have not informed him, we can have dreams that indicate the guru is extremely pleased, dreams in which he is very joyful or gives us presents. In the same way, if we do something negative, even if we do not tell the guru, he can show a negative aspect in dreams, such as appearing very skinny or sick. There is a message for us.

This is mentioned in Pabongka Dechen Nyingpo's commentary on *The Essence of Nectar*,[35] which is an extremely inspiring text by Yeshe Tsöndrü. It has a very good lam-rim outline and I often recommend it as a daily meditation guidebook. There is also a commentary by my guru, Geshe Rabten, a great scholar and meditator, which has been published in English as the *Essential Nectar*.

Kyabje Trijang Rinpoche, His Holiness the Dalai Lama's younger tutor, is the root guru of Geshe Rabten Rinpoche and Lama Yeshe, who took care of me for more than thirty years. Both my gurus have the same level of tantric realizations: the gross and subtle generation stages and five stages of the completion stage; the isolation of body, the isolation of speech, the isolation of mind, the path of unification of clear light and the illusory body, and the path of no more learning. Both of them have clear light realization. Kyabje Trijang Rinpoche mentioned this.

Recently I was lucky enough to receive an oral transmission of the whole collection of Kyabje Trijang Rinpoche's teachings from Kyabje Khyongla Rato Rinpoche, a Drepung Loseling lama who lives in New York and is advanced in both qualities and age. Then, in Sera Monastery after the recent teachings by His Holiness, I also received the complete transmission of Pabongka Rinpoche's collected works from Kyabje Chöden Rinpoche.

---

[35] For the text of the guru devotion section, see *Heart of the Path*, appendix 5, pp. 407–14. Pabongka Rinpoche's commentary on *The Essence of Nectar* has not been published in English.

A monk came to help me with the long-life prayer afterwards. I hadn't met him before but he looked like somebody who was a very sincere practitioner. He was a reincarnation of Yeshe Tsöndrü, the author of *The Essence of Nectar*. When he explained his story I felt his coming to see me was very auspicious.

Anyway, in his commentary, Pabongka Dechen Nyingpo mentioned,

> What are the gurus? They are the embodiment of all the Victorious Ones, those who have gained victory over the four maras. What are called the holy actions of the Victorious Ones and [the holy actions] of the gurus are just names; they are the same thing. And so, disrespecting the guru is disrespecting all the buddhas. There is no heavier negative karma than this. By thinking of the guru as your savior you become the disciple. Then if you belittle the guru you will always experience suffering.

That is the instruction. What are the gurus? We have to think of this quotation as an instruction to us. The buddhas are called the Victorious Ones, those who have gained victory over the four maras: the maras of the delusions, the contaminated aggregates, the Lord of Death and the deva's son. This is victory over the gross and subtle maras, the disturbing-thought obscurations and the obscurations to knowledge.

We are not victorious over the maras but defeated by them. We are under the control of the maras. But the buddhas are victorious over the four maras because they are able to transform the self-cherishing thought into the thought cherishing others. The Buddha was the same as us, having all the problems and negative emotions and the same self-cherishing thought, bound by all the worldly dharmas. But that is what he changed. He was able to transform his mind and develop bodhicitta, and from that he was able to become victorious over all wrong concepts.

This enlightened quality manifests as our own guru, therefore, to disrespect our guru is to disrespect all the buddhas. There are numberless buddhas, not just one—not just Shakyamuni Buddha or just Tara—there are numberless buddhas. Even in this fortunate eon, there are a thousand buddhas who have achieved enlightenment or will do so.

I took some short teachings from Panchen Rinpoche in Tashi Lhunpo in Tibet. Just as His Holiness the Dalai Lama is regarded as Chenrezig, Avalokiteshvara, the Compassion Buddha, Panchen Rinpoche is regarded as Amitabha Buddha. At Tashi Lhunpo Monastery, outside in the court-yard, there are paintings of the thousand buddhas. To generate the cause to achieve bodhicitta and attain enlightenment, people offer flowers and conch shells. There is a particular homage to each buddha, each a cause to generate bodhicitta and, I believe, enlightenment. I asked the Australian monk Max Redlich, who was once director of Tushita Meditation Centre, Dharamsala, to photograph all the thousand buddhas, which he did. There are also texts like the *Sutra of the Fortunate Eon* that talk about each of these buddhas.

Being disrespectful to our own guru means we are being disrespect-ful to all the numberless buddhas. There is no heavier negative ripening karma[36] than that. The quotation says by thinking of the guru as our savior we become his disciple.

Some people don't like the fact I translate *gön* as "savior" because they think this is a Christian term and we should use "protector" instead. I don't accept that at all. If we were to use "protector" as a translation of *gön*, then what about *sung-ma*, which means "protector" in Tibetan? Just as *sung-ma* is not "savior" but "protector" in Tibetan, *gön* is not "protector" but "sav-ior." This is just playing with words. "Savior" is the correct word. In Tibetan these two terms are different and we have to translate according to that. In English the words might have different connotations so we shouldn't make everything solid, mixing everything up together, like making a soup.

Here the quotation tells us that by thinking of our guru as a savior we become his disciple. Then, if we belittle that guru we will always experience suffering and obstacles. It says "always" but that is a shorthand way of saying for many lifetimes, for thousands, hundreds of thousands, millions of life-times. This is because the object we belittle is the highest object. We have to know that. Otherwise we will wonder why this is so, thinking it makes no sense, that it is illogical, just a belief.

THE KINDNESS OF THE PARENTS

The Buddha gave teachings on the kindness of the parents, how our father and mother are unbelievably kind. This text was translated some years ago

---

[36] Ripening karma is the karma that propels us into the next life.

into English and I recently received it from a monk at Nalanda, but I haven't seen the Tibetan translation yet.[37]

Of the unbelievable kindness of the father and mother, there are different types of kindness listed in the texts. There is the *kindness of giving us our body*. In this life our mother bore many hardships, carrying us for nine months in her womb and undergoing much suffering in order to protect us and save us from anything that might harm us.

This is not the first time; she has been doing this from beginningless rebirths. It would be impossible to repay that kindness, even if we were to sacrifice our bodies equaling the particles of dust of the earth. Even if we gave all our human bodies numberless times from numberless rebirths, it would not be enough to repay the kindness of our mother and father.

The second kindness is the *kindness of protecting our life* every day from hundreds of life's dangers. Our mother and our father have both protected us so much. And this is not the first time; they have been doing this from beginningless rebirths. Even if we don't remember, this is what has happened. We cannot remember this because our mind is so ignorant, so defiled, like a dirty cup or cloth that is so dirty that the many nice designs covering it are invisible. To repay that kindness, even if we were to sacrifice our lives for them equaling the number of dust particles of this earth, that is not enough; we cannot finish repaying the kindness.

Then there is the *kindness of bearing hardships*. Parents undergo so many hardships for their children. I just want to tell you about a couple from Hawaii who have now separated. This was at Vajrapani,[38] on the first visit ever from Spain of Ösel Rinpoche, the reincarnation of my guru, Master Lama Yeshe, who was kinder than all the three times' buddhas.

After Lama passed away the Vajrapani students built a stupa and the day it was finished and they were consecrating it the incarnation was able to be there. There was also Lati Rinpoche from Ganden Monastery, Dharamsala, a great lama, a great scholar, a great practitioner. Then there was Geshe Sopa Rinpoche, Lama Yeshe's and my teacher, and the Ganden Shartse geshe, Geshe Gyeltsen, as well as other lamas and geshes who came there to bless

---

[37] The sutra that Rinpoche is probably referring to is the *Filial Piety Sutra*, a sutra revered by Chinese and S.E. Asian Buddhists, in which the Buddha lists ten ways a mother is kind, directly paralleling the Tibetan listing in the kindness of the mother bodhicitta teachings. See www.buddhanet.net/e-learning/filial-sutra.htm

[38] Vajrapani Institute, the FPMT center in California where Lama Yeshe was cremated.

the stupa. And Ösel Rinpoche, the incarnation, was able to come back to see the stupa.

I was staying in a room in a student's house in the bush while the other lamas were down at the center. The student, a carpenter, had the second highest house up the mountain from the center. The highest house was Baba-ji's, a Danish student who once lived in Nepal a long time ago and cooked for Lama Yeshe. He painted thangkas in his house.

This is not to tell the story of Ösel Rinpoche, but he was just at the same place. While I was receiving the oral transmission of the *Lam-rim De-lam, The Path to Bliss Leading to Omniscience*,[39] from Geshe Sopa Rinpoche, Ösel's mother, Maria, was there with Ösel Rinpoche. He was so small. I think he was very handsome, very cute. While we were receiving the *lung*, even though he was very small he suddenly got up and did seven prostrations to Geshe Sopa. It was surprising. I didn't tell him to, nobody told him to; he did it by himself. He was very small but this was the imprint from his past life because he is the incarnation of Master Lama Yeshe. It just shows about past life's imprints.

The main story is about this couple. They had lived in Dharamsala for a long time and the last time Lama Yeshe was there they offered some land they owned in Hawaii. They had just opened the Shantideva Center there, and because of this they invited me for lunch. The man wasn't there but the woman was, with their child. It was amazing. The boy could not sit still for one minute, running everywhere, never still. If his mother had failed to watch him for one minute he would have been dead. I thought about the patience she needed with him, to tolerate him. It was incredible. He gave his mother no peace at all.

I'm sorry; my mind is bad. I watch children at airports or wherever for five minutes, seeing how demanding they are, constantly demanding, demanding all the time from their parents. They never give any peace, always crying, always demanding.

Our mother, too, bore many hardships for us and this is not the first time. Even just as a human mother she has borne hardships from beginningless rebirths. This is without talking about the times she has been an animal mother, having to bear unbelievable hardships, such as a mother bird having

---

[39] Composed by the First Panchen Lama, Lobsang Chökyi Gyaltsen (1570-1662). The outline of this text is included in *Path to Bliss*, by the Dalai Lama.

to guard her eggs against predators coming to eat them. Can you imagine all the sacrifices that animal mothers have to make?

It would be impossible to repay the kindness of this current human mother who had to bear so much hardship for us, even if we gave up our lives equaling the number of dust particles of this earth. We can never finish repaying that kindness.

Then, fourth, there is the *kindness of giving us an education*, also called the "kindness of leading us in the path of the world." Our parents educated us themselves and also sent us to school, right up to university, spending a great deal of money for all that education.

Of course, in this life they have also given us access to the Dharma. We're able to read, write and study Dharma books because of the education they gave us. Then we come to know why we have to get sick, why we have to get old, why we have to die, why we have to be reborn. And we can understand that this is not the first time. For numberless times from beginningless rebirths we have had to go through that. And because of that education we know that if we cannot actualize the path in this life, especially the direct perception of emptiness, then we will have to again endlessly suffer. Through our education we come to know this. We learn the correct teachings from qualified teachers, from the four noble truths onwards.

We are unbelievably fortunate. We can see even this world, the southern world system, just how few people know about this. They do not know about the mind, reincarnation, karma or things like that. Most people have no awareness of death. Because they don't know what to do, they put off thinking about death.

Even though at the moment we have not actualized the path to overcome death by realizing emptiness and so forth, we can still experience an incredibly happy death. We can use death in the happiest way, making it most beneficial for sentient beings, to free sentient beings from the oceans of samsaric suffering and bring them to full enlightenment. So while we have to experience death, we can use it for that through the practice of *lojong* and bodhicitta.

People only think of this life, nothing else, only this life, only this year, this month, this week, just that. We all have to die but probably because they are unable to accept death, because they do not know what to do, they refuse to think about it. To learn about death is the most important subject in life, so it is very strange how people just put it off, just ignore it. It doesn't help.

On the other hand, we are *so* fortunate to have this education and that is due to our mother's kindness. She gave us this education. And this is not the first time. She has shown us the kindness of giving us an education from beginningless rebirths, even just by being our human mother. If we were to sacrifice our lives equaling the number of the dust particles of this earth or the sand grains of the Pacific Ocean for just this life's mother, we could still not finish repaying her kindness.

These are the four kindnesses as explained by Kyabje Khunu Lama Rinpoche, from whom His Holiness received extensive commentary on Shantideva's *Guide to the Bodhisattva's Way of Life*.

Wasting our life, we waste our parents' lives

This life's parents are more powerful objects for us than other people. Ordained people are more powerful objects than our parents, though. By serving the Sangha we collect much merit and purify much negative karma, more than with this life's parents, but still, our parents are very powerful objects for creating merit and negativity as well.

Many older Western students have received teachings and initiations from Kyabje Zong Rinpoche. Now his incarnation is an expert because he was an expert in his past life, like the former past great yogis such as Nagarjuna and Asanga. The incarnation is young but he has already finished his geshe studies in Ganden Shartse Monastery. A long time ago, I was fortunate to able to help with some of the expenses and make offering to the monasteries. I told him that I believed he would be able to offer service to the monastery, to take responsibility like an abbot for all the monks, for their education and their practice in the monastery. It is easy to go to the West to teach, but it is very important in the monastery to look after the discipline and to give the monks an education and take care of them. I said that I felt he would be able to do that. He told me jokingly he would take that as a prediction from me. He is very famous in Ganden Shartse Monastery.

Kyabje Zong Rinpoche was a very high lama in his past life. He became the abbot of Ganden Shartse, where there were many thousand monks. Once, when his parents came from Kham to Lhasa and he was able to stay with them, he wanted to serve them, to clean the house and get rid of the garbage, to make food and so forth. In his heart he really wanted to do everything a servant would do as a way of repaying their great kindness. He told me he was able to do some of those things—not everything, just cleaning the room and the like—but because of his position as a high lama some-how it was not appropriate. In his heart he really wanted to serve his parents because through having learned the Dharma he understood the kindness of the parents.

Understanding the kindness of our parents, we should practice Dharma and use our body, speech and mind to not create negative karma. If we harm other sentient beings and ourselves it completely wastes our parents' lives. For many, many years they served us, took care of us and gave us an educa-tion, and if we then waste all that, we have wasted their lives, made them empty. There has been no positive result from what they have done.

We must serve others. Even if we don't practice Dharma, we must develop a good heart and live a good life. We must become good human beings and serve others with a sincere heart, with compassion. His Holiness emphasizes nowadays that even if we lead a secular life rather than practic-ing Dharma we must still live an ethical life; we must bring happiness to others and ourselves.

We need to explain this to people who don't know or practice Dharma, to show them how to live their life. If we want to bring peace and happiness to others, to not harm them but to benefit them, we need to lead an ethical life. And if we do that it will have made our parents' lives meaningful. They suffered so much for us, therefore we must make it all worthwhile, other-wise we have not given them any meaning in return for all the work they did. That would be very sad. It's very important to think about these things.

THE GURU IS THE MOST POWERFUL OBJECT

As I mentioned, our parents are very powerful objects but the ordained Sangha are even more powerful because of the number of vows they live in. By being of service or making offerings to them we collect much more merit and purify many more defilements than we do with our parents.

After this come arya beings, arhats, who have freed themselves from the oceans of samsaric suffering and attained the blissful state of peace for them-selves. By making material offerings or offering service to them we collect unbelievable merit and purify vast amounts of negative karma and obscu-rations, much more than we would in connection with ordinary ordained people.

Next, when we compare the numberless arhats with one bodhisattva, if we offer service or make offerings to one bodhisattva, we collect much more powerful merit—unbelievable, unbelievable merit—and purify much more negative karma collected from beginningless rebirths. So many eons of negative karma and obscurations are purified. It is unbelievably more powerful offering service or making offerings to one bodhisattva than to numberless arhats.

Now we compare numberless bodhisattvas with just one buddha. By serving or making offerings to one buddha, we purify the most unbelievable negative karma and obscurations collected from beginningless rebirths and collect the most unbelievable merit—more than having served or made offerings to numberless bodhisattvas. That becomes very small compared to serving or making offerings to one buddha even just once.

Finally, we compare the numberless buddhas with one guru. By offering to the numberless buddhas, even just some candy or a glass of water, we collect the most extensive merit and achieve the most powerful purification of negative karma and obscurations collected from beginningless rebirths. So many eons of negative karma and obscurations are purified and so much merit is created by serving or making offerings to numberless buddhas, but even though that is unbelievable, it is tiny compared to serving and making offerings to the guru.

Being able to follow the guru's advice or fulfill one of his wishes just once creates the most powerful merit and is the most powerful purification. Doing the same for the numberless buddhas, although great in itself, becomes very small in comparison.

Having a relationship with a holy being where we are the disciple and he or she is the guru is a dependent arising. The second after that connection is made, the guru becomes the most powerful person in our life and one from whom we can collect the causes of happiness and purify the causes of suffering, negative karma and defilements.

Buddhism came from the Buddha, from India, and then from the great pandits, Nagarjuna, Asanga and all the Nalanda pandits and so forth. Then it went to Tibet, where the four traditions—Nyingma, Kagyü, Sakya and Gelug—developed, depending on the place and the lineage lamas. The essence is the same but there are different presentations according to the minds of the disciples. That is the evolution.

In the Sakya tradition there are five great masters, including Sachen Kunga Nyingpo and Sakya Pandita. I have mentioned that if you please one guru you please all the buddhas. With respect to that, Sakya Pandita said,

Even though sunbeams are very hot,
Without a magnifying glass, they cannot ignite a fire.
It is the same with the blessings of the buddhas:
Without the guru, they cannot enter the disciple.[40]

Just as we need a magnifying glass to ignite wood using the sun's rays, in order to receive the blessings of the buddhas we need a guru. Even though all the buddhas have incredible qualities such as unbelievable compassion, without a guru we cannot receive their blessings.

Sakya Pandita also said,

All the merit you accumulate by practicing the perfection of charity for a thousand eons—giving not only your head and limbs to other sentient beings but even the merit you receive by offering your body in this way—is accumulated in an instant with the path of the guru. Therefore, offer service and feel happy.[41]

We can practice the perfection of charity or any of the six perfections for thousands of eons but fulfilling the guru's wishes for even a second equals this. The merit we gain from practicing the charity of giving our hands, our limbs, our head and so forth for thousands of eons and even giving away the merit we gain from that is much less than what we could accumulate in an instant by following the guru's advice and fulfilling his wishes.

For example, if we are in retreat following our guru's advice to recite OM MANI PADME HUM, then each second we recite it we collect the same amount of merit that we would in a thousand eons of practice in connection with sentient beings. This is because we are following the advice of the guru and fulfilling his wishes. Whether we are ordained or lay, when we keep the vows given to us by our guru, every day, every hour, every minute, every second we purify unbelievable amounts of negativity and collect unbelievable merit.

Say we follow the guru's advice to do the preliminary practices every day. In the morning, when we clean the meditation room—not even the guru's room but just our own—even if the room is spotless, each sweep of the broom we make to purify our own and other sentient beings' negativities, is

---

[40] Quoted in *Heart of the Path*, p. 239.
[41] Quoted in *Heart of the Path*, p. 95.

incredible purification and creates extensive merit because we are following the guru's advice.

Our Dharma study is similar to this. When we are memorizing or reciting texts, because each word we memorize is following the guru's wishes, we collect the most unbelievable merit every day, every hour, every minute, every second. As Sakya Pandita mentioned, what takes a thousand eons to collect in connection with sentient beings, we collect here in connection with the guru in one second. We have to recognize that all this is due to following the guru's wishes and advice.

While going somewhere or returning, if we are following the guru's wishes, his advice, with each step we collect the most powerful merit and purify an unbelievable amount of defilements and obscurations. It's the same thing if we are the guru's secretary, serving him. With each letter we write, we collect the most unbelievable merit and do the most powerful purification, each minute, each second.

Our life is so continuously fortunate. If we think about what Sakya Pandita mentioned I think we can see that. When we recognize what we do as guru yoga practice, our life is only filled with incredible joy all the time. There is no time for depression.

Examples of offering service to the guru

I'll give a few examples of disciples offering service to their guru.

Before he met Marpa, Milarepa followed his mother's wishes and learned black magic from a lama in the area who practiced it. When he had learnt it and gone to the mountains, after digging a hole and doing a seven-day retreat, he returned home to kill his uncle and aunt and their family in revenge for the mistreatment of his mother after his father's death. While his aunt and uncle's family was celebrating a wedding in their house— dancing, drinking and enjoying themselves upstairs—he made the whole house collapse. Stones and rocks fell down on top of them, killing thirty-six people and the many animals that were downstairs. Milarepa himself was not injured and later regretted what he had done, so the black magic lama advised him to go to see Marpa if he wanted to practice the Dharma.

Marpa was an enlightened being but he refused to give teachings to Milarepa, only scolding and beating him. He did this for years. Even if Milarepa came with the other students for teachings, as soon as Marpa would see him he would publicly scold him and kick him out of the teachings.

Marpa asked him to build a nine-story tower by himself, refusing to let other workers help him. When Milarepa had finished, Marpa made him put the stones back where he got them and then build the tower again. I haven't seen the tower yet. I wanted to go to Lhokha to see it when I was in Tibet but it didn't happen.

Marpa made Milarepa build the tower and tear it down three times. The skin on Milarepa's back became thick and bluish in color from carrying so much stone. Then Marpa's wisdom mother—not his real mother—insisted that he give Milarepa teachings, so, because Marpa was the enlightened being Heruka, he immediately manifested a mandala and gave Milarepa all the teachings he needed. He then advised Milarepa to go to the mountains where he could do retreat in different holy places like Lapchi or Sipri. There are the three holy places of Heruka, representing Heruka's holy body, holy speech and holy mind—Mount Kailash, Tsari and Lapchi—and Sipri combines all three.

Living on no other food than nettles in those mountains, Milarepa followed Marpa's advice exactly and was able to complete the path. He ceased not only the disturbing-thought obscurations but also the obscurations to knowledge, the subtle obscurations, and so completed all the realizations and achieved buddhahood in that very brief lifetime of these degenerate times. Even though he had created so much negative karma in his early life, in later life he became enlightened.

Marpa had wanted to make Milarepa bear even more hardships before he gave him teachings so that he would become enlightened even more quickly, but his wisdom mother intervened so he gave the teachings earlier than he wanted to. But still, he made Milarepa build the tower three times. That was extremely harsh.

In the West, if the guru were to speak harshly or use ugly words or do something like strike the disciple, the very next day the disciple would put him into prison. Here, it wasn't like that. Milarepa was able to achieve enlightenment in a brief lifetime of degenerate times because of the incredible, unbelievable purification from Marpa, particularly accepting every scolding and having to build the tower three times.

There is another story that illustrates the guru-disciple relationship. Losang Dhargye Gyatso was a direct disciple of the Sixth Panchen Lama, Losang Palden Yeshe, and Arik Geshe Jampa Özer.[42] He was very learned and gave a commentary to Lama Tsongkhapa's important teaching,

---

[42] See treasuryoflives.org, Shingza Pandita Lobzang Dargye Gyatso (1752–1824).

Drang-nge-legshe-nyingpo, The Heart of the Good Explanation of the Inter-pretive and Definitive Meaning.[43] During the commentary he mentioned this story about how the geshe Chenpo Sumra Mitupa had pleased the Seventh Dalai Lama, Kelsang Gyatso. I think Chenpo Sumra Mitupa is a nickname meaning "one who doesn't have a shortsighted mind." The Seventh Dalai Lama was so pleased with this geshe for not having a shortsighted mind.

In the presence of the Victorious Omniscient One, the Seventh Dalai Lama, this geshe asked him to predict his next rebirth. The Seventh Dalai Lama told him that immediately he died he would be reborn as an ox with blue horns. When Geshe Chenpo Sumra Mitupa heard this he laughed and laughed and laughed. The Seventh Dalai Lama asked him why he had laughed like that and he replied, "O lekso." That's a debating term used when the debater is asking for reasons, meaning "it's not easy to believe." He then went on, "Our path is a path of the reasoning. Even if I were to be reborn as an ox in the next life, first I would have to go through the intermediate stage; then the father and mother ox would have to meet and I would enter into the womb. Then gradually my body would develop and hairs would come out. Then, after all that, I would get horns. You told me I would be reborn as an ox with blue horns 'immediately I died' without any time to do all this—the bardo, the male and female ox meeting, and then developing in the womb. So I was laughing at the absurdity of it. Without time to go through all these processes, to just immediately be born as an ox with blue horns—I was laughing at this."

When he heard this, the Victorious Omniscient One, the Seventh Dalai Lama, also laughed and laughed. He then said, "Now in your next life you will be born as a bhikshu and you will be in my entourage."

Then Geshe Chenpo Sumra Mitupa replied, "Maybe I'm thick-skulled, but this seems unknown and doesn't fit into our path of reasoning. You said before that I will be born as an ox but now you say I will be born a bhikshu. And yet I haven't done any confession, any practice, I haven't collected any merit. There have been no changes, so how can I transform from an ox to a bhikshu?" That is what he said.

His Holiness the Seventh Dalai Lama answered, "For us, for you and me, I have become a special object. I have the blessing of Arya Chenrezig."

---

[43] See Robert Thurman's *The Central Philosophy of Tibet* for a translation of this text.

What that actually means is that he is Chenrezig, but he is expressing it in a humble way.

The main point is this. By laughing so much when he was told he would immediately become an ox and laughing again when he was then told he would become a bhikshu, questioning His Holiness's prediction by using his logic, he made His Holiness very happy. So right there, within that moment, his rebirth changed from animal to human being. He had no need to do many hundreds of thousands of prostrations or mandala offerings or to make many statues or do all the many other practices that are normally needed. No, just there it happened.

Do you understand the point I'm trying to make? Just within that moment, his future rebirth changed because he was able to make the guru happy. The moment we are able to please the guru our rebirth changes, even if we were going to be reborn in the lower realms before. We have to bring stories like that into our life, into our practice. That is my conclusion.

Roger Kunsang

7. A Talk about Dolgyal

❧

RECENTLY I WROTE a foreword to His Holiness the Dalai Lama's book about Dolgyal, or Shugden,[44] for the Mongolian translation of the book made by the monks from the monastery in Ulaanbaatar, Idgaa Choizinling.

Idgaa Choizinling, which is part of Sera Je, was in Mongolia before Russia took over. It was built by an old monk who studied at Sera Je, debating and studying philosophical texts composed by Jetsun Chökyi Gyaltsen.

I went there the first time I was in Mongolia but the door was closed and I didn't see anybody. The second time I went to Mongolia, the monks from the monastery came to the center to call on me but they stayed outside and we never managed to meet even though they waited for five days. Then on my last day there I went to the monastery and was able to meet them. There were twenty young boys of between maybe four and seven, all with their heads shaved, dressed in *chubas* and holding malas. They were sitting in a long room looking very inspired, very enthusiastic to be monks. I did the five precepts with them and gave the *lungs* of the *Guru Puja*, the *Lama Tsongkhapa Guru Yoga* (Tib: *Ganden Lha Gyäma*) and some other practices.

It was crowded because their parents and many other people were there as well. There were only two older monks, maybe eighty or ninety years old, left from before the Russians invaded Mongolia. They were fully ordained monks before but maybe because of the situation they had taken to wearing

[44] Shugden and Dolgyal are names for the same worldly protector. Rinpoche uses both but in this series of teachings seems to prefer Dolgyal. See the foreword Rinpoche refers to in the Dorje Shugden section of LamaYeshe.com.

Mongolian robes, a sort of yellow chuba. It was like a robe for the monks. Maybe they had only taken the five precepts, I'm not sure. One of the old monks was holding the stick wrapped in a lot of Mongolian *khatags* that the disciplinarian holds in a puja, so he might have been the disciplinarian before the Russians came.

After the teaching he offered me a Mongolian carpet and asked me to rebuild the monastery. I accepted and it has worked very well. It seems they have quite good karma because a benefactor in Taiwan, whose father died, offered the money to rebuild it and it was finished a long time ago. Now it is probably an even better place. Usually monasteries in Tibet are not so comfortable and look kind of dark, with tiny windows, but this one has many windows. It's spacious enough to seat thousands of people and is a good place to give teachings. The name, Idgaa Choizinling, means "Joyful Pure Land" or, in Sanskrit, "Tushita." There are between thirty and sixty small monks who can study there, whereas before to study philosophy they had to go to Sera Je, very far away in India.

The monks there could have translated either of two books by His Holiness the Dalai Lama but they decided to translate the one about Dolgyal because although many people in Mongolia have heard His Holiness's advice not to follow Dolgyal, it depends on whom they meet. If they meet somebody who follows His Holiness and doesn't practice Dolgyal, they deny practicing Dolgyal. For instance, if they meet me, they tell me they don't practice.

Some people know about the situation in Dharamsala and what His Holiness says but still think this is His Holiness's advice alone and so they continue to practice. They mainly follow the attachment or anger of their group, their party or their guru, becoming angry at His Holiness without really checking well whether it is correct or incorrect, even though when Tibet was free many other important lamas had already advised the monasteries not to practice Dolgyal.

When His Holiness himself was in a young aspect he was in Domo, southern Tibet, where I became a monk. It was becoming very difficult in Tibet because of China, so there was the question of whether to go to India or remain in Tibet. At that time, my teacher's teacher was the oracle, and he was the one who gave the answer. The governors invoked Dolgyal and asked him whether His Holiness should remain in Tibet or go to India because of the situation. The answer was to stay in Tibet. I heard it helped Tibet for one year.

After His Holiness himself repeatedly checked, using more and more logic, he found out that practicing Dolgyal was wrong and gave up the practice. That was what he also advised other people to do. At the beginning His Holiness was very quiet and didn't tell people directly, but then later on he found more reasons and so he advised that if people were concerned with practicing the correct Dharma they should not follow Dolgyal.

These people who criticize His Holiness are unaware that when Tibet was free there were many other lamas who advised against practicing Dolgyal. In particular this was the advice of six or seven great lamas who were like one sun rising in this world, in this southern continent. These lamas did great benefit for sentient beings, for the teachings of the Buddha. They wrote many teachings on sutra and tantra. They advised what could and couldn't be taught and practiced in the monasteries, and they advised particularly not to practice this one, Dolgyal, Shugden.

They are compared to the sun because when the sun rises it dispels the darkness in the world, allowing crops to grow and people to enjoy themselves. Especially in England! Especially in London! I heard yesterday that when the sun comes out everybody goes to the park. One of the students advertised London weather to me like that.

My life in Phagri and Buxa Duar

I've known about the English weather from the time I lived in Buxa Duar, where I went after I escaped from Tibet.

I went to Tibet from Solu Khumbu in 1956 when I was very small, with my two uncles, who were fully ordained monks and one of whom was also my alphabet teacher, my guru. I went there because one of my other uncles, who became a soldier in the Indian army, had married a lady from the upper part of Tibet who lived in Phagri and had invited us to come.

On our walk from Solu Khumbu there was very little snow, just on some of the mountains. We walked all the time except for one day when two Tibetans on horseback gave me a ride on their donkey for two hours until we reached their house in Sangba in upper Tibet, where we had *thugpa*. My uncles came later with the luggage they were carrying and we spent the night there.

Generally, however, we walked all the way, every day, all day, along a car road, stopping to light a fire on the road to cook food. My teacher made tsampa for me by mixing it with black tea in a leather bag. When it was well mixed we ate it. This is a very simple way of traveling. Sometimes we begged. I was a very small child so, I don't know, maybe I was cute. Families seemed to like us and we were able to beg food on the way. They gave us millet tsampa and *chang* made from grain and so forth.

Eventually we reached Shigatse and stayed at Tashi Lhunpo Monastery, the monastery of the Panchen Lamas, for about ten days. There was a Sherpa khangtsen there and we stayed in the house of a monk from Thangme. As you know, Sherpas are expert mountain climbers and assist in many Himalayan expeditions. One of the previous Panchen Lamas had a very learned Sherpa teacher called Ang something (many Sherpas have Ang as part of their name), that's why there was a Sherpa khangtsen.

Khangtsens are places where monks stay depending on where they come from. A monk will belong to one particular *khangtsen* and stay in that house and be looked after by the teacher there. If the teacher doesn't teach you Dharma he will guide you to somebody who can and you will learn from that person.

So the monk from Thangme insisted very much to my teacher that he wanted me to be his disciple but I really didn't want to be. I don't think he was a monk who had learned the Dharma. He was more into business or something. His *shem-thab* was very black and greasy from the butter used in Tibetan tea. And because it was so cold in Tibet, his *shem-thab* was stiff and made a swishing noise when he walked. He also had a long Tibetan key hanging from his belt. That was the *dob-dob* style.

Finally, the day before my teachers were going to walk the seven days from Tashi Lhunpo to Phagri, they advised me I was to stay behind to become this monk's disciple. I *really* didn't want to become the student of somebody who hadn't studied Dharma.

I didn't get any sleep that night, wondering how I could become free from him. But the next morning as we were having tea and my teachers were preparing to leave they said I could come with them. I was very happy.

One way to understand what happened here is that it's karma, how what's happening in this life is the result of our past actions.

It took seven days to walk from Tashi Lhunpo Monastery to Phagri and every day my uncles had to carry huge loads. I don't remember having to carry anything myself.

After we arrived at the uncle's house in Phagri, my uncles decided to go to Lhasa on pilgrimage to see Ganden, Drepung and Sera monasteries and the most famous Shakyamuni Buddha statue in Tibet, which was made during the Buddha's time and blessed by the Buddha, the "Jowo." But the elder of my teachers said I might have some difficulties if I went with them, like catching a cold or dying, so they didn't take me. Later I saw the statue and the monasteries, but not at that time.

I think that their decision to not take me was actually very skillful. While they were in Lhasa, I was just hanging around, wearing a *chuba* that had lots of lice and lice eggs in its seams. But while I was hanging around I had the chance to go to the many branch monasteries of Ganden, Tashi Lhunpo, Gyüto and Gyüme Tantric Colleges and so forth. And, of course, the monastery of the great yogi Domo Geshe Rinpoche, where I later became a monk.

One morning while my uncles were in Lhasa, I was outside with my uncle's wife and their son, a little monk belonging to a monastery that was part of the Tashi Lhunpo. A tall monk called Losang Gyatso came up to me and asked, "Do you want to be my disciple?" So I said, "Yes." I think this was past life's karma ripening. Then he went inside and told my aunt, "He wants to be my disciple."

She was a very good cook, and the next day she made a thermos of tea, filled a Bhutanese container made of woven bamboo with round breads (she made very good Tibetan bread, served with a lot of butter) and took me to Domo Geshe Rinpoche's monastery, where he lived, about fifteen minutes' walk from our place. (I should keep this story brief. This doesn't need to become an initiation into my story!)

Early the next morning I washed and then we had to go to somebody's house for puja. We used to go to different people's houses to do puja every day; this was kind of a fixed time to do puja. But sometimes we did extra pujas that went all night, like *Praises to the Twenty-one Taras* or the *Four Mandala Offerings to Tara*, and on those nights we got no sleep. But mostly we did protector practices, the major one being Dolgyal, Shugden, because in that area that had been the main practice of Kyabje Domo Geshe Rinpoche in the past. So this practice was well known in Domo and Phagri. They did others as well, such as Mahakala, but this was also very strong and often done for the families.

On that first day there was a puja at the house of the benefactor of Domo Geshe Rinpoche's *labrang*. I was given some pages of the Yamantaka *sadhana* to memorize and told to stay outside where the family dogs were sleeping. I memorized the text and they brought food and tea out to me while the other monks were doing puja inside the prayer hall. That was the first day. I memorized the text for examination by Losang Gyatso, the tall monk who became my teacher.

Then, on the second day, I went to puja together with them because in Solu Khumbu, even though I was very small, I used to attend pujas with many people, like the pujas they did when people died, which extended for many days. However, in the morning, before going out to puja I had to do my memorization.

So, like that, I spent three years in Phagri.

Buxa Duar

Nine months after the Chinese took Tibet I escaped to India through Bhutan. Phagri is near Bhutan and at that time crossing the border was much easier than it became later on. We made our way to Jalpaiguri in West Bengal and from there to a camp called Buxa Duar, where Prime Minister Nehru and Gandhi had been imprisoned during the British time. That's where the Sera Je and Sera Me monks' puja hall and residences had been reestablished.

The monks had beds all the way along the walls of a very long, narrow building. There was a very small courtyard outside surrounded by barbed wire, thorns and a ditch where there were more monks' beds. The house of my teacher Geshe Rabten was also there. The place was very crowded. That's how we lived in Buxa. I was based there for eight years while moving to different places from time to time.

An Englishwoman called Freda Bedi, who was married to an Indian man she met at Oxford University, found me an English pen friend and benefactor. Mrs. Bedi had been a Christian before but became a Buddhist in Burma. Because her son and daughter were best friends with Pandit Jawaharlal Nehru's son and daughter at university, Nehru gave her the job of looking after the Tibetan refugee monks who had been sent to Missamari, in Assam. Everybody said she had strong karma to become a Buddhist. She became a disciple of His Holiness the Sixteenth Karmapa and one of the first Western Tibetan Buddhist nuns, Gelongma Karma Kechog Palmo.

In looking after the monks, Sister Palmo became close friends with them. She came to Buxa three times, looking for all the young incarnate lamas and the old ones as well. The pen friend she found for me, Rachel Levy, was a member of the Buddhist Society in London. I never met her.

During my time at Buxa, many monks died of tuberculosis. There was no cancer at that time, and TB was the main illness. TB became very famous! Looking out from my bed I often saw dead monks being carried to the cemetery by a group of monks from that khangtsen, who would pray for them there. It was like that every week. So many monks got sick and died.

We also heard that food sent by the United Nations was exchanged by the camp's officials for poor quality food. Maybe they did that to give the monks the chance to practice the Dharma well!

The head of the lama camp was a Punjabi Sikh, a soldier from the Second World War. He was a very pompous, arrogant man. My pen friend sent me a book about London, about the weather and the story of London, but the head of the camp wanted to read it and I don't think he gave it back. I don't know what happened to it.

So, anyway, I learned about London weather at that time—how it is always drizzly and always cloudy. I remember that from Buxa all those many years ago. In the past, when I would come to the UK and travel to Cumbria,[45] as we passed Manchester I would see from the train that it was foggy and rainy, just as the book had explained it always was.

ABOUT DOLGYAL

When the Mongolian monks asked me to write the foreword for His Holiness's book I told them it would take many pages. And it did! I have told His Holiness that I am also thinking of writing a book, not about me but about Khadro-la's special experiences, what she sees from her side. It should be very interesting. There is evidently a young lama also working on something similar, so His Holiness said he wanted to see my book before I publish it.

Several years ago, when a new monastery was built at Drepung, His Holiness consecrated it and gave teachings at Sera. At that time, four thousand monks gathered at Sera Je and each monk had to come in front of all the others and swear into the microphone that he would never practice Dolgyal or make any connection with people who were practicing, either with materials, which means money, or by teaching or taking teachings. They then swore, "May you, Most Secret Hayagriva, understand."

They had to say that to make it clear to the Tibetan public, to Tibetan society. This didn't come from Dharamsala; it didn't come from His Holiness. This was from the public's side; they wanted them to do that. Then, after that, those who still practiced Dolgyal were not to return.

[45] There used to be an FPMT center, Manjushri Institute, in Cumbria in the north of England, founded in 1976.

I was not there at that time but Lama Lhundrup, the abbot of Kopan Monastery, was worried. I went there later. I swore in the front of the Hayagriva thangka at Sera Je, with the abbot, the *um-dze*—the puja leader—and the *gekyö* who came a little bit later. They were very happy that I made this promise, but I had stopped practicing a long, long time ago.

As I mentioned, I became a monk at Domo Geshe Rinpoche's monastery in Phagri, where the Dolgyal practice was regarded as very important. They practiced it from the past great yogi and so that is why I didn't know before. That is how it happened.

We followed Dolgyal for many years, even receiving a kind of life initiation, relying on Dolgyal, from Kyabje Trijang Rinpoche, Lama Yeshe's and my root guru. I received my first lam-rim teaching, *Liberation in the Palm of your Hand*, from Kyabje Trijang Rinpoche in Sarnath. We followed Dolgyal for many years but I had stopped long before I went to Sera Je that time.

After I stopped nothing negative happened. The night I stopped I dreamed of the oracle from Ganden Shartse giving me scarf. It was not new but a little bit old, rolled up, and he left it on my table. He said, "Thank you," and then disappeared. That was a good sign. Nothing threatening happened; there were no bad dreams or strange events; the ending was good. Maybe it's because I'm not really a lama who benefits the world but just an ordinary person that Dolgyal let me go!

I'd like to tell you a story so you can get the idea, so you can understand. There was a great lama in Tibet, Trehor Kyörpon Rinpoche, who went to Dalhousie, where he later passed away. He achieved many realizations: guru devotion, renunciation, bodhicitta, emptiness, and also the two stages of tantra, the gross and subtle generation stages and the various stages of completion stage, the isolation of the body, the isolation of the speech, the isolation of the mind, which is clear light, and the union of clear light and illusory body. He achieved the completion stage union of clear light and illusory body a long time ago, so of course he would have achieved all the rest. He was a great lama.

He organized his Dalhousie group by checking whether those who came to him could follow an ascetic life or not. Those who could were allowed to stay to receive his guidance but those who were unable to renounce this life had to leave. He checked up like this. There were many geshes learned in philosophy there.

When Rinpoche was still in Tibet, Dolgyal entered into an oracle monk and came and asked Rinpoche to accept him. He was a high lama with many disciples, so if he accepted Dolgyal many people would trust Dolgyal and do the practice. Trehor Kyörpon Rinpoche asked Dolgyal a question about impermanence, which Dolgyal answered correctly. Then he asked him about the *bum-pa*, the vase. This is a very common object used in debating along with pillars, rabbits' horns and things like that. He asked, "Is this vase truly existent or not?"

Dolgyal, Shugden, who had entered the monk, answered, "Oh yes, yes, yes." Do you understand? Rinpoche asked if the vase was truly existent and Dolgyal replied that is was, so it seems he didn't know about what makes a thing truly existent. He had never been taught. The vase appears to be real, but is that true? If Dolgyal had been an enlightened being, there is no way he would have replied like that. Not even an arya being would have done that, so that proves he was not.

Then Rinpoche did *gek-tor* with three tormas, and by dedicating was able to drive Dolgyal away. Dolgyal had come to ask Rinpoche to accept him but when Rinpoche heard the incorrect answer he was able to drive him away with a gek-tor practice. Dolgyal's motivation was not to benefit sentient beings but for the self. It was an activity of the self-cherishing mind, like wanting to become famous or have great power. Wanting to have great influence, he tried to use a high lama many people trusted so they would accept him and willingly follow him.

In the West I think you call that sort of thing lobbying. At Istituto Lama Tzong Khapa in Italy there had never been a vote in the past, but after Lama Yeshe passed away we needed to appoint a director so I called everybody together to ask them to vote for one. There was a student who went around telling everybody who to vote for; he was lobbying for his friend. In the West, people spend millions and millions of dollars trying to get people to vote for them. They do whatever they can to win the vote. This is kind of what Dolgyal was doing with the high lamas. If you look at it like that, you can understand it. He was trying to cheat the high lamas, the learned geshes, to control them so that many people would practice him.

Having no mistakes but showing mistakes

Many of us are disciples of Kyabje Trijang Rinpoche. He was our root guru and his root guru was Kyabje Pabongka Dechen Nyingpo. We are disciples in the twenty-first century, so this is our special karma, our particular karma, our obstacle. This obstacle has just arisen; it wasn't there before but has now become a particular problem for us twenty-first century disciples.

Now there is great danger from life-to-life for hundreds, thousands, hundreds of thousands, even millions of lifetimes—the great danger of our being led the wrong way.

I gave you the example of Trehor Kyörpon Rinpoche. He saw Pabongka Dechen Nyingpo and Kyabje Trijang Rinpoche as buddhas, as being without mistakes. How could somebody be a buddha and yet at the same time have faults or make mistakes? It is not possible. If he has faults that means he is not an enlightened being. That doesn't happen. If we look at somebody and see he has faults—not *showing* the aspect of having faults but actually *having* faults—then that means he is not an enlightened being but an ordinary being. If he were a buddha he would have no faults.

According to the Mahayana, Guru Shakyamuni Buddha was enlightened numberless eons ago. He had no suffering but he showed us the twelve deeds; he showed us the suffering of rebirth, old age, sickness and death. He showed us those sufferings during his life and in the end he showed us the aspect of passing away. By taking the aspect of having suffering—by pretending in that way—he was showing us that which is true to higher beings, the truth of suffering, so that we can understand and practice Dharma.

And why is there suffering? Because there is the cause of suffering: karma and delusion. That means it is a dependent arising. Suffering is not independent but a dependent arising. If we eliminate the cause, karma and delusion, we are able to eliminate the result, suffering. Understanding the cause of suffering shows us we can achieve the cessation of suffering because there is a true path that leads to the actualization of that cessation. By showing us true suffering—the suffering of rebirth, old age, sickness and death—the Buddha showed us the four noble truths.

The Buddha had none of these sufferings. Even arhats, who are free from delusion and karma, do not have them, so how could a buddha, who is totally free from even subtle obscurations, have them? But he showed us suffering so that we would practice Dharma. Because we dislike suffering, he showed us this to guide us, using himself as an example by enacting the twelve deeds.

There are many stories that illustrate how the buddhas manifest as ordinary beings to guide us. They have no attachment but they show attachment; they have no anger but they show anger; they have no ignorance but they show ignorance.

Like that, because we have this impure karma, Kyabje Trijang Rinpoche and his root guru, Pabongka Dechen Nyingpo, showed us the aspect of practicing Shugden. They did not have faults but due to our impure karma they appeared as if they had faults.

This is like the example I have just mentioned of a buddha pretending to be an ordinary being. Since we are unable to see buddhas in their enlightened aspect they have to appear to us as ordinary beings so that we *can* see them. Buddhas have no faults but they manifest in an ordinary aspect having faults according to our impure karma and in that way are able to communicate with us.

We are also unable to see enlightened beings' deity aspect; we're unable to receive teachings directly from the deity. We do not have the karma. Therefore the buddhas have no choice but to show themselves in an ordinary aspect, where "ordinary" means showing faults. Because of this we are able to receive the pratimoksha, bodhisattva and tantric vows; we are able to receive initiations; we are able to receive commentaries on sutra and tantra and oral transmissions. It is easy for us to directly see and communicate with their ordinary aspect and to directly receive guidance.

Showing the aspect of having faults is unbelievably kind. Because our mind is so impure, so obscured, that is the only way we are able to see them and receive their guidance. This is the kindness of the guru, appearing to us in an ordinary aspect, showing mistakes, so that we can be easily guided by him, we can communicate with him, we can make offerings to him. His kindness is so important, more precious than the whole sky filled with wish-granting jewels. The value of a whole sky filled with wish-granting jewels is nothing compared to the value of the kindness of the guru.

A key element of guru devotion practice is the understanding that the guru shows the aspect of having faults while actually having none. The guru has no delusions, no obscurations, but he shows that aspect for us sentient beings. Ordinary bodhisattvas are able to see a buddha's nirmanakaya aspect; higher bodhisattvas can see the sambhogakaya aspect, but for us ordinary sentient beings, whose minds are so unenlightened, so obscured, so thick skulled, a buddha must show the ordinary aspect, which has faults. It is unbelievably important that they show us this ordinary aspect.

We have to bring this understanding—being without mistakes but showing mistakes—into our guru devotion practice. We have to use that phrase, "showing mistakes," while thinking that they have no mistakes. If we say they have mistakes then they are not buddhas, they are ordinary beings. Then the whole thing changes.

Seeing apparent mistakes in the guru need not become the cause for us to lose our devotion but instead it can become the cause to develop it, to make our devotion stronger. I would also suggest when problems arise that you use the nine thoughts on guru devotion called *Practicing Guru Devotion with the Nine Attitudes* by the great Nyingma lama, Shabkar Tsogdruk Rangdrol.[46] He was non-sectarian and taught lam-rim on the basis of Lama Atisha's teaching, *Lamp for the Path to Enlightenment*, which explains the graduated paths of the lower capable being, the middle capable being and the higher capable being. Lama Tsongkhapa explained the nine attitudes but Lama Shabkar made them into verses.

We have put it into the new FPMT prayer book in the *Guru Puja* lam-rim section. First there is the verse on guru devotion, correctly following the guru, then the prayer *Practicing Guru Devotion with the Nine Attitudes*. I have translated it so it can be recited during the *Guru Puja*.

When you have a negative thought in relation to the guru, one solution is to recite that prayer. If you do so, it cuts that negative thought off immediately, clearing it away just like a horrible black fog that fills whole sky suddenly dispersing.

The need to renounce Dolgyal practice

Kyabje Pabongka Dechen Nyingpo practiced Most Secret Hayagriva, the Circle of Dharma, from the pure appearance of the Fifth Dalai Lama and many other things. One day he made a prediction to his attendant that the next day a fat monk would come to see him. He told the attendant, "Don't allow him into my room."

But, as I mentioned, the karma of us present-day sentient beings is to deal with this problem, to get involved with the Dolgyal problem. So the next day, when the fat monk arrived, the attendant forgot Pabongka's instruction and admitted him. I think he spent quite a long time in the room and when the attendant entered after the fat monk had left it seemed that Pabongka Dechen Nyingpo's aspect was not well, like something had entered, had occupied him. Pabongka seemed changed and the thangkas of Most Secret Hayagriva, the deity he had practiced before, which were hanging behind him, had been taken down. So this is the start.

---

[46] *Heart of the Path*, appendix 8, pp. 429–31. See also *Lamrim Chenmo*, vol. 1, pp. 78–81. Shabkar Tsogdruk Rangdrol (1781–1851) was a tantric practitioner and prolific writer and said to be an emanation of Milarepa. See *The Life of Shabkar: The Autobiography of a Tibetan Yogin*.

If we understand the beginning, this is what happened. Pabongka Dechen Nyingpo was a great bodhisattva and a great tantric practitioner, a great yogi, Heruka. Because of that, his holy actions were able to bring so much benefit to Tibet. Many people believed it was because he practiced Dolgyal that he became so famous and was able to extensively benefit Tibet. Because many high lamas and geshes have so much devotion to Pabongka, without analysis it is very easy to think this.

There are many others who question this. For example, Kyabje Ling Rinpoche, His Holiness the Dalai Lama's elder guru, was a heart disciple of Kyabje Pabongka but did not practice Dolgyal. There are many other high lamas as well who have questions about it and do not practice, feeling uneasy about it. They reject the practice and advise us not to practice it. There are also others who are very devoted to Pabongka and who do practice Dolgyal, the basic reason being that they have not checked the guru's activities.

As I said before, the guru has no faults but he shows the aspect of having faults according to our karma.

When we check we can see that in reality all the gurus are one—His Holiness the Dalai Lama, Pabongka Rinpoche, Kyabje Trijang Rinpoche, Kyabje Zong Rinpoche—all the gurus are one. We can see they are all one, all Buddha Vajradhara. In the prayer *Namo Gurubhya, Namo Buddhaya, Namo Dharmaya, Namo Sanghaya*, the guru comes first before the Buddha, the Dharma and the Sangha because the guru is kinder than all the buddhas. That is why we take refuge in the guru first, then in the Buddha, the Dharma and the Sangha.

The main reason the guru comes first is not the kindness, however, but because in reality the guru is *that* guru, Buddha Vajradhara. We find no contradiction there. Otherwise, saying Pabongka Rinpoche is mistaken is saying the Guru Vajradhara is mistaken. That means he is not a buddha but an ordinary being. That changes everything.

I mentioned Trehor Kyörpon Rinpoche. Think about what he did and you will understand. This is similar to Kyabje Pabongka Rinpoche. He had many followers, many learned lamas in Tibet who were his heart disciples and did not practice Dolgyal, but there were others who did not check but practiced it because they had so much devotion to him.

This is not just about practicing Dolgyal. There are many examples of the guru showing mistakes. He might lead an unhealthy lifestyle such as eating harmful food or not exercising and we, as his disciples, need to explain to him what might happen if he keeps doing that. He might get sick or have to go to the hospital and so forth. There are so many mundane things we need to explain to our guru. Although the guru does not have ignorance, he shows that aspect because of our impure karma.

Those great Indian pandits were enlightened. They had actualized the path; they knew everything the Buddha taught—the entire Kangyur and Tengyur—and were not only experts in the meaning, they had also actualized it. However, when they reincarnated, they showed an ordinary aspect, like any small child, crying, making pipi and kaka, playing and so forth. They needed to be looked after.

When His Holiness the Dalai Lama, who is Chenrezig, was growing up he had to study in the monastery just as normal monks do. He had two main tutors, Kyabje Ling Rinpoche and Kyabje Trijang Rinpoche, and seven *tsenshabs*, who were not gurus but expert, learned monks who helped with his education, his debating, and came from each of the main monasteries, Sera (Je and Me colleges), Ganden (Shartse and Jangtse colleges) and Drepung (Gomang and Loseling colleges).

His Holiness undertook much study and then sat examinations. So, even though he is Chenrezig, an enlightened being, to benefit us ordinary sentient beings he acted in an ordinary aspect. An enlightened being who manifests as a dog must then eat like a dog and bark like a dog. Manifesting as a dog, he would have a dog's hairy body, a dog's eyes, a dog's nose and so forth and do everything a dog does, all to guide us sentient beings.

One of Lama Tsongkhapa's closest disciples was a monk called Duldzin Dragpa Gyaltsen,[47] who some say was reborn at the time of the Fifth Dalai Lama as Tulku Dragpa Gyaltsen.[48] He was said to have been murdered by a government official and to have reincarnated in the wrathful aspect of Dol Gyalchen, Dolgyal. In that aspect he went to Tashi Lhunpo Monastery as he was a disciple of the Panchen Lama but he was prevented from entering by the eight guardian Dharma protectors of the monastery.[49] If Dolgyal, appearing as Dragpa Gyaltsen, had in actuality been a buddha, an enlightened being, or even an arya bodhisattva, there is no question that he would have been allowed in. So it's a *huge* question why he was not. A *huge* ques-

---

[47] 1374–1434. He actually resides in Maitreya's Yiga Chödzin Palace in the pure land of Tushita. There are several versions of the Dolgyal origin story.

[48] 1619–56. The Dalai Lama says it is doubtful that Tulku Dragpa Gyaltsen was the reincarnation of Duldzin Dragpa Gyaltsen.

[49] Tib: *nam-se ta-dag gyä*, the eight keepers of the horses of Vaishravana, who is one of the four directional guardians.

tion. According to one version, he then went off to offer a torma to the head of the Sakya order, but the lama put the torma on a very low shelf.

What happens is that practicing Dolgyal creates a problem in your relationship with His Holiness, who is Chenrezig. It stops you working for and offering service to His Holiness. That's what has happened with many lamas who are very devoted to Dolgyal.

It interferes with your guru devotion. In particular it breaks your *samaya* with His Holiness and that harms not only this life but life after life for hundreds, thousands, hundreds of thousands and even millions of lives and it causes you to be reborn in hell and suffer for eons and eons. Then, even if you are born human, you cannot find a guru for hundreds or thousands of years. It goes on like that.

It also causes problems at the end of your life. There are stories of people who strongly practiced Dolgyal but were harmed terribly at the end of their life. Dolgyal has common powers and can manifest in many forms but at the end of a practitioner's life it shows its own form, its spirit form. When that happens the person sees clearly what he has done and how Dolgyal has cheated him his whole life and he becomes extremely repentant.

There was a man in Tibet, not a monk, who practiced Dolgyal intensely but even his wife didn't know. When he was gravely ill and nearing death he asked his wife to have a puja done, a tea offering in the temple where they practiced Dolgyal. It was only then that she came to realize he had been a follower of Dolgyal.

He had practiced Dolgyal so much but then, at his last breath, the spirit manifested, not in its usual form but in its true form, the real spirit, so ugly, so terrifying. Seeing this with his last breath the man realized he had been completely deceived by this spirit his whole life. He had unbelievable regret and felt strong repentance. This story is in the foreword I wrote.

There are other stories, like a very learned geshe who died falling from a car that crashed. Nobody else in the car was thrown out but he was catapulted over a precipice and died, having great regret. And there are other such stories of catastrophes that happened to geshes at the time of death. So, it seems there is great harm at the very end.

When my master, Lama Yeshe, who was kinder than all the past, present and future buddhas, was passing away, he went to Los Angeles for an operation in a good hospital but they didn't operate because the doctors said the heart was too old to do the operation. What they did, though, was put a hole in it and attach some tubes using a new technique. We were not allowed to go into the room while that was happening because there were machines there but when Lama came out he said it was quite difficult, almost like he had passed away.

We were in America but it was the Tibetan New Year, early in the morning, around two thirty or three o'clock.[50] Whenever obstacles occurred I was used to reciting the request to Dolgyal for help, so I was reciting that. Lama's belly seemed to be moving around and I was reciting the prayer requesting help when Lama's eyes opened wide, like he was seeing some unpleasant aspect. It was like he was surprised, seeing some form there. It didn't seem positive; it was like there was some negative aspect there. I'm not saying that Lama had made a mistake but the aspect was like that. So, as I recited the request for Dolgyal's help it was like he was seeing something fearful. His eyes were big and had a kind of surprised, fearful look.

Dolgyal was the main protector he relied on. That is my view. He commonly used Dolgyal, for example, during the Kopan courses whenever somebody went crazy. Not everybody went crazy there, of course. Actually, I suppose it depends on your definition of craziness. On one level I'm crazy, you're crazy, everybody is crazy. On one level it's like that, but at the level we worldly people are on only a few people become crazy with *lung* or things like that. Lama would do the Dolgyal puja before each one-month Kopan course started and then whenever there was something important. However, at the end of a person's life the aspect that Dolgyal shows is not good, as I said before. I mentioned Lama's external aspect in the foreword I wrote.

Another danger of following Dolgyal is that the person criticizes His Holiness. When somebody who is not a bodhisattva gets angry with a bodhisattva for even one second it destroys all the merit he has collected over a thousand eons making charity, making offerings to the buddhas and so forth. So if somebody criticizes or gets angry with His Holiness, can you imagine? For however long the person is angry and criticizes His Holiness—however many weeks, months or years—countless eons of merit are destroyed.

Of the many bodhisattvas, the Buddha predicted that the bodhisattva Limitless Supreme Awareness, attaining the state of Chenrezig, would be in Tibet in the aspect of His Holiness the Dalai Lama to benefit the Tibetan people and spread the Dharma. There were four great prayers done for sentient beings in Tibet and people generated refuge in their heart in the Bud-

---

[50] This was the morning of 3 March 1984.

dha, Dharma and Sangha, so it happened as the Buddha has predicted. Getting angry with a buddha like His Holiness destroys the merit created in the past over millions, probably hundreds of millions of eons. These very heavy things happen.

In short, practicing Dolgyal is harmful to Tibet, harmful to Buddhism, harmful to our own life and harmful to the world because it destroys this life. And it is not only harmful to this life; it affects the next life and the life after that for hundreds and thousands of lifetimes. The harm, the negative result, goes on and on, for many, many lifetimes. The essence is that we destroy ourselves.

His Holiness is the one to reveal the complete teachings

The last time I visited His Holiness in Dharamsala I thanked him on behalf of Tibet and the Tibetan people and also on behalf of practitioners of Buddhism and I think I thanked him on behalf of the world. I thanked His Holiness even though many learned lamas and geshes continuously criticize him so much. From His Holiness's side, he bears all the difficulties with much compassion. And His Holiness continuously advises us to not practice Dolgyal, no matter how much those people are against him, how much they criticize him. I think it is so important to thank His Holiness, who is the one to correct our life, showing us the unmistaken Dharma we should practice and the mistaken Dharma we should avoid.

He is the one to do this, not just because of his Nobel Peace Prize but because in the world he reveals not only the Hinayana teachings but also Mahayana sutra and the Mahayana tantra teachings. In reality, he is the Buddha. In the past there have been buddhas and now there is Shakyamuni Buddha in the aspect of His Holiness. What was in the aspect of Shakyamuni when the Buddha was giving teachings in India is now in this aspect, as His Holiness.

He is the one who has complete Dharma understanding, so he is the one who can correct us, correct our life and explain what is right and wrong. He's the one to show us logically what path to follow instead of just doing whatever we like and not doing what we don't like.

I gave the example at the beginning of Dolgyal in the aspect of the oracle monk who went to see Trehor Kyörpon Rinpoche and asked to be accepted by him. This is what Dolgyal did with Pabongka and many other lamas. That is according to our impure karma. The gurus don't have mistakes, but the aspect of practicing this is our projection that decorates the reality; it is our hallucination. It is decorated by ignorance, as I mentioned yesterday. Decorating is such a good term, like decorating with paint, putting white color on the wall so you don't see the bricks.

Can I ask that you please read the foreword I wrote for the Mongolian book. Please read it well, not just like reading through a puja or something in order to finish it but thoroughly, thinking about what I have written.

8. Khadro-la

KHADRO-LA AND EARTHQUAKES

Although Khadro-la, the young Tibetan lady, has been publicly recognized as an oracle she is much more than that. She is beyond that; she is beyond all of us. The story of what she saw when she went to Mount Kailash is just unbelievable. It is not at all what we common people normally see.

When she was in Chamdo, in Kham, she had been unaware of the big problem of Dolgyal but when she reached Mount Kailash this problem appeared everywhere, in all the four traditions. So, when she was at Mount Kailash she went to Tushita, the Joyful Pure Land, Lama Tsongkhapa's and Maitreya Buddha's pure land, to find Thagpo Dorje Chang. Not many people would have heard of Thagpo Dorje Chang but he was a great, great lama and one of Pabongka Rinpoche's gurus. In his past lives he used to see Tara Cittamani all the time, and receive initiations, commentaries and all the various activities of Tara Cittamani from Tara herself.

Because Thagpo Dorje Chang was in Tushita, Khadro-la went there to ask him about Dolgyal. She has a totally free mind so she can do that. His Holiness has said that the previous beliefs were incorrect, that he had never seen the explanation about following Dolgyal in the collections of teachings Thagpo Dorje Chang received from Tibet. I think Lama Tsongkhapa asked who would protect his teachings and Thagpo Dorje Chang in the pure land said that he would do it.

Thagpo Dorje Chang was giving teachings to hundreds of dakinis, highly realized female sky-goers, and Khadro-la went to him and asked this question, "What did people believe in, in the past? Did you say it was correct to practice Dolgyal before or not?" He replied he had not, that this was incorrect. This concurred with what His Holiness had said. By going to the pure land Khadro-la was able to confirm this.

What she told me is something not known by common people but, in order to believe these stories, you need to understand her capacity.

In Dharamsala quite a number of years ago she told me there was going to be a huge earthquake endangering hundreds of thousands or even millions of people. It involved the whole Himalayan range of mountains. I think there was probably going to be a volcanic eruption or something and so many people would die. She could see everything and could see that there was great danger.

After she told His Holiness, he gave her the responsibility to prevent it. She wanted to build several stupas around His Holiness's palace. They were not exactly the same as normal stupas; they looked much the same on the outside but there were some differences on the inside. Because these were not normal stupas His Holiness's Private Office and his attendants didn't listen to her and so for a long time they refused permission. In the end His Holiness told them to do whatever Khadro-la said. She explained the stupa to His Holiness's attendants and that its details were in a particular text by a great lama, which was confirmed when they checked. Without ever having looked at the text herself she knew exactly where this was mentioned, even giving the page number. They were very surprised when they found it was there as she had said. Generally Khadro-la does not read scriptures quickly because she has never been trained, or so it appears externally.

She was finally able to complete all the stupas in different colors. One was built at the Tibetan nursery school and another one at Norbulingka in lower Dharamsala where the Tibetans who have come from Tibet have art and handicraft shops and restaurants. There are many statues there.

She explained this to me in detail, how although the major earthquake could be prevented there would be a very small one that could not be stopped. That has already happened in lower Dharamsala and I think one cow died, but the major earthquake with the volcanic eruption has been stopped.

Once, when she was on a beach in Taiwan, there was about to be a typhoon. She did some prayers, nothing long at all, and the typhoon stopped. The students who were around her at the time actually saw this happen and they told me.

She is very powerful. The nagas and worldly protectors who cause violent weather—all those hail storms and winds and such things—react depending on what people do. If people do positive things the weather is subdued but violent weather is the result of people's negative, violent minds, their violent thoughts.

I'm telling you this in case you are wondering whether it is possible for Khadro-la to go to a pure land. Maybe you believe it or maybe not, but I can tell you other things so you can understand what she can do.

The power of the bodhisattvas

Of course, such powers as being able to influence the weather are as yet unknown by Western scientists. They attribute bad weather to other causes. They can see the physical conditions but they have yet to understand the most important thing, the inner cause, karma. Not even the most expert Western scientists have discovered this but it seems their thinking is getting more subtle and they are getting closer to the Buddhist views.

For example, they used to believe that there were no sentient beings on Mars but then—before I left America for India last year or the year before—it was announced that they had discovered the potential for life there.[51] So, it is changing, and it will continue to change the deeper they check.

Karma has yet to be discovered by the scientists. But once it is discovered—how all suffering comes from negative karma and all happiness comes from positive karma—it will blow their minds! It will be such an unbelievable shock. This is what I think. At the moment, because it is not within the scope of scientific thought, people in the West don't think about it. Some people might even think that concepts like karma and reincarnation are crazy, that they come from people's imagination. Such people either don't think about future lives or what death means or their thoughts are very vague.

One time, on an airplane, I was watching my fellow passengers put their luggage up before the flight. They were well-dressed, maybe in clothes worth a thousand dollars, and talking about nothing but this life, nothing else, about how they made ten million dollars and things like that. But they had no idea at all about the life after this. They had never heard that the result of negative karma is rebirth in the suffering lower realms—the hells, the hungry ghost realm or the animal realm—or that the result of positive

---

[51] As of March 2016, the Mars rover, Curiosity, is discovering more and more evidence of all the factors needed to have life, such as running water, methane and the five principal elements.

karma is the happiness of the human and god realms. And this is without talking about what is beyond samsara, about nirvana, the total cessation of the oceans of samsaric suffering and the five paths that lead to liberation and enlightenment.

There are five paths to peerless happiness, buddhahood, the state of the omniscient mind, the elimination of all obscurations and the completion of all realizations—*sang-gyä*. Even before reaching that goal, simply progressing through the five paths and the ten *bhumis* brings unbelievable happiness and bliss.

Even on the first bhumi a bodhisattva is able to go to a hundred different buddha pure lands and receive teaching from the buddhas there at the same time and with a hundred different bodies do prostrations to the buddhas there. Then, when he achieves the second bodhisattva bhumi, he is able to go to a thousand different buddha pure lands and receive teachings and manifest in a thousand bodies and give teachings to sentient beings. With each succeeding bhumi the numbers increase and with the eighth, ninth and tenth bhumis the bodhisattva can go to billions and zillions of pure lands and receive teachings and do prostrations there and is able to manifest in billions and zillions and trillions of forms and give teachings, getting ever closer to enlightenment like that. He can manifest as a river, a bridge, a mountain, as all kinds of things to benefit sentient being. What a bodhisattva can do to benefit sentient beings is so amazing it doesn't fit our ordinary, limited concepts. If this is what a bodhisattva can do, there is no question what a buddha can do.

Saving animals and humans

There are many stories about Khadro-la that I have heard as well as many stories I have yet to hear. Besides the earthquake that Khadro-la predicted in Dharamsala, there's also the huge California earthquake that Western scientists predicted a long time ago and announced again at the beginning of 2014. She has also spoken about that one.

Normally our organization liberates animals. The FPMT center in Singapore has already liberated almost two hundred million. They don't liberate them the way we normally do, just buying them from where they are going to be killed and releasing them. What they do is put small insects and shellfish into sacks and frogs in containers and circumambulate them around many stupas filled with mantras, including the four dharmakaya relic mantras, and also many texts, such as the entire collection of teachings by Lama

Tsongkhapa and his disciples. There are also the Kangyur and Tengyur and many collections of all the teachings.[52]

Carrying the animals by hand, all the children, parents and grandparents circumambulate the holy objects. With each circumambulation they all create the karma to achieve highest enlightenment, even the insects. In one plastic bag there may be a thousand crickets. As many times as that bag is taken around, the closer to enlightenment those thousand crickets come. That includes nirvana, the blissful state of peace, liberation from the oceans of samsaric suffering as well, and a good rebirth in the next life and temporary happiness—all those things are contained in that. So it has amazing benefit.

Then everybody blesses the buckets of water by reciting different mantras, beginning with OM MANI PADME HUM of course and many other different mantras, and then blowing on the water. They then sprinkle it over all the animals and birds, or, with the sacks containing the shellfish, they pour the water over them. That way the animals get a higher rebirth, and possibly, hopefully, meet the Dharma. The third thing is to recite the mantras to those beings who can hear, to plant the seed of enlightenment in their minds. So at least we should try to do those three things to benefit them as much as possible.

I tell people who have cancer to dedicate and donate some money to those doing animal liberation and sometimes it is able to cure that cancer. Cancer causes a shortening of life so by liberating animals we are causing them to have a long life and that in turn causes us to have a long life. By giving others a long life, we can have a long life. And it affects our life for hundreds and thousands of future lifetimes.

This is how it is done in Singapore, not just buying and releasing them but trying to help them as much as possible. We also do that in Hong Kong and from time to time in Taiwan. Later I'm hoping we can do it in China and Malaysia as well.

I thought if we do that with animals, why not also save human beings? If the big earthquake is going to happen, why not try to help the human beings there? I wanted to do something before it happened because once it has

---

[52] This topic is covered extensively in Rinpoche's *Liberating Animals from the Danger of Death and Other Ways to Benefit Them*. There is also a CD of Rinpoche's *Recitations for Animals*. Both are available from the FPMT. See also *Practices for Benefiting Animals* on the LYWA website.

happened so many people will have died. Places that have been developed over hundreds of years at a cost of billions, zillions or trillions of dollars can be destroyed in an hour by something like an earthquake.

A few years ago in Dharamsala I asked Khadro-la about preventing the Californian earthquake and she predicted so quickly, like a waterfall, what stupas we needed to build, how and where we should build them and so forth. I marked where she said on a map but the map was very small. At first, the American Embassy in Delhi rejected her visa, even when we tried a second time. She even had a letter from His Holiness's Private Office but they didn't want to read it. They probably do this to other people as well.

Then she tried to go to Canada but they rejected her there as well. We spent about ten thousand dollars in America applying many, many times to the government before she finally got a visa.

When she flew to California and was landing in San Francisco, she felt this was the place to build a stupa. She stayed at the Aptos house. One day, as we went across the Golden Gate Bridge she saw that the nearer of the two mountains close to the bridge was the better location for a stupa. So at the moment we are looking for the place to build it. One time, when we were in a Zen restaurant, I thought maybe we could build it inside the restaurant so many people could see it. One of the places is a government park called The Presidio. Venerable Roger has appointed an ex-director of Tse Chen Ling, our San Francisco center, to look for a suitable place.

After the place has been found, Khadro-la has to come to purify the land, to bless it before building the stupa. Hopefully, this will prevent that huge earthquake and save hundreds of thousands or even millions of people's lives.

Publicly she is like an ordinary person

Khadro-la's main purpose for coming from Tibet to India was to serve and protect His Holiness.

A few years ago, when His Holiness was ill, all the Tibetan doctors agreed that His Holiness should not have an operation. Even the Nechung oracle agreed. Nechung, who has been the Tibetan government's protector from ancient times, appears in a worldly aspect but is, in reality, the five buddha families, or five Dhyani Buddhas. They invoked the protector and asked him and even he said not to do the operation. Finally, when His Holiness was in Delhi he asked his attendants to ask Khadro-la. She said he must have surgery immediately, it was very important. When the doctor in Delhi operated he discovered gallstones and was shocked because it was unbelievably dangerous. So Khadro-la's insisting on the operation was correct. This is one example of her capacity.

She has also saved several Tibetan people who were about to die, as they were drawing their last breath. By coming from Tibet she has been able to save the lives of many people, allowing them to live for several years longer.

Her main responsibility is to look after His Holiness, to protect His Holiness's life, to help His Holiness fulfill his holy wishes in the world. That is the most important thing in the world, to benefit the world. Publicly, she is just like an ordinary person, but in reality she is beyond that. I have an inner offering from her. Basically, I asked for it. It contains her blessing, a blessing from the real Vajrayogini.

I think she might have obtained the inner offering in Kullu Manali, one of the two places in India famous for hot springs. One seems good for the knees and one for the belly. Once I went there with her. We had arranged a hotel but she didn't stay there; she stayed at the hot spring, where the rooms were much cheaper. Many people came day and night.

While she was there she had a competition with Shiva, the Hindu god. Because of Shiva's powers, he was carrying unbelievable weapons like in the many stories you hear about him. He can manifest all kinds of weapons but Khadro-la can also manifest all kinds of weapons as well, so they were competing. Of course, to the other people in the room it probably seemed like she was sleeping or something, but in reality this is what happened; she was in the aspect of Vajrayogini, with her hair standing straight up terrifyingly, competing with Shiva.

Whatever she did, however she transformed or whatever miraculous power she displayed, Shiva also did. However, when she sang the hymns of the guru, the hymns of emptiness, Shiva knelt down and put his head on Khadro-la's knee. Until then, she was manifesting all kinds of things and he was able to do the same, but finally manifesting in Vajrayogini's form and singing of emptiness was so unimaginable that Shiva knelt down and respected her.

The next day, before she left, she went down to a Shiva temple just to say goodbye. The blue drawing of Shiva was there just the same so she said goodbye before she left. I think this also happened at the hotel as well. She explained that this is a very secret story.

I think in the future I will ask her to go to the Land of Joy.[53] It will be good to get her to bless the land. She did that at Mahamudra Centre in New Zealand and at Chenrezig Institute in Australia the first time she went there. She did a retreat for seven days and everybody cried for two days! Everybody cried.

At Chenrezig Institute they have done the Basic Program several times and were just starting another round.[54] Some nuns have done the Basic Program several times. There are maybe twenty-five or twenty-six nuns at Chenrezig—a lot of nuns—but not so many monks. Geshe Tashi Tsering—not the Geshe Tashi in London but another one—was there for many years and he was very kind, pushing the nuns to study a lot. He did this because in his life in the monastery he saw the importance of studying and working very hard for the monastery, and he saw that this was also true for Chenrezig Institute.

When Khadro-la went there, for the first two days everybody cried through her teachings as she brought everybody's mind into the Dharma. Then she went to Mahamudra Centre in New Zealand and all two hundred students also cried for the first two days as she brought their minds into the Dharma as well.

Now she is unable to travel for a year because she had a Tibetan yellow passport,[55] which is a lot of trouble, so she gave that to the Indian Government and has applied for an Indian passport, which takes a year. She could get the refugee paper back but I advised her to stay there and try to get the passport.

At the moment we are so fortunate. We have this human rebirth, we have met Buddhism and we can meet great beings like Khadro-la. So we are unbelievably fortunate.

In the "dream experience" Khadro-la received many teachings on emptiness from Kyabje Trijang Rinpoche in his past life aspect. He told her that Dolgyal totally cheated him and this has interfered with the activities of his present incarnation. Ling Rinpoche lives in India quite publicly because he doesn't practice Dolgyal but Trijang Rinpoche is sort of in hiding.

---

[53] The FPMT retreat center in the far north of England that was purchased during Rinpoche's 2014 visit.
[54] The Basic Program is an FPMT course of study that has been taught at Chenrezig Institute since 1997. Three full rounds have been completed and the fourth started in 2015.
[55] A refugee identification card that few countries recognize.

THE GURU APPEARS IN AN ORDINARY FORM BECAUSE OF OUR IMPURE MIND

The tantric text *Vajra Tent* says,

> In these degenerate times, I, who am called Vajrasattva, will abide in the form of the spiritual master. With the aim of benefiting sentient beings, I will abide in an ordinary form.

In these times of the five degenerations, Vajrasattva, or Vajradhara—the names differ but they're the same being—has taken the holy form of the spiritual master, or guru, to abide in an ordinary form in order to benefit sentient beings. We should understand this and generate faith and respect for the guru. This is also mentioned in the *Fifty Verses of Guru Devotion*.[56]

Once the bodhisattva Meaningful to Behold asked the Buddha, "When you, Guru Shakyamuni Buddha, have passed away, who will there be to guide us?" To that the Buddha replied, "Hi, Meaningful to Behold, when that time comes I will manifest in the form of an abbot, a master, a *lob-pön*. In order to ripen the minds of sentient beings, in order to benefit them, I will show the aspect of having birth, old age, sickness and death."

There are other quotations but that is enough. As I have already mentioned, for arya bodhisattvas—"arya" meaning exalted bodhisattvas who have a direct perception of emptiness—the Buddha manifests in the sambhogakaya aspect. Ordinary bodhisattvas who have achieved the great stage of the path of merit can see countless buddhas in their nirmanakaya aspect. Of the five Mahayana paths, the first one, the path of merit has three stages, small, medium and great, and it is when the bodhisattva reaches the great stage of the path of merit that he is able to see numberless buddhas in nirmanakaya aspect.

For us ordinary beings, whose minds are obscured, the Buddha manifests as an ordinary being, in a human form, like His Holiness, or he manifests as a king or as a beggar to allow us sentient beings to collect merit. He can manifest as a child, a crazy person, a butcher, a prostitute or a judge. He can manifest in all kinds of forms.

---

[56] Find the root text and commentary at LamaYeshe.com. See also Tsongkhapa's *The Fulfillment of All Hopes*.

An abbot of a monastery in Tibet who had clairvoyance recently passed away. He seemed to have been a very important lama. I was able to help somebody he knew well in Switzerland, a monk who was at Buxa, who wanted to build a large covered Padmasambhava statue that would cost a hundred thousand dollars.

Once, this lama went into a market in Kathmandu and, seeing a butcher there—just an ordinary butcher living his life selling meat—the lama made a throne for him and had him sit on it. So, even in the marketplace we never know who is a buddha and who isn't. We have to know that. We have to be careful to not harm others, to not get angry and to practice patience, otherwise we might create the cause to suffer for hundreds of thousands or millions of years. When this clairvoyant lama saw the butcher he made a throne.

There is also the story of a teacher, a monk, in Tibet who buried his money in the ground outside his room. From time to time he would go to where it was buried and look at it. Then one day he died and his disciples needed money to make an offering. They couldn't find any money in his room so they went outside to where they had seen their teacher often go. When they saw a small mound of earth they dug it up and discovered the money, but there was a scorpion holding tightly onto the entire big bundle of money.

A young monk took the scorpion to his teacher's guru, Chösang Rinpoche, and asked him what to do. The guru told him he must take it and give it to a butcher behind the Potala. When the disciple did this, the butcher placed the animal on the chopping block and chopped it in half, eating one half and throwing the other half in the air. When the young monk told the teacher's guru what had happened, he said, "Oh, now that is very good!" This was because the butcher was the deity, the enlightened being, Red Yamantaka, and throwing half the body into the air meant his consciousness had been transferred to a pure land.

His Holiness Serkong Tsenshab Rinpoche told me many times that although he had not seen this happen he had heard this story. Rinpoche was the incarnation of Marpa's son, Darma Dodé. One day Marpa told Darma Dodé not to leave the house but he went anyway to look at some scenery, fell off his horse, knocked his head on a stone and died. Anyway, Serkong Tsenshab Rinpoche was his incarnation. This great holy being is among my kind teachers. Any small break he had—even while he was eating—he would give teachings and answer questions. He was so kind. He told me this story many times. He passed away in Ladakh and his incarnation was born in Spiti in 1984.

That butcher behind the Potala was the enlightened deity Red Yamantaka. So an enlightened being doesn't have to be some being we see radiating light in the sky whereas somebody we see elsewhere—on the ground, in the bathroom, where meat is sold and so forth—could not be an enlightened being. Any of those people could be enlightened.

Buddhas manifest as gods or demigods, as all kinds of human beings. For example, when we are having problems and somebody suddenly appears and helps us, telling us what we need to hear, showing us the path, that could be a buddha or a bodhisattva manifesting to help us. This happens many times.

We may think a person is ridiculous, that she doesn't know any Dharma, but we cannot judge by the appearance. In reality, what appears to us is totally a projection, or decoration, of our own karma, our ordinary impure mind. We really cannot say. The way something appears to us and what we believe to be real can be the complete opposite of what is actually real. The ordinary person can in reality be an enlightened being. Many times unknown people have helped or guided us and we have not known who they were.

Buddhas can manifest as hungry ghosts to help hungry ghosts. They are not hungry ghosts but they manifest in that form in order to help them. They can manifest as all kinds of animals to help animals. They are buddhas, not animals, but they manifest as animals or insects or whatever. They can manifest as hell protectors or hell beings. They can manifest as maras; they are not maras but they show that aspect to help others. There are all kinds of ways they manifest to help beings.

Because of our deluded mind we find it difficult to know reality and always believe that what appears to us exists the way it appears. Somebody ordinary appears to us and we believe in that appearance; we think that that is the reality. We cannot see the reality, that that is a buddha.

In the Heruka body mandala there are twenty-four holy places. When we do the sadhana we have to visualize those holy places on the body as they are on earth, in Nepal, Tibet and India. They are there, but we also visualize them on our body. At that time numberless dakas and dakinis immediately come and enter our body, blessing our winds, chakras and drops to make them functional while we are meditating, as in the *Six Yogas of Naropa*.[57] They enter our central channel, abide and absorb, and then, after the gross mind is absorbed and the subtle mind is absorbed, the most subtle mind, the clear light, arises. Then we experience the great bliss of non-duality with emptiness, ceasing the dualistic mind, the dualistic view, the superstitions, ceasing the ordinary mind-wind. This is like an atomic bomb. This is the practice of Highest Yoga Tantra.

At those holy places there are numberless dakas and dakinis with different levels of realization. There are those who have just achieved the unification of clear light and illusory body and also enlightened beings. When we go to those holy places we will definitely meet those holy beings, but the question is whether or not we will be able to recognize them as such. That is the biggest problem, especially in those places. Of course, this is not something to speak about in public, but it's just to get the idea.

Once in Nepal I dreamed of a small four- or five-year-old girl who was Vajrayogini. The next day we went to Pharping,[58] not because of the dream, it's just something we do from time-to-time. Pharping is where two brothers, two yogis, the Phamtingpas, achieved Vajrayogini's enlightenment. There is a main Vajrayogini statue there and also a small one—a natural one not made by man—that might have belonged to the Phamtingpas. The caretakers show it from time-to-time, if they are happy. Anyway, that day the girl was there—exactly the same girl I saw in my dream. She was with some Nepalese ladies who had come to worship the statue. Although she was so young she put some *sindura* on Lobsang Nyima, Lama Yeshe's disciple from Tibet who served him at Buxa, Lawudo and Kopan. He had good guru devotion but sometimes got angry while he was working. This little girl didn't know him and he didn't know her but she put some sindura on him. She didn't put it on me. It was very interesting and very strange.

Even though I had seen this very clearly in my dream, still my mind is so bad. Because the way it appeared was a projection of my mind, so ordinary, what she did was still hard to believe. I should have done what it says to do in the Vajrayogini commentary—go around her three times anticlockwise,

---

[57] In Highest Yoga Tantra the practitioner learns to control the winds (the psychic energy that flows through the body), chakras (the energy wheels located along the central psychic channel) and drops (subtle substances within the body).

[58] A small village and pilgrimage site near Kathmandu where Padmasambhava is said to have attained high tantric realizations. It is also the site of an important Vajrayogini temple and a self-emanating Tara.

grab her feet and say the verses, "You are my mother" and so forth, and then one-pointedly pray for her to guide me. Nobody stopped me from doing that, only my own mind. My very strong ordinary mind would not let me. My mind is very thick-skulled, full of very ordinary concepts and I followed it.

The guru's kindness in guiding us in this life is really unbelievable. It's inexpressible. This has been happening from beginningless rebirths. For countless lifetimes the guru has guided us, manifesting in all kinds of ways in pure and impure forms. He has manifested not only as a Buddhist teacher but also as Brahma, Indra and Shiva, benefiting sentient beings by taking their form and then guiding them. He has manifested as a Christian priest, a nun or monk, or as a Muslim practitioner. There are all kinds of ways he manifests. From beginningless rebirths we have been guided.

In 1983 Lama Yeshe and I went to Assisi, where Saint Francis had died and where his holy body is kept along with that of his chief disciple, the nun who had three hundred disciples. Her very long body is well preserved in a glass-topped coffin but Saint Francis' body is covered in a black iron coffin. When we visited there, Lama Yeshe sat down in front of his body and meditated.

At that time I thought that because his mind was so pure, Saint Francis was the same as a Kadampa geshe, with bodhicitta, with no self-cherishing thought and no attachment to this life. I don't know how, but he was a completely pure Dharma practitioner in his mind. He dressed differently from the other monks, so renounced, with many patches in his *chuba*-like robes. In India and Tibet and also among the Kadampa geshes, there are monks who practice renouncing this life who have many patches in their robes, even though they have great realizations and are great tantric practitioners. Saint Francis was like a Kadampa geshe in this.

He was very humble and he always recited "God, God" in the same way we recite "Tara, Tara." All his disciples were also very humble. The other priests who lived higher up would spit on him and say bad things about him because of his humility and patched robes and because he was so different from them.

I saw on his table a picture of Jesus Christ that had spoken to Saint Francis. I think, when your mind is pure, statues speak to you. All the statues at Bodhgaya spoke to Lama Atisha. Some of the statues there now are new because they took away the old statues to sell and put others in their place. Even the Buddha statue is not that old. When Lama Atisha was there, all the statues, not just the Tara, gave him the answers as to the best way to quickly achieve enlightenment for sentient beings. In Tibet, Nepal and India there are many holy objects that have spoken to meditators, to practitioners who have strong devotion. I think this is similar to Jesus Christ's picture speaking to Saint Francis because of the purity of his mind.

The absolute and conventional guru

This time we have been born as human beings and, not only that, we have met the holy Dharma, which means we have been able to learn and practice that much. For many past lives we have been creating the cause, praying for this to happen, and now it has happened. This is incredibly precious. We must not just take it for granted. That English term, "take it for granted" is a nice term.

Due to the kindness of the guru guiding us from beginningless rebirths and continuing to guide us up until the time we achieve enlightenment, we are able to do all this, to become enlightened, to free numberless sentient beings from suffering—numberless hell beings, hungry ghosts, animals, humans, gods, demigods and intermediate state beings. We are able to bring them all to peerless happiness, the state of omniscient mind, due to the kindness of the guru. We are able to repay the kindness of all the numberless mother sentient beings.

I have already talked about the kindness of the guru but I just want to mention this advice from Gyalwa Ensapa, who said,

> Until you are free from negative karma and obscurations, even if every single buddha were to descend in front of you, you would not have the fortune to be able to see their supreme holy bodies adorned with the thirty-two major marks and eighty minor signs. All you could see would be the ordinary view, just an ordinary being.

This is a great teaching. Until we are free from our negative karma and obscurations, even if all the buddhas descended in front of us all we would see would be ordinary beings, nothing special. Even though the buddhas have the thirty-two major marks and eighty minor signs, we are unable to see this. We do not have the fortune to see the buddhas in the aspect of a buddha.

As I mentioned before, when we say the prayer *Namo Gurubhya, Namo*

Buddhaya, Namo Dharmaya, Namo Sanghaya, the guru comes before the Buddha, Dharma and Sangha. We take refuge in the guru first. Why? There is a very important reason that we need to understand. It is not just because the guru is kinder than all the buddhas. Yes, this is true, but it is not only that.

I saw in the Heruka sadhana—it may be the same in other sadhanas too—the inner offering starts from Vajradhara: Vajradhara, Vajrayogini, the great yogi Tilopa, Ghantapa and all the lineage lamas. But at the very beginning is the root guru. Even before Vajradhara, first there is the kind root guru. Then it starts from Vajradhara and all the lineage lamas and at the end it mentions the root guru again. Why? That is very important.

Here, "guru" means that all these lineage lamas, including Vajradhara, Vajrayogini and so forth, come from the root guru. As Padmasambhava said,

> The root guru is the essence of all the three times', ten directions'
> *tathagatas.*
> He is the originator of the heaps of the 84,000 teachings.
> He is the possessor of all the arya Sangha.
> To the holy mouth of my kind root guru I make offerings.

Tathagatas means all the numberless buddhas of the ten directions, all the past, present and future buddhas' holy body, holy speech and holy mind, their qualities and actions. The root guru is the essence of all that. This is what Padmasambhava said. The second line says he is the originator of the heaps of the 84,000 teachings, from where all the teachings come. Then the quote says that whatever qualities the arya Sangha have, the root guru also has.

Finally, he says, "To the holy mouth of my kind root guru I make offerings." This is before we make offerings to Vajradhara and Vajrayogini. When we understand why this is so, we can understand what the guru is. Otherwise we really can't.

That we will be able to enlighten all sentient beings depends on the kindness of the guru. Who is the guru? Who is the guru who has guided us from beginningless rebirths and will guide us all the way until we reach enlightenment?

There are the ultimate, or absolute, guru and the conventional guru. The absolute guru takes the ordinary form, the conventional guru. The conventional guru is just a manifestation but the main thing is the absolute guru. The absolute guru is eternal; it is the primordial mind, with no beginning and no end, free from all gross and subtle obscurations.

And next, it is very important to understand that the absolute guru pervades all existence. We say that there is no place where there is no buddha—which is also stated in the sutra teachings—therefore there is no place where there is no absolute guru. Just as we think of the buddha, the omniscient mind, pervading all existence, so too does the ultimate guru.

The guru manifests everywhere to do the work of benefiting sentient beings, in a pure form to those whose mind is pure and in an impure form to those sentient beings whose mind is impure. The guru works to benefit every single sentient being, so it's infinite.

For example, in this world only one sun rises, but whether it's an ocean, a river, a spring or just a drop, wherever there is water it can reflect the sun. As long as it's not obscured, the sun can be reflected in water everywhere. When the sun rises, its reflection also rises everywhere, naturally and without effort, even in a drop of water.

A being needs to have motivation before becoming enlightened but after that there is no need for effortful motivation. Until each and every single sentient being has been enlightened—every hell being, hungry ghost, animal, human, god and demigod—until each has been brought to enlightenment, the guru continuously works for sentient beings.

The *Guru Puja* mentions,

> Arising from the play of omniscient transcendental wisdom,
> You are the essence of ten million mandala cycles.
> Pervading lord of a hundred buddha families, foremost vajra
>   holder,
> Unified primordial savior, I make requests to you.
>
> Unobscured, inseparable from the play of simultaneous joy,
> Pervading everything in motion and at rest;
> The nature of all things, free from beginning or end,
> All good actual ultimate bodhicitta; I make requests to you.[59]

---

[59] Vv. 51 & 52.

The guru is the one who manifests as numberless mandalas. Even just one mandala manifests many deities such as Yamantaka or Guhyasamaja. There are many, many details within the mandala, but the guru manifest as all the numberless mandalas, all the numberless deities. This absolute guru, this primordial mind, has no beginning or end; it pervades all existence and has been guiding us to enlightenment from beginningless rebirths.

The absolute guru is without obscurations, experiencing simultaneously-born bliss, the greatest bliss. Pervading all existence, the numberless buddhas and the numberless mandalas are all absorbed into the one, the absolute owner of all, the absolute guru. The absolute guru is all good, absolute bodhicitta. This is not the usual bodhicitta but the bodhicitta of the absolute mind, the primordial mind.

The prayer continues,

> You are the guru, you are the yidam,
> You are the dakinis and Dharma protectors.
> From now until enlightenment I shall seek no other refuge
>   than you.
> In this life, the bardo and all future lives,
> Hold me with the hook of your compassion;
> Free me from samsara and nirvana's fears,
> Grant all attainments,
> Be my constant friend and guard me from interferences.[60]

With this request we recognize what the guru is. This is the real guru but for us he must manifest in the ordinary aspect. This is the way to understand that the absolute and conventional gurus are not two separate things. The absolute guru manifests as the conventional guru to guide us easily. We need to think like that, that only with the conventional, ordinary aspect can we be guided to enlightenment. That is the guru's kindness.

Even if we were dying today, even this hour or this minute, this is what we must request, that the guru holds us with the hook of his compassion.

It is as the quote says,

> Before the guru there is not even the name "buddha."

---

[60] V. 53.

So, all the buddhas come from the guru. Can you see that? That is why the root guru comes even before Vajradhara in the lineage lama prayer, *then* Vajradhara, Vajrayogini and so forth. Without the root guru there can be none of these lineage lamas—no Vajradhara, no Vajrayogini, nothing. There cannot be the Buddha. They are all a manifestation of the root guru. For that reason the prayer *Namo Gurubhya, Namo Buddhaya, Namo Dharmaya, Namo Sanghaya* has great meaning.

9. The Importance of Guru Devotion

I N THE BUDDHA'S TIME artists could not draw the Buddha by looking at him because he was so glorious, so they painted him by looking at his reflection in water. There is a standing Buddha statue I have seen all covered with wrinkles, especially on the robe, that is a copy of his reflection in water.

When I was in Mongolia I wanted to see the Buddha statue that was made during his time. When the Buddha descended from Tushita, the Land of Joy, to Sankasya in India, this Buddha statue walked seven steps without touching the ground and greeted the Buddha by sort of bowing three times. Then the Buddha predicted which countries this statue would go to in order to benefit them: first India, then China, and then different countries.

There is a story that the Mongolians or Russians stole it from China. The stolen statue was supposed to be sandalwood, but the one I saw in Mongolia seemed to be made of bronze. The abbot of Ganden Monastery in Ulaanbaatar also thought the same, that it was bronze. Somehow, when I saw the picture of the statue, I didn't think it was made in the Buddha's time. It seemed more like how statues are made in other places like Japan and it looked more contemporary. So I kind of lost hope that this was the real statue from the Buddha's time, but I went because Kyabje Kirti Tsenshab Rinpoche wanted to go there to meditate and pray.

It seems the statue was still in China, but the temple was never open. So I asked a student, Dr. Chiu Nan Lai, if she could find out about it and then see if I could meet it in the future, maybe secretly or something.

In Mongolia I was told how the abbots, monks and other people went to see an old lama who had passed away before the Russian invasion but his subtle mind was still there; he was still meditating. He predicted he would continue to meditate and told them to bury him under the ground because the Russian Communists were coming and then open the grave after they had left and return him to the monastery.

After the Russians left Mongolia they dug him up. I think they were careless and cut his nose so they put something there in its place but his body was preserved despite being in the ground the whole time of the Russian invasion, some seventy years.

Just as he had predicted, they took him out of the ground and placed him back in the monastery, still meditating. When they do protector practices such as Palden Lhamo, sweat comes from his face, so he is still in meditation, continuing to meditate in that way to benefit the world. That he's not just a skeleton and his body is still intact clearly shows the capacity of the mind, how it can develop by practicing tantra. We have to know more about the different levels of mind: the gross mind, the subtle mind and the extremely subtle mind.

If the Buddha statue had been there, I would have gone to see it, but I was not able to get a visa. But I think that particular Buddha statue was made in Beijing. That's the real story.

THE IMPORTANCE OF GURU DEVOTION

Padampa Sangye advised the people of Tingri,[61]

> You should regard the guru as more exalted than the Buddha. If you do that, realization will come in this life, people of Tingri.[62]

Kadampa Geshe Chayülwa[63] was an incomparable practitioner and disciple who correctly devoted to the virtuous friend, following his guru Geshe Chengawa perfectly. If he was doing his mandala offering, piling up the mandala to collect merit, and his guru called him, the moment he heard his guru's voice, he would immediately stop his mandala offering and run to his guru. If he was writing something, for example, the Tibetan letter *na*, the moment he heard his guru's voice, he wouldn't even wait to finish that letter but would immediately run to his guru's room to offer service. He had unbelievable devotion.

---

[61] A town in southern Tibet not far from the Nepalese border.
[62] Quoted in *Heart of the Path*, p. 176.
[63] See also *Heart of the Path*, pp. 109–10.

He cleaned his guru's room every day, collecting the garbage in his lower robe, his *shem-thab*, holding the robe in one hand and going down the steps to throw it out. Cleaning was part of his practice. It was not a question of cleaning if there was garbage and not cleaning if there was none. It was a preliminary practice, a daily practice he did every day before sitting to meditate, whether there was garbage or not.

One day he collected the garbage, put it in his shem-thab and went down the stairs as usual, but when he reached the third step he gained a realization. We think that we can attain realizations only by doing formal meditation, with our eyes closed, but it's not like that. There have been many practitioners who have attained vast numbers of realizations while actively practicing guru yoga, busy serving their guru. In his great commentary Pabongka Rinpoche has cited many stories of guru devotion, correctly devoting to the virtuous friend, that illustrate how many practitioners have achieved realizations by actively serving their guru rather than by sitting on a meditation cushion. My memory's very bad, so some stories I don't remember very clearly.

Anyway, on the third step Geshe Chayülwa's level of mind reached the path of merit and of that path's three levels—lower, middle and great—the great path of merit. Then, just there, because his mind had become purer, he was able to see numberless buddhas—not on the altar or somewhere else but from that step, just as he was going to throw out the garbage. He suddenly saw numberless buddhas in their nirmanakaya aspect.

This incomparable practitioner who correctly devoted to the guru, correctly followed the guru, said,

> If you wish to attain something special *separate* from the guru—
> Vajradhara or a mind-seal deity—no attainment will happen in
> your mental continuum. You have to keep this in mind.

This was his own experience. He had the realization and was expressing what he knew. If we think that something special, like Vajradhara or our mind-seal deity, is other than the guru, then we will not attain it. Mind-seal is how I translate *yidam*. I don't know what other people do.[64]

---

[64] In other teachings Rinpoche has explained that "seal," as in mahamudra, or "great seal," refers to sealing the mind, as one does an envelope, making it inseparable with the meditational deity, or *yidam*.

Also, the *Sutra of the Stainless Sky* gives very clear advice:

> Regard the virtuous friend as more special
> Than the tathagatas who have gone beyond,
> Who see emptiness as it is.
> No matter how skillful and compassionate the buddhas are,
>
> Without the self-condition of the guru,
> In the mental continuum of sentient beings to be tamed
> The buddhas' holy actions and blessings cannot be received.
> Without the guru, even the buddhas themselves cannot occur.[65]

We should regard the guru as more special than the tathagatas. The Tibetan for tathagata, *de-zhin sheg-pa*, literally means that they have gone beyond both disturbing-thought obscurations and subtle obscurations to knowledge (*sheg-pa*) and that they see emptiness as it is (*de-zhin*). They see all phenomena as empty, as *tong-pa*. Here, we do not say *tong-pa-nyi*, "emptiness only," that all phenomena are emptiness only; we say phenomena are *tong-pa*, empty of being truly existent. Tathagatas see everything directly "as it is," *de-zhin*, which is one part of the term, the other being *sheg-pa*, "gone beyond."

Why should we hold the guru more special than the tathagatas? Even though a buddha is so skillful, so compassionate, if there is no self-condition,[66] if there is no guru in the mental continuum of sentient beings who are the objects to be subdued, they cannot receive the buddhas' holy actions, the buddhas' blessings. And then, even a buddha himself or herself cannot happen. (In English you have to say "him or her" but in Tibetan you don't need to. *Sang-gyä* can refer to a buddha in a male and female aspect.)

Because a buddha cannot happen without a guru, we must hold the guru as more precious than the buddhas. As the quotation from the *Sutra of Stainless Sky* proves, that is what Guru Shakyamuni Buddha himself said very clearly.

---

[65] Also known as *The Sutra of Immaculate Space* (Tib: *nam-kha dri-ma me-pä do*). See a similar quote in *A Cascading Waterfall of Nectar*, p. 32.

[66] Tib: *dag-kyen*, also called dominant or main condition; one of the four conditions giving rise to a moment of consciousness, the others being the focal condition (*mig-kyen*), the immediately preceding condition (*de-ma-thag-kyen*) and the causal condition (*gyu-kyen*). See *How Karma Works*, p. 135, n. 49.

The first time Lama Yeshe and I went to Australia there were two hundred people at the course in Diamond Valley, Queensland, near Chenrezig Institute. Our hut was some distance from the main tent and the kitchen, which were next to the mountain. The outside of the hut was made of logs cut in half whereas inside was neat and fresh, with the walls made of the stuff you make take-away cups from, Styrofoam. It was all white, except for the floor.

There was Lama's room, my room and then, through a door, the kitchen. Although we usually had meals from the main kitchen there was a small stove where we made tea and cooked some food. Lama made it. He usually made food really quickly.[67]

At that time there was a tall man[68] with a long nose who was supposed to practice Ganapati—not the Hindu Ganapati but the Buddhist Ganapati, the manifestation of Chenrezig. I think Lama had found a Ganapati statue for him somewhere in Australia. Lama had him help put together a Four-arm Chenrezig meditation for Lama's upcoming visit to the Chinese Buddhist Society in Sydney. Anyway, he told Lama, "I don't know who Chenrezig is but I know you, I can see a lama." I just remembered that.

So now, this is a real story. At Buxa, there was a monk called Jamyang, who was Pabongka Dechen Nyingpo's attendant in Tibet. Even though he couldn't read texts because he was illiterate—he couldn't even read the Tibetan alphabet—Rinpoche had told him that in the future he would be able to read the *Guru Puja* by himself, without anybody teaching him. Then, one day in Buxa, he was suddenly able to read the entire *Guru Puja* from beginning to end. This was the blessing of having served Pabongka Dechen Nyingpo in Tibet. By serving him he purified his mind and it happened exactly as Pabongka Rinpoche had predicted. This was the great benefit of having impeccable guru devotion to Pabongka Rinpoche. He didn't tell me this himself; Lama Lhundrup told me.

Lama Lhundrup and Jamyang both stayed at Lal Bangla, which was not within the grounds of the Buxa camp itself but on the hill just outside. This was also where Pabongka Dechen Nyingpo's incarnation stayed, so Jamyang was again able to serve him in his next incarnation. I went up there to do Dolgyal puja with them a couple of times. While we were doing the protector practices there was a wind blowing and he was able to see the different protectors coming.

Dromtönpa was Lama Atisha's translator in Tibet, translating Sanskrit into Tibetan. Toward the end of his time in Tibet, Lama Atisha showed the aspect of having sickness. He was sick for quite some time, making kaka and pipi in the bed. Dromtönpa cleaned it up with his hands with no thought of its being dirty. It was unbelievable purification; he purified many eons' obscurations and collected extensive merit. Suddenly one day Dromtönpa was able to read the minds of sentient beings—even insects like ants—for a distance as far as an eagle can fly in eighteen days.

There are many other stories of people serving the guru who have suddenly realized emptiness or seen deities. That is the power, the benefit of showing devotion to and serving our guru. Our mind is not oneness with ignorance, with obscurations. It is only temporarily obscured and by serving our guru we can purify many eons of negative karma and develop higher realizations such as a direct perception of emptiness.

Correctly devoting to the virtuous friend is the root of the path to enlightenment. If we don't know how important it is, nothing can happen. It is the root of all realizations from here up to enlightenment, on the Hinayana path to achieve nirvana and the Mahayana sutra and tantra paths to achieve enlightenment. If we correctly follow the virtuous friend with thought and action, if the root is there, we can have success up to enlightenment. Everything depends on this practice, on how much we know of it. This is the reason I have spent a bit of time explaining it, even though I got distracted here and there.

Otherwise we might have done this retreat or that retreat, this practice or that practice, received this teaching or that teaching, this initiation or that initiation, this and this and this, but *nothing* happens in our mind. Our mind is still like an empty container. Maybe we know the Dharma intellectually, but when a problem comes it looks like we don't know it at all, like we have never learned it. This is why correctly devoting to the spiritual friend is called the root of the path to enlightenment.

Feeling regret purifies mistakes made in the past but in the West regret is considered bad. Therefore, since we don't feel regret for the negative things we have done, our mind never changes. Regret can be negative or positive. Positive regret is like healing—when we regret all our past mistakes we naturally purify our negative karma; it becomes thinner. This is a very important aspect of the confession practice. Another is to determine not to commit negative actions again. This gives us the power or energy to destroy the habit of repeatedly creating negative actions. We can reduce and then destroy that habit. It takes time to do, and at the beginning there is still the chance that we will repeat that particular action, but by continuously trying to overcome it, the habit becomes weaker and weaker.

I always feel that if we don't know the Dharma we don't know how to enjoy life, whereas if we know the Dharma we can enjoy our life. And especially if we practice bodhicitta—*especially* if we practice bodhicitta—that is the real enjoyment in life, that is how to enjoy our life the most, to make it most beneficial for sentient beings and for ourselves.

THE REAL BEGINNING IS GURU DEVOTION

Fifty Verses of Guru Devotion says,

> A guru should be subdued in his action, cultivated in his speech, wise, patient and honest. He should neither conceal his shortcomings nor pretend to possess qualities he lacks. He should be an expert in the meanings of the tantra and in its ritual procedures of medicine and turning back obstacles. He should also have loving compassion and a complete knowledge of the scriptures.[69]

A spiritual friend needs to be wise in leading the disciple on the path to future lives' happiness, to a perfect human rebirth and then to nirvana and full enlightenment. To do so he must be subdued in mind and manner.

Then also, from the disciple's side, we have to have firm devotion, enjoy meditation and like virtue very much. I don't remember the other qualities but anyway, those are the three main ones.[70]

Kadampa Geshe Chengawa mentioned,

> A disciple who practices correct devotion to the virtuous friend, even if he is as foolish as a dog or a pig, will have no difficulty in becoming like Manjushri.[71]

[69] V. 8.
[70] For extended teachings on the qualities of the guru and of the disciple, see *Heart of the Path*, pp. 29–48.
[71] Quoted in *Heart of the Path*, p. 114.

The real meaning is that if the only thing we have is guru devotion and we know nothing about anything else—even if we are "as foolish as a dog or a pig"—because of that devotion we will have no difficulties in becoming like Manjushri. We can be completely foolish, knowing nothing other than guru devotion, but that will be enough.

With correct guru devotion, whatever we do in this life also becomes a preparation for our future lives, determining whether we will meet a qualified guru or not. This is extraordinary. This is not just for this one life but also for life after life. As we improve in following the guru correctly, as we come closer to becoming an arya bodhisattva and then a buddha, we have progressively fewer difficulties.

In my view, even if a person knows nothing but has very strong guru devotion, that person is the luckiest person. Even though somebody is very clever and knows many things—even if he is a great scholar who knows both the Kangyur and Tengyur by heart and can explain them perfectly—and even if he has a guru, if he has no guru devotion, if he fails to take care of that most vital practice, his life will not improve. The luckier of the two, the one who will achieve enlightenment quicker, is the one who has strong, stable guru devotion.

The other person, the knowledgeable one who fails to take care of his practice, will be unable to integrate all he knows into the lam-rim, the three principal aspects of the path to enlightenment, and will be unable to achieve the realizations of the two stages of tantra.

Then, when he tries to do *shamatha* meditation it goes wrong and he gets lots of *lung*, wind disease, and lots of sicknesses. Life becomes like that. He might look very clever, but not taking good care of his guru devotion practice robs him of any real success in life.

Kadampa Geshe Potowa advised that the guru who leads us should at least emphasize attaining the happiness of the next life so that the aim of the disciple is not just this life's happiness. We need to renounce this life's happiness but it should not stop there. There are numberless future lives. More important is to free ourselves from karma and delusion and to no longer need reincarnation, although I myself have no idea how long that takes!

One time, Lama Yeshe and Geshe Thubten were discussing the definition of Dharma, the definition of the renunciation of this life. Geshe Thubten said it was that in your heart you felt that future lives were more important than this life. Here "important" means making more effort for future lives than this life. Lama said maybe that's not enough; he added that you should be free from the self-cherishing thought as well. Something like that.

The texts then go on to say that the happiness of future lives is still samsaric pleasure and so there is still samsaric suffering, albeit the suffering of change rather than the suffering of pain. Therefore, it is better that the guru emphasizes that nirvana is more important than that. Better still is the guru who emphasizes *sang-gyä*, the state of the complete elimination of all obscurations and the attainment of all realizations. Achieving enlightenment for the sake of other sentient beings is better than achieving nirvana, the state of lower peace for oneself alone. That ultimate level of practice is the most important one.

ALL HAPPINESS COMES FROM DHARMA

People who have attained the most precious human body but don't know Dharma do not know how to make this life useful. They have no idea of anything except how to create the cause of suffering day and night. Whenever they move, whenever they think, they create negative karma. It makes having a good heart difficult. Life is *so* full of positive things. Even not practicing Dharma, there are many good things they can do to benefit others and themselves but, because their mind is very weak, they cannot think of them.

After many lifetimes of praying and practicing morality they have attained this human body, but for what? What do they have this human body for? It's so they can again create the cause of the lower realms, nothing else. Whether they are billionaires or zillionaires or whether they are beggars, it's like that. It's very sad.

An example is an Indian billionaire I was told about. He had a lot of money but didn't know what to do with it, so he built a house in Bombay for more than a billion dollars with somewhere between fifty and sixty stories. There were quite a few swimming pools and a rooftop helipad. He needed six hundred people to take care of the house for him.

After the house was completed he had a *feng shui* expert come to check out the house. The expert said that the house was very harmful; it was not good for him. So then the whole family moved out, leaving the house empty.

If we were billionaires we could help a lot of poor people even just in India, without talking about other countries. There are many poor people who are suffering, who are homeless, without food, and there are many ways in which we could help bring them happiness. We could build houses for them or we could give them food. This man had an unbelievable amount of money and all he could think of doing was to build something for his family. That's so poor, so sad.

If we were like that man and were to suddenly die in our sleep from a heart attack or something, what then? Many people die. They go to bed alive and the next morning they cannot get up because they've become a corpse. This happens to millions of people in the world every day. If we were to suddenly die like that, what is the connection between this life and the next? We collected all that wealth but only our mind continues into the next life. We cherished our body more than we cherished the buddhas and bodhisattvas, more than we cherished all the sentient beings, but even that has to be left.

It is very difficult to feel confident that our next rebirth will be in the upper realms. It depends on whether we have created virtue or nonvirtue, and the nonvirtue we collect every day is very strong—it is perfect—whereas whatever virtue we might collect is very weak. Even if we do manage to create some virtue, we destroy it by getting angry and having ill will. Whenever we fail to practice patience and compassion, anger arises and blows away our merit. Since whatever little virtue we have created is not dedicated for enlightenment, our merit is completely destroyed by anger and the result is rebirth in the lower realms, which is utterly unimaginable.

When we look at the sentient beings in this world, including ourselves, our entire life is spent working for attachment, and not attachment to a good rebirth and the samsaric pleasure of the next life but attachment to this life, attachment only to this life. Except for those who are practicing Dharma, everybody in the world—billionaires, zillionaires, beggars—is working for attachment to this life, the eight worldly dharmas. We have become servants to money, servants to work, servants to attachment to this life.

Furthermore, we also get angry, so we are servants to anger too. And ignorance is there all the time, especially the ignorance that holds the I and the aggregates as truly existent, the ignorance that is the root of samsara. Day and night, all the time, we are completely servants to that as well. This is our life.

Happiness comes from Dharma; our job comes from Dharma; money comes from Dharma. That is the main cause, good karma, the positive mind, the positive actions of body, speech and mind. This is something that normally only people who know Dharma would understand. Worldly people do not know this; they do not know that everything positive, all happiness, comes from Dharma.

Practicing Dharma is more important than anything else but it is so difficult for the majority of people in the world to practice it. They are unable to create virtuous actions—the positive, pure, healthy actions that are the cause of happiness—because they do not know about the mind, they do not know about karma. Whether they are billionaires, zillionaires or beggars, they do not know about Dharma, and so day and night, whatever they do with their body, speech and mind becomes an action of attachment; it becomes nonvirtue.

There are people who are ignorant of Dharma but who naturally have a good heart. People who think of others can possibly collect merit, but without dedicating or practicing patience and compassion, that merit can easily be destroyed.

If, on the other hand, we dedicate whatever merit we create to achieving the state of the omniscient mind, then even if anger or heresy arise, that merit might become weaker but cannot be completely destroyed. As Pabongka Dechen Nyingpo said, even though you can remove many rocks from a big mountain, the mountain itself will remain. Merit that has been dedicated for enlightenment can be harmed but not completely destroyed. When it has not been dedicated it can very easily be totally destroyed.

The best way to dedicate is with emptiness. That is why, when I do the dedications at the end of a teaching, I do them with emptiness. If we dedicate our merit by meditating on emptiness—not just saying the word "emptiness" but meditating on emptiness—the merit will not be destroyed and later, if heresy or anger arise, they will not even weaken it.

Kyabje Kirti Tsenshab Rinpoche said only emptiness, and nothing else, can directly eliminate the root of samsara, the ignorance holding the I as truly existent. Although it can help, even bodhicitta does not have the power to do this.

The importance of the Dharma and Dharma centers

Just a little investigation will show clearly how much suffering sentient beings are experiencing. Even if we don't consider all sentient beings and simply look at the people in this world, we can see how much suffering they must endure by being ignorant of Dharma and how much not knowing Dharma harms them in this life. Even here in this world, where the Buddha descended in the past and where Buddhism still exists, human beings are still suffering so much. It hasn't stopped yet. Looking at the plight of others, we should appreciate how greatly fortunate we are to not only know Dharma but be able to continue to study and assimilate it into our life.

From that perspective we can see how important a Dharma center is; a place with a teacher, a translator and a good, functioning organization. That is unbelievably important. It is so beneficial and so needed.

I want to use this opportunity to thank everybody who works for the Dharma centers in the different countries and here in England, at Jamyang London and Jamyang Leeds and the other study groups. I want to emphasize how important it is. Even small study groups are very important. Even just one person volunteering at a center is very important.

This is how a person's connection with the Dharma begins. At the very beginning, her mind is totally closed and she has no idea what to do. But then she has a chance conversation with a center volunteer in the street or in the center's café and that leads to her coming to classes and reading books. Just being able to see Dharma books opens the mind to think about new phenomena, to think about new ideas in life. From that she can discover new ways to attain happiness. Even just by chatting to somebody on a bus about compassion you are able to open that person's mind. You take that opportunity and it starts from there.

When you simply talk to people about Dharma or Buddhist philosophy and they get interested, you can gradually help guide them. You are able to benefit sentient beings one-by-one like that. You can give them Dharma books or show them how to find teachings online. Nowadays there are so many more possibilities than there were before. There are many different ways of helping, so many different books they can read according to their particular problem. That's how even small study groups are very important.

All of us came to Buddhism through somebody's introducing us to it. Of course, this is all on the basis of previous karma, our past lives' karma. Then we went on to learn and practice and become more involved. There are many ways of helping and, of course, because we can't stand seeing all sentient beings suffering so much, we need to achieve enlightenment ourselves.

So, I would like to take this opportunity to thank everybody from the depths of my heart, especially the people who have been serving the FPMT organization, working for centers in different countries, and especially everybody in England. You have been helping others, teaching, giving happiness to others. That is vital. Others have helped us, so now we should help them. On behalf of Lama Yeshe, His Holiness the Dalai Lama, all the buddhas and bodhisattvas and all sentient beings, I would like to thank everybody from the bottom of my heart.

Rinpoche learns English

We all need enlightenment. I don't know who used the word "enlightenment" as a translation for *jang-chub*. It might have been the Sikkimese person who made the very old dictionary I had in Buxa.[72] It was very old and was printed on very bad paper; even if you put a paper clip on it, it would tear.

I tried to memorize the dictionary. Lama Yeshe and I tried to learn English the way we learnt Dharma texts, by memorizing the whole book. There was no other way because at Buxa we had no opportunity to use English. When I met the head of the lama camp, the Punjabi Sikh from the Second World War that I mentioned before, I would say, "How are you?" or something. There was no other conversation.

There were two lower caste Indians working in the khangtsen kitchen. One of them was called Pokang Babu, but I don't remember the name of the other one. Anyway, there wasn't much conversation with them either. Because we didn't have a chance to use it, we forgot it. I could memorize most texts well but not that dictionary! The husband of a relative in Ghoom gave me some English books.[73] He taught at St. Joseph's School, a very good quality Christian school in Darjeeling. I checked the meanings of various words and tried to memorize them but then forgot them and had to memorize them again. I did that a few times. Otherwise, the books were of no use.

And of course there was the pronunciation. Because I didn't learn from somebody, when I tried to use a word it just didn't work, like the word "ritual." Freda Bedi, who I also mentioned earlier, ran a school in Delhi for young lamas and invited me to go there many times, but I didn't go until I got TB. Then I went and stayed there for six months. Later on she moved the school to Dalhousie, which I also attended. Once she asked me about His Holiness Zong Rinpoche, but when I tried to say he was doing many

---

[72] Kazi Dawa Samdup (1868–1923), who published *An English-Tibetan Dictionary* in Calcutta in 1919. He also translated and published with W. Y. Evans Wentz as editor the *Tibetan Book of the Dead*, *Tibet's Great Yogi Milarepa* and *Tibetan Yoga and Secret Doctrines*. See his very interesting entry in Wikipedia.

[73] Ghoom is a small hilly locality five miles from Darjeeling, West Bengal, where Samten Chöling, Domo Geshe Rinpoche's monastery, is located. This is where in 1967 the Lamas met Zina Rachevsky, their first Western student.

pujas and used the word "rites," she didn't understand at all. She thought I'd said he was writing! So then we had to look for a translator.

It's very strange how life turns out; very, very strange. I must tell you this. When I was in Darjeeling somebody took me to see an English movie, the only time I saw one. English movies were shown in the evenings, while the Hindi ones played in the daytime. Sometimes an elder monk from Tibet would take us to see a Hindi movie and they were OK, but the night I was taken to see the English movie and saw how busy people were, going all over the place in airplanes and running around so busily, I made many prayers to never be reborn in the West! Even the Tibetan ladies who were sitting behind me watching the movie could hear me praying. I remember that, my very first Western movie. But now I live in the West! I'm in Asia from time to time but I live in the West. That's why I said it's strange the way the life turns out.

VAJRAYANA IS LIKE THE SUN AND MOON

As Lama Tsongkhapa, the omniscient one, explained, there are two vehicles, or *yanas*, that can take us to enlightenment, the fully purified and completely realized state. They are the Paramitayana and the profound Vajrayana. Of those, the Vajrayana, or Secret Mantra, is more special, more exalted than the Paramitayana. He said it's like the sun and the moon, which means it's supreme, the best, in terms of attaining enlightenment.

If we don't have bodhicitta, we can still develop renunciation of samsara and achieve the five paths of the Hinayana, or Lesser Vehicle. In this way we can free ourselves from the oceans of samsaric suffering and attain the ultimate happiness of lower nirvana, the blissful state of peace for oneself alone. But we can't attain enlightenment for the sake of all sentient beings. For that, we need bodhicitta.

It's said that we can attain full enlightenment by following the Paramitayana path, practicing the bodhicitta aspect of the three principal paths. In reality, by following this path, when we're about to attain enlightenment, without receiving initiation and actualizing the clear light, we can't.

So finally, even though we've collected all the merit—the merit of wisdom and the merit of virtue—and purified all the defilements necessary to attain the dharmakaya, the buddha's holy mind, and the rupakaya, the buddha's holy body, and it has taken us three countless great eons to do so, when we're close to enlightenment we still can't get there without the Vajrayana.

As the great lay pandit, the great holy being Lobpön Chandragomin pointed out, during the three countless great eons that we're accumulating the merit of wisdom and the merit of virtue, sentient beings are undergoing sufferings in samsara, and that's unbearable. It takes so long to reach enlightenment following the Paramitayana path. It's unbearable that the transmigratory beings have to suffer that much and for that long.

Therefore we should practice the quick path of tantra, but not with the attitude, "Great! I can get enlightened quickly and then I can relax. I can bliss out," like taking LSD or some other drug. It's not like that, where you're totally hallucinated and spaced out and don't know what's going on in the world or even if it's day or night. There are many people like this. They either don't know Dharma or don't practice it. But even if you practice just a little Dharma, it reduces attachment, you have some renunciation and it helps bring peace.

If you don't know the Dharma or don't practice it, you have no protection and no method to bring happiness into your life. Then all you see is problems. The only life you know is one of dissatisfaction. And then, like many other people in the world, you get fed up and perhaps even commit suicide. This probably happens every day. People don't know what to do, they don't know how to bring themselves happiness and are overwhelmed by problems. It's such a pity; this is very sad.

So, we must help sentient beings but we cannot wait the three countless great eons that it takes to become enlightened following the Paramitayana path. Therefore we have to practice tantra, the Vajrayana, which allows us to become enlightened in an incredibly short time.

As the omniscient Lama Tsongkhapa said,

> Please bless me to enter
> The holy gateway of the fortunate ones:
> The supreme vajra vehicle.[74]

Of the three vehicles, Hinayana, Mahayana Paramitayana and Mahayana Vajrayana, the latter is supreme. It is the holy gateway of the fortunate capable beings, who, among sentient beings who are objects to be subdued, are like jewels, with so much merit and intelligence. To achieve full

---

[74] *The Foundation of All Good Qualities.*

enlightenment in one life, this is the holy gateway we must enter, so, "Please grant me blessings to enter that."

We must practice the various levels of tantra: Kriya Tantra, Charya Tantra, Yoga Tantra and Maha-anuttara Yoga Tantra (or Highest Yoga Tantra). Doing so will give us the skillful means we need to achieve enlightenment in one lifetime.

As I mentioned before, transmigratory beings are completely under the control of delusion and karma, totally without freedom. All the time they migrate through the six realms again and again and again, and suffer and suffer and suffer unbelievably, continuously. There is nothing new that they have not already done from beginningless rebirths but they are unable to remember.

To free these transmigratory beings from the oceans of samsaric suffering and bring them to full enlightenment, we must practice tantra to achieve enlightenment in one lifetime. This is the motivation for practicing any of the four classes of tantra. But with the lower tantras, we begin by achieving a long life, where we can live for hundreds and thousands of years, and eventually achieve enlightenment.

With Highest Yoga Tantra, however, there is no need to do that. Even though the practices of the lower tantras are more skillful than those of the Mahayana Paramitayana, the sutra vehicle, Highest Yoga Tantra is even more skillful than those, and through it we can achieve full enlightenment, the unified state of Vajradhara, in one brief lifetime of these degenerated times, with no need to prolong our life. So, because of that, it has the greatest skill.

How can we be happy while others suffer?

As the bodhisattva Thogme Zangpo mentioned in his *Thirty-seven Practices of a Bodhisattva,*

> When your mothers, who've loved you since time without
>   beginning,
> Are suffering, what use is your own happiness?
> Therefore to free limitless living beings
> Develop the altruistic intention—
> This is the practice of bodhisattvas.[75]

[75] V. 10.

Totally ignorant of the cause of happiness and the cause of suffering, we worldly beings think we're always working for happiness but in reality we are constantly creating the cause of suffering. We keep ourselves totally busy, day and night, like ants frantically running around, up and down trees or whatever. Because our motivation is not even attachment to future lives but just attachment to this life, every action of our body, speech and mind becomes negative karma.

In that, we are no different from insects, spiders, crickets, ants and so forth. Our motivation is identical to theirs. Likewise the billionaire, the zillionaire, the trillionaire—there is no difference; their motivation is identical. We have all been billionaires, zillionaires, trillionaires, kings in the god and human realms, Indra and Brahma, numberless times.

We are just like those slugs that come out when it rains. Just like them, we work only for this life, so every action we do is nonvirtuous. And even if we do collect a little virtue, because we have so many enemies, anger arises frequently and very easily due to the habituation of our mind, and whatever merit we might have accumulated is continuously destroyed.

We might intellectually know about merit, thinking, "I've done this retreat; I've done that preliminary practice; I've studied this and studied that; I've done so much, so much," but, as I mentioned, our mind is the same as it ever was or even worse. It's as if we never met the Dharma. Problems still come. Before they meet the Dharma, some people have very few negative emotions, but the more they engage in intellectual study of the Dharma, if they don't practice, the stronger their negative emotions grow. More pride, anger and so forth arise, causing constant suffering now and in the future.

So, Thogme Zangpo asks how can we be happy while numberless sentient beings are suffering? What use is being happy like that? He then says that in order to free others from the oceans of samsaric suffering we must generate bodhicitta, the practice of the bodhisattvas.

Until we are free from the control of karma and delusion we must constantly suffer: the suffering of pain, the suffering of change and pervasive compounding suffering. We encounter the suffering of the six realms and suffer again and again, endlessly. Therefore, we need to be free from the whole of samsara and achieve lower nirvana, the blissful state of peace.

But that alone is not sufficient. Rather, we must achieve great nirvana, full enlightenment. We must free ourselves from even the subtle obscurations, the obscurations to knowledge, especially for all sentient beings, to free them from the oceans of samsaric suffering and bring them to full enlightenment as quickly as possible. We must achieve full enlightenment as quickly as possible. This is why we must practice Highest Yoga Tantra.

10. Seeing the Guru as a Buddha

THE HARM DOLGYAL HAS DONE

I WANT TO MENTION this story so you can get a better understanding of the damage Dolgyal does to the world, to Buddhism, to Tibetan Buddhism, and in particular to Lama Tsongkhapa's teachings. Some stories are from many years ago but this particular story is from recent years.

This incident happened in Ganden Monastery. There was a geshe, Jangtse Geshe Drati, who was an expert in philosophy. When we were in Buxa he was well known for his understanding of the five major sutra texts—*Abhisamayalamkara, Vinaya, Madhyamaka, Abhidharmakosha* and *Pramanavarttika*—and I think he became even better known in south India. He came to our class in Buxa to explain one of the texts.

After Buxa he was advised by His Holiness's office in Dharamsala to change the way the monks studied into that of a school, like a university. Previously the subjects ran sequentially, one by one, with a different number of years for each subject, so what was studied depended on time. So he transformed the course of study into a university-type curriculum, where the five major sutra texts were taught simultaneously.

When Geshe Tsephel, who now has a center in America,[76] was the abbot of Ganden Jangtse, he wanted to take teachings from Geshe Drati, especially because he was an expert in Madhyamaka, even though Geshe Tsephel himself is also very learned. He had prepared all the offerings in order to request the teachings the next day but, that night, he had very bad dream, so he did not go.

What happened was that Geshe Drati had criticized His Holiness. He

---

[76] Land of Compassion Buddha in West Covina, California.

said there were many learned lamas who were practicing Dolgyal and that they were very good, something like that. I didn't see details of his criticism but Khadro-la told His Holiness that it was the worst criticism so far.

Ganden Monastery has two divisions, Shartse and Jangtse, and the letter criticizing His Holiness was read in public to the Ganden Jangtse assembly. I don't know how many thousands of monks were in Jangtse but they were all there for a puja. Because of that, the staff and abbots of the monasteries gathered to decide whether to expel Geshe Drati from Ganden Jangtse Monastery, even though he was a great teacher with a thousand disciples.

They decided to ask Kalarupa, the main protector of Ganden Monastery, for advice. The power of all the buddhas is manifested in Yamantaka, Vajrabhairava, who is the most wrathful aspect of Manjushri. Kalarupa is the protector that Yamantaka orders to do activities. But this protector is not a worldly being; he is beyond samsara. There are three aspects of Kalarupa: outer Kalarupa, inner Kalarupa and secret Kalarupa. Of Lama Tsongkhapa's two protectors, Kalarupa and Six-arm Mahakala, Kalarupa is the main one. Lama Tsongkhapa gave them orders and they fulfilled them.

The requesting ceremony to Kalarupa, which requires using small bowls, takes time because every bowl has to be weighed exactly, like when you buy gold. The answer to the question is inside the bowls—you ask the question mentally. So, each bowl has to be of equal weight; if any are lighter or heavier the answer becomes incorrect.

After the abbots and staff of the monastery did pujas and prayers asking whether this geshe should be expelled from the monastery or not it came out he should be expelled. His criticism of His Holiness was then read out to all the monks, who clapped their hands. Clapping hands in the West means joy and approval, like in football, to show you are happy. In Tibet, clapping hands in this way means the opposite of being happy or welcoming somebody. In the monasteries it's something wrathful.

We also did it at Buxa in the very early times. A huge pot of black tea was made for the monks and they tipped all of it out, which was a sort of wrathful action, showing the unbelievable suffering of the whole of Tibet turned upside down. In the very early Buxa days the monks tipped the tea out and then beat it with the end of their *zens*.

The monks did that, but of course, although the action can be wrathful, it has to fit into Buddhist practice and be motivated by compassion, otherwise it becomes a worldly activity, which is the same as most countries do— fighting each other, killing each other. There is nothing different.

I heard that in Iraq, while Saddam Hussein was president, when somebody did something wrong they took him to the place of execution and laid him on the ground. His parents and relatives had to be there and when his head was chopped off they had to clap their hands as if they were happy with the execution.

The original motivation must fit with Buddhism; it must be great compassion for others, even for the enemy. Then, even if the action is wrathful, it is like parents punishing their child in order to help him. They send him to school to educate him so he can have a good life in the future, but if the child refuses to go they scold and beat him with compassion because they have concern for his future and they don't want him to suffer later. This is like the monks tipping out the tea.

In Ganden, when the letter was read publicly, all the monks clapped their hands, indicating they wanted to expel that geshe even though he was an expert, especially in the Madhyamaka teachings on emptiness. They clapped their hands and kicked him out. Now he is in France.

We ordinary people don't understand the extent of the harm that Dolgyal can do through the great lamas, those learned in philosophy. He harms them from the top and then they spread his influence to many people, getting them to practice him. He wants many people to practice him, to follow him, so he influences the geshes, the lamas, like this.

This has even spread to Lama Tsongkhapa's main monastery, Ganden, where his teachings are preserved; where the monks not only study the texts but practice their meaning as well. This was a great Lama Tsongkhapa tradition monastery in Tibet and is now located in south India. They preserve the excellent Buddhist education, which is like the Pacific Ocean, deep and vast, but it is not just faith. It is not like you are forbidden to check anything, to ask questions, that you must just believe what you are told. The monks are perfectly qualified to explain the Dharma to sentient beings, whether it is the vast teachings, the middle-level teachings or just the very essence of the lam-rim, depending on the level of the students' minds. These monasteries—Ganden, Sera and Drepung—always produced highly qualified teachers and continue to do so.

So you can see that the harm Dolgyal can do is huge. If the top teachers, those who are expert in Dharma, succumb to Dolgyal's influence, then many students, if they don't check what their guru does, can easily follow. They might even think the reason the guru is so successful is because of Dolgyal.

But the guru is already successful; he already has great knowledge. The great lamas like Kyabje Trijang Rinpoche, Kyabje Zong Rinpoche, Pabongka Rinpoche and all the other lamas have renunciation, bodhicitta, the right view of emptiness, and tantric realizations of the generation and completion stages. Even by just having bodhicitta, of course, they can benefit others greatly. Just by giving a spoonful of food to a dog with bodhicitta purifies the dog's negative karma and makes a connection with that dog so that it will be able to meet the bodhisattva again and again in future lives. So, it's not only by teaching that these great lamas benefit sentient beings. But so many people think that they're of benefit because of Dolgyal.

The conclusion is that Dolgyal wants to harm others. He himself has no guru connection with His Holiness because he broke his samaya in the past, so he wants to make other people like that. He is harming Buddhism—particularly Lama Tsongkhapa's teachings—and harming the world.

Even though we might have learned the words of Dharma well by studying the scriptures, we can still make big mistakes in our practice by not correctly following our virtuous friend and even criticizing him. We might be experts in all the extremely difficult texts but because we have not done proper analysis we can easily believe things like that.

In that way Dolgyal particularly tries to harm Lama Tsongkhapa's teachings and create disharmony within Lama Tsongkhapa's tradition. He is very sectarian; very, very sectarian. He wants to cause disharmony between the Tibetan Buddhist traditions, the Nyingma, Kagyü, Sakya and Gelug. To not make a connection with the other traditions, to not take teachings from them, is very sectarian; it brings great disharmony. Lama Tsongkhapa took the full ordination vows from the eighth Karmapa, Mikyö Dorje, and he took different teachings from lamas of the other traditions.

We must investigate any guru we want to follow

The root of enlightenment is correctly devoting to the virtuous friend. If that is done well, it brings every success up to enlightenment, to be able to free all sentient beings from the oceans of samsaric suffering and bring them to full enlightenment. If the root is wrong, if we are mistaken in how we devote to the virtuous friend, then there is no success and there is great suffering in this life and from life to life, for hundreds of thousands, or even millions of lives. For example, we have to experience the unbearable suffering of the inexhaustible hell realm for an intermediate eon.[77]

---

[77] See *Heart of the Path*, p. 155.

But even then our karma is not finished. Even when this world ends, even when this world becomes empty, which after a great eon it will, we must be born in the hell realm of another universe. There are numberless universes and in those universes there are hell realms, so we will be born there and suffer until our karma has finished.

Even in recent times it has happened that Dolgyal has caused incredible danger, particularly to Lama Tsongkhapa's teachings. For instance, many disciples have become angry or developed heresy to their guru, so he creates harm like this. In one second they have destroyed their ability to attain enlightenment, their realizations, their merit. Although I haven't yet seen it with my own eyes, I have heard that the scriptures say that heresy toward the guru destroys hundreds of thousands of eons of merit.

The lam-rim outline is a bit different. It says that if we get angry with our guru, for however many seconds we are angry with him, we have to be reborn and suffer in the lower realms for that many eons. There is a contradiction in this outline. What I mentioned was that if we are not a bodhisattva and we get angry with a bodhisattva for one second, we destroy one thousand eons of virtue created by cherishing sentient beings and making offerings to the buddhas. That is also mentioned in the *Lamrim Chenmo* and *A Guide to the Bodhisattva's Way of Life*. I asked Jangtse Chöje, who thought it might be a minute but I think it's a second.

These things are not small matters. Dolgyal destroys the root of the path to enlightenment, correctly following the virtuous friend, the most important thing in our life. You should know this. You should not think, "Oh, this is a Tibetan problem." You have to know how harmful it is, otherwise you can get drawn in and then you won't know you are getting cheated.

I have heard that Dolgyal followers in Singapore stick the Dolgyal mantra on their cars and leave them outside. They actually believe that by putting the mantra on a car or reciting it they can be successful in business.

We can very easily be cheated, so we must check everything. Guru Shakyamuni Buddha said,

> Oh bhikshus and wise men, as one assays gold by rubbing, cutting and melting, so examine well my words and accept them, but not because you respect me.

The Buddha himself said that.[78] We have to examine his teachings just as

---

[78] A well-known saying of the Buddha from the *Ghanavyuha Sutra*, this version is found

we would examine a metal to see if it is gold, to see whether it is false, mixed or pure. There are three ways you test for gold, by cutting it, rubbing it and burning it. He said we should accept his teachings only after examining them and seeing they are correct. That means we are most welcome to investigate whatever question we have. Once we have investigated and found the teachings to be correct and, on the strength of that, have decided to follow them, then we are not doing so through blind faith. It's my view that, among all the religions, only Buddhism gives us the opportunity, the freedom, to examine the path completely.

In the monasteries the special way of studying is debate. Acceptance of the Buddhadharma is not just through belief but also through debate, through questioning—you can ask any question and then decide for yourself whether the answer is correct or incorrect. Even if it *is* correct, you can still debate. If you are good debater, even if somebody has given a correct answer you can still try to change that person's mind.

Buddhism is very logical, very perfect, and examination of it leads to a deep, clear understanding of the teachings. We are not asked to accept something on blind faith. We are never told we are not allowed to ask questions but must just accept what we hear. This is how it can become when somebody doesn't have an answer.

I'm bringing this up in the context of Dolgyal. What I'm saying is that if we are allowed to check what has been revealed by the guru, then why not with Dolgyal? That is my question. A Dolgyal practitioner might be an expert in debate but has never checked on Dolgyal. That is very strange. Especially seeing how Dolgyal is clearly so harmful to the world, to Buddhism, to the success of Tibet, to His Holiness's wishes and, particularly, to Lama Tsongkhapa's teaching. This is extremely clear. That is what Dolgyal's influence is like, even for learned lamas and geshes. It leads many people to no longer follow His Holiness but to follow Dolgyal instead, to go in the wrong direction.

If you are following Tibetan Buddhism, learning and practicing tantra, you have to understand this. If, as a non-Tibetan, you think that this is purely a Tibetan problem, you are mistaken. Tibetan Buddhism originated from the Buddha himself and from those who were like second Buddhas—Nagarjuna and all the great pandits from Nalanda and the many enlight-

---

on a plaque next to the Buddha statue in the Tsuglhakhang, His Holiness the Dalai Lama's temple in Dharamsala.

ened Tibetan lamas, such as Lama Tsongkhapa. Because what you are learning comes from this great lineage, the Dolgyal problem is also yours.

SEEING THE GURU AS A BUDDHA

A sutra says,

> From your side as the disciple, think that the guru who reveals the Dharma to you is a buddha, always abiding in front of you, blessing your heart. By thinking this way, the buddha constantly blesses your mind, liberating you from all wrong conceptions and mistaken ways of thinking.

It is very important to remember these words whenever we do the guru devotion meditation. Think that the virtuous friend who reveals the Dharma is a buddha. From our side as a disciple, we should think of him as a buddha. Then the buddha is always abiding in front of us in the form of the one who reveals the Dharma to us, as the guru. Even if we have only received an oral transmission of OM MANI PADME HUM or one verse of teaching, still the connection has been made. We are the disciple; he or she is the guru.

Any time we think "buddha," the buddha is always there in front of us, blessing our mind, our heart. This is not our physical beating heart but where the mind is. Scientists often talk about the brain. That is quite natural, isn't it? Don't you sometimes feel that thinking happens in the brain? When you think of some problem or something, don't you feel it's in the brain rather than anywhere else?

On the other hand, emotions such as compassion, patience and anger don't seem to come from the brain but from the heart. When strong negative emotions come, that is where we feel them. So my question is, why do we feel them there? Why not in the brain, when scientists talk about the brain as being everything? I think many of you have investigated and rejected the scientific notion that the brain is everything. There are even instances where a person has been able to remain alive without a brain.

In Phagri, where I lived for three years, Kyabje Zong Rinpoche—who gave me many initiations and teachings—saw a person without a head, with only a neck. To feed him the family spooned the tsampa in through his neck. He managed to communicate. When he wanted to be out in the sun or when he was hungry he talked with his fingers, like rubbing his stomach for hunger. He had no head but he lived. This sounds unbelievable but you should know that my guru, Kyabje Zong Rinpoche, actually saw this in Phagri. There is no reason why my guru would lie to me.

He also told me that he had heard about a chicken that lived without a head for two or three years. Perhaps he saw it on TV. The person who fed the chicken took it all around the world to make money but then after three years it died because he forgot to give it food or something. It means that even without a brain there is still a basis for the mind to function in the body; it is still possible to be a living being.

Later, I saw something similar in a text by a great lama from Amdo, who had many collections of sutra and tantra teachings. He said in the teachings that in Amdo he saw a person without head. I don't know what scientists would say. If I were in a meeting with them, I would ask that question.

This is all just to do with the notion that the mind is the brain. These examples show that there is more to reality than what scientists believe. They need to change their ideas, to refine them so that they become closer to reality.

Wherever we consider the mind to be, think of the guru as a buddha who always abides there, blessing us and liberating us from all the wrong concepts, especially the ignorance that is the creator of samsara, believing that the I and the aggregates are truly existent. This is a very important practice. If we want to achieve enlightenment and liberate sentient beings from the oceans of samsaric suffering, if we want to lead them all to *sang-gyä*, the total elimination of all obscurations and the completion of all realizations, we must practice seeing the guru as a buddha.

This is the very essence of how to follow the virtuous friend, how to devote to the virtuous friend through thought and action. Devoting through thought is looking at the guru as a buddha and devoting through action is receiving the guru's advice and fulfilling his wishes.

When we invited Kyabje Chöden Rinpoche to Vajrapani Institute[79] he said that the reason we, as disciples, see the guru as a buddha and follow his advice is because this is the sole way to enlightenment. If we are able to fulfill these two things, correct thought and action toward the guru, the result must be that we will achieve *sang-gyä*. Otherwise it is impossible; there can be no *sang-gyä*. That was his conclusion. Rinpoche did not use that term, but that is what it is, *sang-gyä*.

---

[79] The FPMT retreat center in Boulder Creek, California.

Many people think that to serve the guru we have to be with the guru. This is not so. Whether we are far from the guru or near we can still serve the guru. It doesn't matter whether we're living in his house or on the other side of the world. We could be on the moon or the sun and still be serving the guru by keeping purely the vows he has given us: refuge vows, pratimoksha vows, like the five lay vows or the eight Mahayana precepts, and higher vows, such as those of monastic ordination or the bodhisattva or tantric vows. If we are keeping those vows we are following the guru's advice, fulfilling his wishes; we are serving the guru.

Also, meditating, studying such things as the lam-rim, the commentaries and the philosophical teachings—learning the Dharma and integrating it into our practice—is what the guru wishes us to do, and doing all that is also serving the guru, fulfilling his advice. Whatever else the guru has advised us to do, such as retreat or to teach the Dharma, is also service to the guru. So we do not have to be with the guru. We can be far away, on another planet or wherever.

In general, anything that benefits sentient beings and helps liberate them from suffering is service to the guru because that is exactly what he advises. That is fulfilling the guru's wishes.

We also need to recognize any physical or verbal action of the guru, even dancing, as an action of the buddha's holy body. Whatever the guru does is the holy action of a buddha; whatever the guru says is the holy speech of a buddha.

Rather than having a mind thick with attachment, we have to shake our mind, we have to be aware. We have to enlighten our mind. When the guru talks to us, we need to see it as the holy speech of all the buddhas. This is Shakyamuni Buddha talking to us, this is Maitreya Buddha talking to us, this is Tara talking to us, this is Manjushri talking to us, this is Heruka talking to us, this is our own particular deity talking to us. This is our practice. This is what we have to do.

We also have to think that whatever the guru says or does, which is the action of the guru's mind, is the action of *all* the numberless buddhas' holy minds.

Every single atom of the guru's holy body is all the buddhas' holy bodies. We have to think like that; we have to meditate on that; we have to realize that. If we do, then it is like the sutra says—any guru we think of as a buddha in that way, the buddha always abides there and always blesses our heart, liberating our mind from all the wrong concepts.

If we want enlightenment, then this is how and why we should practice. We shouldn't practice just so that we can space out like we do on drugs, on LSD—not that I know if anybody here has taken LSD or not.

In the very early times at Kopan, before we built the monastery, Lama Yeshe and I were staying in the old British-style house built for the Nepalese king's astrologer. We had a small room, just big enough to fit two people, with Lama on one side and me on the other. There was a door and a window, but I can't remember whether there was a table or not. I remember a Western student at that time was smoking what he called "Buddha grass." There were many drugs around then. LSD had just come out. Everywhere you went in Kathmandu, on every corner you could see Western people, coming from here, coming from there, their faces unhealthy and pale because of the drugs they were taking. Once a student gave us some bread with LSD in it but we didn't eat it. If we had taken it, I would be able to describe our experience, singing the mandala or maybe visiting hell, I'm not sure.

Offering to the pores of His Holiness

Even though you have read many other lam-rim texts, when you read any of Lama Tsongkhapa's teachings you think, "Oh, I should have read this at the very beginning, as my first teaching. I wish I had seen this when I first encountered Buddhism." When I read one of his texts it strikes me like that. His advice is very concise but so vast, so deep. That is the way Lama Tsongkhapa explains the teachings. For example, with the mandala offering, he said it is very important to make a good-quality visualization. Good quality means visualizing the mandala in the most extensive way we can and then making the offering.

Offering the mandala is one of the exceptional methods of collecting extensive merit, so doing it purely, doing a good-quality one—the best quality—is very important, as is doing the greatest number of mandala offerings possible. He mentions that these are the two ways to collect the most merit, the quality of the mandala offering and the number of times it's made. Other lam-rim texts describe the details of the visualizations but Lama Tsongkhapa just makes this main point.

Those meditators who have achieved the eighth, ninth or tenth bodhisattva bhumi can manifest billions, zillions, trillions of mandalas. They can do prostrations in the pure land of the buddhas. They can do so much, while we are unable to manifest even one. We have mountains of obscurations and negative karma, which high-level bodhisattvas do not.

Lama Tsongkhapa said doing prostrations is another way of collecting extensive merit. He said we should visualize many bodies, as if we have numberless bodies covering the whole ground, and then, with those millions of bodies, prostrate to the merit field.

Visualizing two bodies prostrating gains us the same merit as if two bodies were actually prostrating; visualizing ten bodies prostrating gains us the same merit as ten bodies doing it. If we are able to visualize the whole earth full of our bodies, filling the four directions and the intermediate ones, all prostrating, we get the same merit as that many of our bodies prostrating. This creates unbelievable merit.

Lama Tsongkhapa explains things like this so concisely, giving just the essence. Just using one or two words he explains the contradictions in the arguments of many famous contemporary and previous meditators. Then he spends more pages on practices such as the preliminary practices.

Just as visualizing countless bodies prostrating brings great merit, so too does thinking that, while offering something as small as a cup of water to the guru, we are offering it to the numberless buddhas; we get the benefit of actually offering water to numberless buddhas. We can think how every atom of our guru's holy body contains numberless buddhas and we are offering to all of them. Whatever we are doing—offering service, offering robes, cleaning or washing—if we think we are doing it for the numberless buddhas, we get that amount of merit. Even if we do not consciously think that, we still get much merit.

For example, when attending our guru's teachings we can think that this is Tara giving the teaching, this is Guru Shakyamuni Buddha giving the teaching, this is Manjushri giving the teaching, this is our deity giving the teaching, this is the numberless buddhas giving us the teaching. Similarly, whenever our guru gives us advice, whatever it is, we should think that this advice is coming from all the numberless buddhas. This is Tara giving us advice, this is Maitreya Buddha giving us advice, this is Guru Shakyamuni Buddha giving us advice, this is Mahakala giving us advice, this is all the thousand buddhas of the fortunate eon giving us advice. All the merit field, all the dakas and dakinis, all the arhats, including the sixteen who are buddhas, the Dharma protectors—everyone is giving us advice. The guru's advice is everybody giving us advice.

In that way, we never feel abandoned; we are always connected with all the numberless buddhas, up to the Dharma protectors of the merit field. In the same way, the merits are unbelievable when we make offerings to the guru's disciples, the guru's "pores."

This is an example you can keep in mind. When I make offerings to people who have received teachings from His Holiness, even lay people, even Westerners, but especially in the monasteries such as Sera, Ganden, Drepung or Kopan, first of all I try to generate bodhicitta motivation, thinking, "To achieve enlightenment to free the numberless sentient beings from the oceans of samsaric suffering and bring them to full enlightenment I am going to make these offerings." Even without bodhicitta, the merit of offering to the many fully ordained monks is unbelievable. The higher number of vows they live in, the more unbelievable merit we collect by making offerings of food, tea, money or whatever.

Even offering to one monk with bodhicitta motivation collects skies of merit. There are thousands of monks in each monastery—Sera Me, Sera Je, Ganden Shartse, Ganden Jangtse, Drepung Gomang and Drepung Loseling—so after generating bodhicitta, I think, "I make this offering to achieve enlightenment for sentient beings." If you offer to each monk in this way you collect more than skies of merit.

After that, I think they are all His Holiness the Dalai Lama's pores. Literally, pores are tiny holes in the skin of the body but these pores are different. Pores here means not only the disciples of the guru but, if the guru is a layperson, it can also mean his or her spouse, children and any animals he or she has, dogs, horses and so forth. Even the guru's neighbors are pores.

After generating bodhicitta, while making the offering, I think wherever they are, whatever college or khangtsen they belong to, they are His Holiness's pores. So I offer to all the thousands of monks in Sera Je and Sera Me thinking that they are all His Holiness's pores.

By generating bodhicitta at the beginning and thinking of the monk to whom we are making an offering as one of His Holiness's pores, we collect inconceivable merit. The merit of offering to just one statue of the Buddha is utterly beyond our comprehension, yet we collect far more merit by offering a glass of water, tea, money or whatever to a monk we see as a pore of His Holiness than we do by making offerings to the numberless Buddhas, the numberless Dharma, the numberless Sangha, the numberless statues, the numberless scriptures and the numberless stupas combined.

Now that is by thinking of just *one* monk as a pore of His Holiness and making an offering to him. Of course, this is multiplied when offered in this way to all the other monks. They are all disciples, or pores, of His Holiness, so when we make offerings to them we can think that we are making offerings to the guru's pores. If offering to just one monk brings greater merit than offering to the numberless holy objects in all the universes, *now* there is not just one monk but thousands of monks and many of them are fully ordained. By thinking of them all as the pores of the guru and making offerings, the merit we create is utterly unimaginable.

It's the same at the centers, even in the West, when we make offerings to students who are disciples of His Holiness. If they have received teachings or initiations from His Holiness and see him as their guru, can you imagine the merit we create by offering them just one cup of tea? Or a milkshake! In the West there are many things we can offer, not just momos. We can offer ice cream or hot apple pie. By thinking of those students at your center as pores of His Holiness and offering them something, you create incredible merit, even if there are only three students. So it's not just in faraway monasteries that you can create this kind of merit.

What a great opportunity we have to make ourselves beneficial for sentient beings, to help free them from the oceans of samsaric suffering and bring them to enlightenment. Even if we just offer a little candy, the merit can be unbelievable. The opportunity is always there.

When I was in Tibet I visited Tsurphu, the Karmapa's monastery. I had not planned to go there because the Karmapa had fled to India some months earlier, but our Sherpa travel guide included it in the itinerary because he usually took tourists there. Since I'm a Sherpa the guides made Sherpa food for us, millet tsampa mixed with water.

We were actually on our way to Reting, Dromtönpa's monastery where many of the Kadampa geshes had their hermitages, and the road passed through Tölung Dechen, the place west of Lhasa where Lama Yeshe was born and where his family still lives. The Karmapa's monastery was not far from there, so they arranged for us to go for a day to visit. The monastery is situated in a narrow valley, with a hermitage on the hill. We camped where there was running water.

We went into the monastery and made money offerings. I tried to offer the money to each monk myself and I was wondering what to think when suddenly I decided to think of each one as my guru. They were not my guru but I thought of each one as Kyabje Trijang Rinpoche, my root guru, and then made the money offering to them as my guru. They were not my guru's pores, but by thinking like this, thinking of offering to the guru, can you imagine the merit? As I mentioned, the guru is the most powerful object, the most holy object, so offering in this way becomes the most powerful purification and the best way to collect the most extensive merit, much more than by making offerings to the numberless Buddhas, Dharma and Sangha. Offering to the guru creates unbelievably more merit than that. I'm just telling you this so you know how to think to collect the most merit. This is just a small good experience I had.

We also visited Tashi Lhunpo, His Holiness the Panchen Lama's monastery. When we circumambulated the monastery there were many dogs, each with its own place, like a personal hermitage, and a pot to eat its food from. The old mothers from Shigatse carried tsampa and water in buckets to give them. Sometimes they gave the dogs big pieces of the tsampa from their home. By going around the monastery giving food and water to the dogs they were also circumambulating all the unbelievable number of holy objects and holy beings inside. I was really happy seeing those mothers being so kind and compassionate, giving food like that. They were very, very kind.

Before visiting Tshurpu we had been to Tashi Lhunpo, His Holiness the Panchen Lama's monastery. I had taken a short teaching from the Panchen Lama in Dechen Ling, which is just below Tashi Lhunpo, during the previous trip to Tibet with Geshe Lama Konchog. At that time Gen Wangdu, a meditator from Sera Me, was there and he was the main person who wanted to meet the Panchen Lama and ask for teachings. I had to lead the mandala offering before the interview and, as I had never taken teachings from the Panchen Lama before, I was wondering whether to make the guru-disciple connection or not as I began chanting the prayer. It was in my hand whether to take him as guru or not. I did not want to feel that His Holiness had one view and Panchen Rinpoche another, because then you get into difficulty and can create heavy negative karma. Then I thought they are one in essence. His Holiness the Dalai Lama and Panchen Rinpoche are one in essence, one buddha, so there was no problem. Toward the end of the mandala I had decided to take the teaching and take him as a guru. It was a short teaching based on the Buddha's advice that we often recite, the verse that starts, "Do not commit any unwholesome actions." He gave a very powerful teaching on it.

Anyway, I wanted to tell you about the dogs. When we were circumambulating the Panchen Lama's monastery we saw that there were many dogs, each with its own place, like a personal hermitage, and a pot to eat its food from. The old mothers from Shigatse carried tsampa and water in buckets to give them. Sometimes they gave the dogs big pieces of the tsampa from their home. By going around the monastery giving food and water to the dogs they were also circumambulating all the unbelievable number of holy objects and holy beings inside. I was really happy seeing those mothers being so kind and compassionate, giving food like that. They were very, very kind.

In the same way that I visualized the Tsurphu monks as my guru, you can do that whenever you throw a party for your family or friends. If you can also invite your enemy, that is the best party! That is something that worldly people don't do. Worldly people usually harm the enemy, insulting him, shooting him and things like that. If you are a Dharma practitioner, you can invite your enemy and offer him apple pie or momos or whatever.

At a party, if you think of each guest as your guru or His Holiness the Dalai Lama when you offer them food or drink, you are making offerings to your guru or His Holiness. In that way you collect the greatest merit and make the most powerful purification. It is much greater than making offerings to the numberless Buddhas, Dharma and Sangha and the numberless statues, stupas and scriptures. Such merit is comparatively small. As I mentioned, in themselves, such offerings are unbelievable—even offering a small grain of rice or a tiny flower to a stupa, a statue or a picture of a buddha, the benefits are beyond our concept, just like the sky. But now, offering to the guru, the merit is much greater than offering to all those holy objects. You collect the highest merit, the most powerful merit.

So, by imagining all the guests at your party as your guru, as His Holiness, that is your Dharma practice, your guru devotion practice. Not everybody can go to the Karmapa's monastery in Tibet and make offerings to the monks while seeing them as the guru, but you can collect a huge amount of merit even in your own home by having a party and serving your guests food or drink, seeing that as an offering to your guru; that becomes your Dharma practice. It is such a quick way to achieve enlightenment.

The guru is more precious than a wish-granting jewel

The *Kalachakra Tantra* says,

> Even making offerings to the Three Rare Sublime Ones of the
> three times for eons

Or saving tens of millions of creatures,
You will still not attain enlightenment in this lifetime,
But if you please the guru by devoting yourself with a devotional
    mind,
Then you will definitely attain the common and sublime qualities
    in this lifetime.

This is something you should know. The usual translation of *kon-chog sum* is "Three Jewels" but I think that is a very poor meaning of the term. I prefer to translate it as exactly as I can according to the Tibetan because it is very important. We say the "Three Jewels" in relation to the Buddha, Dharma and Sangha but "three jewels" what? Three jewels what? It's nothing; it doesn't give us anything. I prefer to translate *kon-chog sum* as "Three Rare Sublime Ones"—the exact Tibetan translation—because it has great meaning.

Why should they be called *kon-chog sum*? Among all material objects, gold, silver, diamonds and sapphires are the most precious. But rarer than these is the wish-granting jewel. After being in the world a long time, at the end, the buddhas' relics go into the ocean and become wish-granting jewels. I saw this evolution mentioned in a medicine book. That is one explanation; I don't know if there are any others.

A universal king is a bodhisattva who has collected the most unbelievable merit. They only appear in the world one at a time, never two, and when a king does appear his people are able to live their lives in the ten virtues.[80] This happens by the power of the universal king.

Universal, or wheel-turning, kings—great bodhisattvas who have unbelievable merit—are able to find wish-granting jewels in the ocean. The jewels are cleansed of mud in three ways and on the fifteenth of the month are placed on top of a banner. Then, whatever material needs of this life you pray for you can have.

This is something Sai Baba was said to be able to do. He made a hand gesture and produced gold chains, watches or things like that for people to have. These were not magicians' hallucinations, things you took back home and they then disappeared. You could use them for a long time. Because Sai Baba had a lot of merit he was able to produce material gifts for people.

---

[80] The ten virtues are the opposites of the ten nonvirtues and so, instead of killing, the first virtue is not killing or saving lives and so forth. See Rinpoche's forthcoming book on karma.

For example, Ming Ming, one of my students and the godmother of Sangye from our *labrang* in Sera, had a special connection with Sai Baba. She has been inviting the monks in Sera to do puja every year on Sai Baba's birthday for ten years. She also invites them to do puja on Chinese New Year. I heard that Sai Baba produced a gold chain or something for the head monk.

It's very strange, because usually, in other places, Muslims would never think of reciting mantras; they might even become infuriated. But many Christians and Muslims come to Singapore and her son recites the mantra of the bodhisattva Ksitigarbha, which I gave to him and his mother to chant. They have special karma. They made a CD of their chanting, but they recite it so fast I couldn't follow. It is very interesting how the mother and children do this. One time when the son chanted it there were thirty-one thousand people there. Everybody, including all the Muslims, chanted. That is very special. There was no discrimination, no sectarianism, just everybody chanting the mantra. For Muslims, chanting is the most difficult thing in the world. And after they left Singapore they continued to chant the mantras.

Even though a wish-granting jewel is much rarer than diamonds, sapphires or gold, it cannot purify our past negative karma, the cause of lower realms. Only the Buddha, Dharma and Sangha can guide us from the lower realms to the upper realms, from the upper realms to nirvana, liberation from the oceans of samsara, ultimate happiness, and from there to *sang-gyä*, the total elimination of all obscurations and the completion of all realizations. Wish-granting jewels can give us whatever material comfort of this life we ask for but they cannot do what the Buddha, Dharma and Sangha can.

So, *kon-chog sum*, the Buddha, Dharma and Sangha, is much rarer than a wish-granting jewel, much rarer than numberless wish-granting jewels. Even skies of wish-granting jewels are nothing compared to the value of the Buddha, Dharma and Sangha and what they can do for us. *Kon-chog sum* has a very deep meaning, but "Three Jewels" is very loose; it becomes like a plastic apple.

I don't know if they do this in the West, but in Pathankot[81] there is a shop that sells fruit. Above the fruit there is a big mirror that reflects all the fruit back. From a distance it looks like there is a lot of fruit but when you

---

[81] The railway town in the Punjab where you alight for the bus to Dharamsala.

look closer you seen that the top part is only a reflection. Anyway, it's kind of like that.

It says in the teachings that even making offerings to the Three Rare Sublime Ones, *kon-chog sum*, for three eons and saving the lives of ten of millions of creatures isn't enough to achieve enlightenment in this lifetime, but if we devote ourselves to the guru who has oceans of qualities we can definitely attain both common and supreme qualities—"supreme" here means mahamudra, enlightenment—in this lifetime.

The tantric text *Yeshe Gyatso, Ocean of Transcendental Wisdom,* says,

> For the wise fortunate one, skill in doing activities for the guru is much more meaningful than doing prostrations to all the past, present and future buddhas for ten million, six hundred thousand eons. If you accomplish whatever your guru advises, all your desires will succeed.[82]

Compared with doing prostrations to all the past, present and future buddhas for ten million, six hundred thousand eons, being expert in serving the guru and fortunate and wise enough to do so is much more greatly meaningful. If we can accomplish whatever the guru advises us to do, all our wishes, our desires, will succeed just like that and we will collect unimaginable merit.

Seeing apparent mistakes in the guru

There is also a very important practice to remember that helps you develop your mind and prevents what has already developed from degenerating. A verse by the Fifth Dalai Lama explains how important it is:

> When mistakes appear in the guru's actions you should recognize them as your own distorted, hallucinated mind, which sees the opposite of reality. Understand these as your own mistakes and abandon such thinking like poison.[83]

---

[82] See *Heart of the Path*, pp. 97–98, for the rest of this verse and a commentary upon it.
[83] See also *Heart of the Path*, pp. 194–95.

This is such an important guru devotion practice. Our mind is hallucinated, distorted, and sees the very opposite of reality. To that mind, our own faults appear as faults in the actions of the guru. We must recognize this, understand how these are all our own mistakes and abandon the mind that sees them as faults in the guru.

We must abandon that mind like poison. If we encountered poisonous food and knew that by eating it we would die, we would immediately throw it away, without a second's delay. Like this, we must recognize the mistakes we see in our guru as results of our hallucinated mind and abandon that mind immediately.

When we see an apparent mistake we cannot see that it is completely the reflection of our own mistaken thinking. We are unaware of that and see it as coming from the guru's side, that it is his mistake. It is like having dirt on our forehead and being unaware of it until we look in the mirror and then blame the mirror for the dirt. That way of thinking is totally false; the reality is not like that. This is exactly what the Fifth Dalai Lama said: we must recognize that this is our mistake and abandon such wrong thinking like poison.

Guru devotion is like a jewel; it's the most important jewel in our life and we can destroy it in an instant by seeing any apparent mistakes of the guru as coming from him. For as many seconds as we think like that, we must suffer for that many eons in the lower realms; for that many eons our virtue is destroyed. Even though we might be just about to attain bodhicitta or renunciation or the realization of emptiness, that is delayed for the number of eons equivalent to the number of seconds we had heresy or anger.

When mistakes in the actions of the guru appear to our hallucinated mind, there are two ways of utilizing this. The first way is described in this verse from the Fifth Dalai Lama. When we recognize that the appearance of a mistake is our own mistake, instead of destroying our guru devotion, it strengthens it. We use apparent mistakes to develop our devotion. We see that the mistake is a projection of our hallucinated mind, our negative karma, and there is no mistake from the guru's side. Because the guru is a buddha, the mistake cannot be from the guru's side. If we think like that our devotion will not be disturbed and will, in fact, be made stronger.

The second way is to see that in order to guide us to liberation, to free us from the oceans of samsaric suffering of the lower realms, the guru manifests in an ordinary aspect, as having mistakes, especially for us. Showing an ordinary aspect is his method of helping us.

When His Holiness the Dalai Lama first gave the mahamudra commentary[84] I asked him what "showing an ordinary aspect" meant. He explained that showing an ordinary aspect means showing mistakes. It is very important for the guru to show us an ordinary aspect and appear to have mistakes in order to guide us. If he were to show himself in the aspect of a buddha we would not be able to see him because our mind is so impure. Without pure karma we cannot see him in an enlightened aspect. With a mind such as ours, a mind full of obscurations, we can only see mistakes. As His Holiness said, the guru can only guide us by appearing to have mistakes. But it is a manifestation of our own mistakes, our hallucinated mind. Therefore, showing the ordinary aspect, showing mistakes, is unbelievably important to us. It is mentioned in the *Lama Chöpa,*

> Adorned with a *sugata's* three bodies and ornamental wheels,
> You manifest from an alluring net of skillful means
> In ordinary form to lead all beings.
> Compassionate refuge savior, I make requests to you.[85]

That is very important. The guru is the essence of the three bodies of all the buddhas gone to bliss, the sugatas, the skillful means that is like a net cutting through appearance. His actions, like a blissful dancing gait, guide transmigratory beings to enlightenment in an ordinary form, not in a pure form.

This means that when the guru appears, he purposely shows us this mistaken, ordinary aspect in order to guide us and all other transmigratory beings to enlightenment. The conclusion is that without the guru guiding us in this ordinary aspect, we would be without a guide, totally lost in samsara. We would be like a baby left out in a hot desert with no food or water, surrounded by dangerous animals. Or we would be like somebody lost in the nighttime in a forest full of tigers and many other animals around that could eat us at any time. We would be totally lost in samsara, totally without a guide, without a protector.

Because of that we live our life creating only negative karma, nothing else, creating only the cause to be born in the lower realms. It is terribly sad, just living our whole life day and night to create the karma to be born in the

---

[84] In Dharamsala at the FPMT's first Enlightened Experience Celebration, March, 1982. Published as *The Gelug/Kagyü Tradition of Mahamudra.*
[85] V.49.

lower realms. The lower realms are where we have just come from and now all we are doing is creating the cause to go back there and to suffer for eons.

Every second that the guru appears to us in an ordinary, mistaken aspect to guide us is more precious than the whole sky filled with wish-granting jewels. This is a very important meditation.

Robin Bath

11. More Precious than a Wish-granting Jewel

LAMA TSONGKHAPA AND MÖNLAM

WE CHANT the Palden Lhamo prayer during the great prayer festival, the *Mönlam Chenmo*. Establishing the Mönlam Chenmo in Lhasa was one of Lama Tsongkhapa's four great holy deeds in Tibet. Another was the construction of the Maitreya Buddha statue in the Dzingchi Monastery, which I have yet to see.[86] Although now many different monasteries or organizations do mönlams at Bodhgaya, it previously referred to just the prayer ceremony initiated by Lama Tsongkhapa.

There were many thousands of monks in the six colleges of the three main monasteries of the Lama Tsongkhapa, or Gelug, tradition in Tibet: over seven thousand at Drepung, over five thousand at Sera and over three thousand at Ganden. Obviously the numbers are different now in India.

Anyway, these large monasteries, the very top monasteries where the monks do extensive study on Buddhist philosophy, are like huge universities. They resemble the huge factories that make all the different parts of a plane—every single screw, every single engine component, everything that is needed. Without missing anything, the monks learn the whole path to enlightenment, both method and wisdom sides, the qualities of the Buddha, the different levels of the Hinayana and the Mahayana sutra and tantra

---

[86] The festival (the third great deed) was established in 1409. The Maitreya statue (the first great deed) was renovated during Tibetan New Year in 1400, during the time Lama Tsongkhapa was doing his long retreat at Wolka; Dzinchi is not far from there, in the general region of Lake Lhamo Latsho. The other two great deeds were giving an extensive Vinaya teaching with Jetsun Rendawa and Kyabchog Pal Zangpo at Namtse Deng in 1402, thereby revitalizing the monastic tradition (the second great deed), and constructing Ganden Monastery, which was completed in 1410 (the fourth great deed).

paths, the five paths to liberation, the thirty-seven aids to enlightenment and so forth. What they study is truly amazing; so extensive, as deep and as vast as the Pacific Ocean.

Besides studying the sutra path, the tantra they learn and practice is much more than just reciting mantras or doing sadhanas, as people with little knowledge might think. Even though reciting mantras greatly purifies the mind and prepares it for achieving enlightenment, the practice of tantra is so much more than that. It contains the entire path to enlightenment. In tantra there are many skillful techniques that are not found in the practice of sutra. The study of the mind in sutra lacks the great profundity of tantra, where we learn about the gross, subtle and extremely subtle mind, the pure mind.

When Lama Tsongkhapa organized the Mönlam Chenmo, all the main monasteries and many other monasteries gathered together, and this continued up until His Holiness the Fourteenth Dalai Lama left Tibet. Now we do it in exile. The festival lasts for fifteen days, from Losar[87] until the Day of Miracles.[88] Many people think it is just the Day of Miracles, but in fact it lasts the entire fifteen days.

Lama Tsongkhapa was extremely skillful. During the fifteen days of Mönlam Chenmo we start each day with puja. Lay people come from all over to ask for prayers for those who have died, are sick or have difficulties. They make food, money and tea offerings because during this period, the merit of offerings made to each monk is increased a hundred million times. Monks also come to ask for success in their Dharma studies and practice or for help in overcoming obstacles.

Then the monks debate on the *Pramanavarttika*, logical teachings on mind, reincarnation, the trustworthiness of the Buddha because his teachings are pure and so forth. Then there is another puja followed by debate on the *Prajnaparamita* or the *Abhisamayalamkara*. After another puja or meditation there's debate on the *Madhyamaka* and in the evening there is another puja and then debate on the *Vinaya* or the *Abhidharmakosha*.

The debates are between geshes who have finished their study of these five major texts. Each day they gather in groups and two of them are chosen to reply to questions. They are also examined and their answers checked by

---

[87] Tibetan New Year's day, determined by the lunar calendar, it usually falls in February or March. See fpmt.org for more details.
[88] Tib: *Chö-trul Dü-chen.*

somebody like the Ganden Tripa, His Holiness's regent or the abbots of the monasteries.

After the early morning puja the Ganden Tripa reads the Buddha's life stories in order to inspire the monks to follow the path he practiced, with the six paramitas of charity, morality, patience, perseverance, meditation and wisdom. Besides the famous story of when the Buddha gave his body to the tiger, there are many stories of how he made charity of his limbs, eyes and so forth for three countless great eons. Listening to those stories told by Ganden Tripa, the monks and laypeople are inspired to follow in the footsteps of the Buddha.

In that way Lama Tsongkhapa integrated so many things for everybody to collect merit. It was an incredibly skillful way to benefit sentient beings.

As with offerings made to the monks, on any of those fifteen days, reciting one Vajrasattva mantra becomes the equivalent of a hundred million Vajrasattva mantras, giving one rupee of charity to a beggar becomes the equivalent of giving a hundred million rupees, making offerings of one light becomes the equivalent of making a hundred million light offerings and so forth. This is also the best time to do a retreat or a *nyung-nä*, the extensive two-day lower tantra retreat on Chenrezig with many prostrations to the Thirty-five Buddhas and Chenrezig and extensive mantra recitation. All this creates the most unbelievable merit.

The benefits of prostrations

During a nyung-nä people generally do full-length prostrations, like a tree lying down, but it is also possible to do the five-limb, or half, prostration.

Doing prostrations correctly brings many benefits. As you go down onto the floor you must be aware that you're prostrating to the Buddha, Dharma and Sangha, otherwise it just becomes exercise. Mindlessly going up and down might make you fit but it doesn't become prostration. Prostration means purifying your body, speech and mind, wiping off the garbage, the obscurations and negative karma collected through the actions of your body, speech and mind from beginningless rebirths. I don't know what the English word "prostration" means, but in Tibetan, *chag* has this meaning. If you think of the Guru, Buddha, Dharma and Sangha and pay homage to them, it becomes a prostration. Otherwise you are just mimicking prostration and it doesn't become purification.

After I'd had my stroke, a lady who came to the Aptos house didn't know what to do. My stroke was a light one and the paralysis was not severe but it was difficult to walk. She asked, "What do you want? What do you expect?" She often asked that when she came. There was quite a famous man in New York who taught meditation by email or through a website that many people followed. I can't say whether he is a realized person or not but he seems to have a connection to many people and had put his meditation on the Internet.

She got the idea of doing prostrations from him and told me to do them in order to get the movement back in my legs. When I said I would do prostrations to the Buddha she was a little bit surprised. I didn't do them every day, but with the exercise I slowly got better.

For every atom of ground your body covers when you go down you create the karma to be born as a wheel-turning king a thousand times. Wheel-turning kings arise only one at a time; there can't be two at once. They have unbelievable power. It takes infinite merit to be born as a wheel-turning king just once, yet with your body covering just one atom of ground you create the karma to be born as a wheel-turning king for a thousand lifetimes.

From your head down to your feet, when you do prostrations you cover so many atoms. Now, if you keep your ankle flexed so that the tips of your toes touch the ground, you lose covering many atoms, so when you do prostrations you should point your toes. In that way you cover countless more atoms. I need to explain this because if you don't know about it you're in danger of thinking prostration is simply a Tibetan custom and not prostrating properly. Then you fail to collect all that unbelievable merit. Due to ignorance, you cheat yourself.

Even though my body is short, when I do prostrations I still cover numberless atoms between here and the bottom of the earth. Even atoms that our fingers and toes cover are uncountable, especially for us beings who don't have omniscient minds or even ordinary clairvoyance. So, for each atom of ground we cover, from the surface of the earth down to its bottom, we create the good karma to be born as a wheel-turning king for a thousand lifetimes. That is mentioned in the *Lankavatara Sutra*, where it says a "golden base," but it means the bottom of the earth. The merits that the Buddha explained in that sutra are beyond comprehension.

People who are tall or fat cover even more atoms, as do people with long hair. If you have long hair, when you do prostrations you should let it loose so that it spreads out on the ground and covers even more atoms. Having long hair or being tall or fat has huge benefits when doing prostrations; you create so much more unbelievable merit, like generating a greater income. I have to do two prostrations for every one a tall or a fat person does! Americans tend to be tall, so they are very fortunate because when they do prostrations they collect unbelievable merit.

Reciting the names of the Thirty-five Buddhas while doing lots of prostrations purifies many eons of negative karma; for example, reciting just Guru Shakyamuni Buddha's name purifies eighty thousand eons of negativity. Students who come to Kopan and learn to chant *Lama tön-pa chom-dän-dä* [89] in the mornings are unbelievably fortunate. The lam-rim lineage lamas normally say that ten thousand eons of negative karma are purified, but in the Kangyur I have seen that number cited as ten *million* eons. Not only that, I have even seen it said that it can be a hundred *billion* eons of negative karma.[90] That is how much negative karma is purified by reciting the buddhas' names, Guru Shakyamuni's mantra TADYATHA OM MUNÉ MUNÉ MAHAMUNAYÉ SOHA or a few words of the *Heart Sutra*. It's unbelievable. We are so fortunate that we are able to know this.

When Lama Tsongkhapa first did seven hundred thousand prostrations at Wolka he saw the Thirty-five Buddhas without their heads. This was because he had recited the Thirty-five Buddhas prayer omitting the words *de-zhin sheg-pa*, *tathagata*, which explains the qualities of a buddha. Afterwards, however, when he added *de-zhin sheg-pa* to the beginning of each buddha's name, he saw them with heads.

So in the Lama Tsongkhapa tradition we include *de-zhin sheg-pa*, whereas some other traditions don't. If you have seen this you might wonder why there are different forms of the practice, but it is not that they are different texts, it's just that some omit the *de-zhin sheg-pa*.

There is also unbelievable merit in doing many prostrations to the Thousand-arm Compassion Buddha with the mantra OM MANI PADME HUM. The number of atoms of dust of this earth can be counted, the number of raindrops can be counted, the number of drops of water in the oceans can be counted, but we cannot count the benefits of reciting this mantra. It

---

[89] A prayer of prostration, offering, refuge and a request for blessings containing several epithets of the Buddha: *La ma tön pa chom dän dä de zhin sheg pa dra chom pa yang dag par dzog pä sang gyä päl gyäl wa shakya thub pa la/chhag tshäl lo chhö do kyab su chhi wo/jin gyi lab tu söl.*

[90] Tib: *trag-trig.* In the Tibetan system the large numbers are as follows: 100,000, *bum*; 1 million, *sa-ya*; 10 million, *je-wa*; 100 million, *dung-chur*; 1,000 million (US billion), *ter-bum*; 10 billion, *ter-bum-chen-po*; 100 billion, *trag-trig*; 1 trillion (Euro billion), *trag-trig chen-po*. See *Teachings from the Vajrasattva Retreat*, p. 531. See also "Tibetan numbers" at LamaYeshe.com.

is so unbelievable, especially if you recite it with bodhicitta. Each time you recite the mantra OM MANI PADME HUM once, each time you recite one buddha's name, you collect more than skies of merit. And besides powerfully purifying obscurations collected from beginningless rebirths and collecting extensive merit, it generates compassion within your heart for the numberless sentient beings: the human beings, the gods, the demigods, the hell beings, the hungry ghosts, the animals—for every sentient being, without leaving out even one insect. You develop the most amazing compassion.

Without generating compassion for sentient beings, there is no enlightenment; by generating compassion for others, there is enlightenment. That is one hundred percent sure. The benefit of generating compassion for even one sentient being—whether it is a mosquito, an ant, any kind of insect or whatever, no matter how big or small it is, even as big as a mountain—generating compassion for even one sentient being brings you to enlightenment.

I must tell you this. In Solu Khumbu, lay people quite often do *nyung-näs* at the small temples in the different villages but, although they have the text, the sadhana, they cannot read it at all, because they have not even learned *ka kha ga nga*, the Tibetan alphabet. Those who can read do so, but they are very few. What most people do is go there with great faith and recite OM MANI PADME HUM, OM MANI PADME HUM, doing the sessions with prostrations. They also take the eight Mahayana precepts on both days of the nyung-nä. Each precept you take with bodhicitta, you benefit numberless sentient beings. You are a great source of happiness and success, an unbelievable source of enlightenment for every being. Doing such practices combines many powerful things.

KHADRO-LA'S STORY

Chanting the Palden Lhamo prayer is an important aspect of Mönlam Chenmo. When Khadro-la and I are in different places we chant this prayer. Once she made the comment that the prayer actually makes Palden Lhamo come, which is why she likes chanting it.

Sorry! Again there's a story. Palden Lhamo is a servant to Khadro-la. She serves Khadro-la. When Khadro-la was going to Mt. Kailash she rode on Palden Lhamo's mule. That is just the essence of the story.

When Khadro-la first went to Dharamsala it took her a year to see His Holiness because, coming from lower Kham, Chamdo, so far away, she had the appearance of a villager, with very messy hair and so forth. Of course, that was just her external appearance and no indication of the level of her mind and the realizations she had. On the outside she appeared as a very ordinary Tibetan village girl, kind of disheveled, whereas in reality she was something else entirely. If I tell you some of her story—I don't need to tell it all—that will show you.

She worked in a Tibetan government restaurant in Dharamsala but because of her appearance they made her clean the toilets. Not having any tools, she had to clean them by scratching the kaka off with her fingernails. That's what she said, but I think maybe this is not public talk.

One day the manager of the restaurant was possibly thinking of having physical contact with her, maybe sex, I'm not sure, and she pushed him away—just a little shove—but he was flung really far. Then his mind completely changed. He said, "Now, whenever you want something from the refrigerator, Coca-Cola or anything, please take it any time you want." Her wrathful aspect had so shocked him that his mind completely changed.

She tried to meet His Holiness for a year but a lay lama who was a religious head wouldn't let her. That happened at the beginning of her troubles. She may have told me before not to mention this but anyway, she went to a place in Dharamsala where the water comes down—I don't know what it's called—and picked up a stone. After she touched the stone it became water, like nectar. She took this to offer to His Holiness. She often went into a trance, outside looking like a *ten-ma*,[91] and then something like blood would come.

Kirti Tsenshab Rinpoche was the one who helped her meet His Holiness. He told her, "I myself will make the golden bridge connecting you and His Holiness." Once he had made that connection she was able to meet him. She told me that she went to see Kirti Tsenshab Rinpoche a few times and he told her, "Even at the very end of my life, you are the object of refuge I rely on."

From that time on she was given a house to stay in and an old lady to take care of her. Early one morning the old lady saw a lot of mule prints on the floor of her room. It seems that during the night Palden Lhamo had come to protect or serve her.

And similarly, in the middle of the night an old Nyingma lama—I can't say whether he was enlightened or not but he was very highly realized—

---

[91] The *ten-ma* goddesses are the twelve guardian deities of the Gelug tradition, associated with Palden Lhamo.

who had just passed away came to speak with her. The old lady who cared for her was in the next room and she could hear talking, blah, blah, blah, blah, blah, so the next morning she scolded Khadro-la. "You have a boy-friend! You have a boyfriend. You are a complete liar!" I think she scolded Khadro-la for a few mornings, not only the one time. Khadro-la just said, "No boyfriend." The lama came in middle of the night to speak with her, to give her teachings or something like that. He had other powers, so I think His Holiness also knew. But to the old lady listening from the next room it seemed that Khadro-la had a boyfriend so she scolded her, saying she was a total liar. Then afterwards she realized it wasn't like that, that in reality Palden Lhamo was Khadro-la's servant. That is what I wanted to tell you.

BENEFITING SENTIENT BEINGS

At this time we have received not just a human rebirth but a perfect human rebirth. Each day, each hour, each minute, even each second, how many sentient beings from the intermediate state are reborn in the hell realm? It's as many as the specks of dust of this earth. Each day, each hour, each min-ute, each second how many sentient beings from the intermediate state are reborn as hungry ghosts? It's like the number of the sand grains of the Pacific Ocean. Each day, each hour, each minute, each second, how many sentient beings from the intermediate state are reborn as animals? It's as many as the blades of grass growing on all the mountains and the ground everywhere— and of course there are numberless universes—so it's uncountable. We have to think about these things really well.

There are so many kinds of animals in the oceans. Some, like whales, are as huge as mountains; others are so small that we can see them only through a microscope. I remember we were once crossing a short bridge on a beach overlooking the ocean. Due to a combination of sun and shade we saw so many incredibly tiny insects in the water under the bridge. Because of the way the light hit the water the number of creatures we saw was unbelievable. If you look at a drop of water under a microscope you can see all the small creatures you cannot see by eye.

As I have mentioned, although the ocean is very blue, very calm, very peaceful looking, just below the surface there are all kinds of sentient beings, large and small, swimming everywhere trying to eat each other while at the same time trying to avoid being eaten, all the time full of fear.

Like this, there are numberless animal realm beings in each of the oceans and numberless animal realm beings in the air and on and under the ground. Every time you walk on grass, so many tiny insects run away.

That's why we recite the mantra to bless the feet in the prayers we say at the beginning of each day.[92] Traditionally, we recite this mantra seven times and then blow on the soles of our feet, but because we all wear shoes I think we should blow on the soles of our shoes. This will help any insects, like ants, that we kill while walking around. When we recite the mantra and blow on the soles of our feet or shoes, any insect we step on will get reborn in the Heaven of Thirty-three. That's the benefit of this mantra.

Before we travel by car we can also recite the mantra and spit or blow on the tires. That way, any animal or insect that is crushed by the wheels gets a higher rebirth. I have already mentioned the benefits of having the Namgyälma mantra in your car.

How to help somebody who is dying or dead

Whenever you yourself, a family member, a friend or an animal is dying or dead, one of the most powerful things that can be done is for a Namgyälma card to be put on top of the body for a little while. Then that being will definitely be protected from going to the lower realms and will definitely get a higher rebirth with the possibility of meeting the Dharma. That is a vital practice when somebody suddenly dies and you don't know what to do.

When I was in France leading the Four Kadam Deities retreat at Institut Vajrayogini in 2003 the father of one of our German students died. She had been a Buddhist for ten years, but when her father suddenly died she didn't know what to do. So I spent a few days during the retreat talking about how to help a dying or dead person. Some things were my own ideas and others were based on a book.

The Tibetan way of benefiting dead or dying people may be traditional but it is certainly not a meaningless custom. It really benefits. I explained ways of helping both yourself and others at the time of death. If you know how to do that properly you can help dying or dead people very effectively.

A book based on these talks at Institut Vajrayogini is now available.[93] I also gave some teachings several years ago about the five powers near the

---

[92] OM KRECHA RAGHANA HUM HRI SVAHA.
[93] *How to Enjoy Death: Preparing to Meet Life's Final Challenge without Fear.* Also available as a free download from fpmt.org as *How to Help Your Loved Ones Enjoy Death and Go Happily to Their Next Rebirth: A Handbook by Lama Zopa Rinpoche.*

time of death because I was getting so many messages about people who were dying, asking for advice.[94] One person I mentioned this to was Linda Rose, in Hong Kong, who had cancer. I talked for more than an hour but I still wasn't finished. I told her that she would die if she stayed in Hong Kong and that according to my observation, or *mo*, it would be better for her to go to America. So she went to California and lived for another three years.

Some years ago the FPMT created a "Liberation Box,"[95] which contains all the things needed to help somebody who is dying or already dead. For example, if somebody is still capable of comprehending, you can give them advice, but if that is not possible, like with children and very old people, you need to help externally in order for them to not be reborn in the lower realms. When somebody is dying you can make all these things available to help that person, to guide the mind—all the mantras and other things, such as *po-wa* pills. This is very important.

The Liberation Box already contains all the external things to put on people to bless them, to save their consciousness from being reborn in the lower realms. Everything is explained; everything is prepared. I don't think other organizations have something like this yet. The FPMT also has other books of practices, with different mantras, different pujas and prayers. Those who are familiar with these practices can do them. When a person dies you really don't know about the dying person's mind; you just know your own thoughts, so these practices can guide you.

It is extremely important to be able to help a dying person and, if you can, the dying person's family as well. Like us, they are not yet dead but they are dying. There are only a certain number of in-breaths and out-breaths in a lifetime. Every day, every hour, every minute, every second, that number is constantly diminishing. In reality, we too are dying. The intuitive feeling we have, that the person with cancer is dying but we are not, is totally incorrect.

No matter how many days, how many hours, how many minutes, how many seconds we have left in this life, they are constantly finishing. Life is getting shorter and shorter. We too are dying and are therefore the same as the person we label as dying. We could even die before that person.

I'm extremely happy that the organization and the centers can provide such things. It's really good. We should develop these tools even more, showing how to guide others to avoid rebirth in the lower realms and to

---

[94] Published as *Practicing Five Powers Near the Time of Death*.
[95] Available from the Foundation Store as the *Liberation Box: Tools for a Fortunate Rebirth*.

gain a higher rebirth, in a pure land or as a god or human being, and especially to receive a perfect human rebirth and meet the Dharma. Most people don't think in that way.

HAVING A PERFECT HUMAN REBIRTH IS LIKE A DREAM

The Buddha compared the number of human beings to the number of other beings. He said that if we scratch the ground, the amount of dirt we collect under our fingernails is like the number of human beings whereas all the dirt of this entire earth is like the number of animals.[96] That there are so few human beings compared to even the animals is because it is very difficult to create the cause to be born human, which is to have not just morality but pure morality. Morality alone is not enough to be born as a human being or a god; it must be pure morality.

There are so many animals. There are uncountable gnats in the swarms that fly up when we walk on the grass; there are so many ants in just one nest. The number of human beings compared to the number of ants living in all the ant nests is tiny. We need to make such comparisons in case we think that the number of human beings is so huge.

However, we do not just have a human rebirth but a *perfect* human rebirth, this life in which we have met not just Buddhism but the Mahayana teachings, and of the Mahayana teachings, both sutra and tantra. We have this perfect human rebirth because in past lives we observed the pratimoksha, bodhisattva and tantric vows purely. Therefore in this life we are again able to meet all these different levels of teachings and have the opportunity to take these vows again. This is almost the only time we will ever receive such a perfect human rebirth. We have this opportunity now, but the future depends on what we do with it.

Having received this perfect human rebirth is like a dream. Achieving the eight freedoms and the ten richnesses seems impossible but it has happened. I don't need to detail the eight freedoms and the ten richnesses here. If you are unfamiliar with the teachings on the perfect human rebirth, please study them. There are many lam-rim books that cover this topic. If you don't know how precious this precious human body is you will not value it.

Besides seeing the rarity of this perfect human rebirth by comparing it

[96] See also *The Perfect Human Rebirth: Freedom and Richness on the Path to Enlightenment*, p. 115.

to the number of other beings, we can also understand its rarity by investigating its causes and seeing that they are incredibly difficult to create. It is difficult to find even a human rebirth in general let alone a perfect human rebirth. Reflecting on such things over and over again dispels negative states of mind such as laziness, anger, attachment and ignorance, all those things that waste this life.

There is also this example.[97] A golden ring floats on the ocean. It is not a wooden ring that would float easily but a golden ring, something that would normally sink. Somehow it remains afloat but not in one place. It is constantly moved about by the wind and waves.

The golden ring represents pure Buddhism, not corrupted Buddhism. I think without studying much Dharma it is difficult to understand what "pure" means, what is pure Buddhism and what is corrupted. If you study the world, however, and the Dharma you have been practicing, you will understand how other people suffer and how difficult it is to find the correct Dharma. Then you will understand the whole situation. Otherwise you can just run to anybody who teaches meditation and never check whether he or she is a meditator or not.

It's like the quote from Panchen Losang Chökyi Gyaltsen that I have already mentioned. We should not be like an old dog looking for food in the street, grabbing it from anybody and gobbling it down as quickly as possible. This quote relates to finding a guru but it applies to the teachings in general as well. A dog sees somebody handing out food and just runs to him. Even if there are no other dogs around, he eats the food without first checking whether it is good for his health or not. You should not be like that dog, running to somebody teaching meditation without checking the person or the teachings. You need to learn more, especially Lama Tsongkhapa's teaching, but also look at other teachings. Then you will know.

So, the golden ring represents pure, unmistaken Buddhism—not just the pure morality needed to get a higher rebirth but also the higher trainings of morality, concentration and wisdom required to achieve nirvana, liberation from the ocean of samsara. It also means developing compassion, bodhicitta, to achieve full enlightenment, the elimination of all obscurations and the completion of all realizations for sentient beings. This is what

[97] These are the three ways to understand the rarity of the perfect human rebirth: by numbers, by cause and by example.

the golden ring signifies. Although the ring is somehow able to stay on top, it is moved back and forth by the winds and tides.

Anyway, in this example, swimming in the depths of the ocean is a blind turtle that comes to the surface once every hundred years. Not only does it come up rarely, it is also blind, so it cannot see the golden ring. This time we have received the perfect human rebirth with eight freedoms and ten richnesses, which gives us the opportunity to practice Dharma and achieve full enlightenment for sentient beings. But we have received this perfect human rebirth just this once. This is like the blind turtle coming up and putting its head through the golden ring. This is an example of something that seems to be impossible but has somehow happened. So, this perfect human rebirth that we have received this one time is like a dream—a seemingly impossible thing that has somehow happened.

We must not waste one moment

Therefore we must not waste this perfect human rebirth. We must not waste one day, one hour, one minute. We must not use our whole life to create nonvirtue, to create the cause to be born back where we came from, where we have been most of the time, the lower realms. Wasting our life means more than just leading an empty life; it means using our life to create the causes of the lower realms.

Without ever having met the Dharma, the Buddha's legacy to the world, and without having developed a good heart, everything we do can only be the cause of the lower realms. Our education is solely for this purpose. We go to kindergarten, primary school, high school and then college and university just to create the causes of the lower realms. I don't think I have ever put it this way before.

Unless our mind changes we are in no way different to the insects. We have the same attachment to this life, just working for the pleasure of this life. We are the same as the ants, the same as the worms, the same as the lice. How we spend our life is so poor, even if we are a billionaire, a zillionaire, a trillionaire. No matter how much power we have in the world, how many people we have working under us, in reality there is no difference in the motivation, in the way of thinking. It is just cherishing the I, just thinking of this life's happiness.

We might be human beings, with a better brain and a better education, but even if we've been to university and have been extensively educated, unless we know and practice Dharma, in essence our way of thinking is the same as that of an insect. Mosquitoes need to look for blood, but we are no different, needing to eat meat, another being's flesh and blood. If we kill and eat animals, how are we any different from mosquitoes? If we don't practice compassion for the beings of the lower realms, how are we different from them?

Whether or not we eat animals is in our hands

While I was in hospital in Australia,[98] I saw on TV that Australia was selling huge numbers of sheep and cows to Indonesia. They showed sheep all lined up, so tiny, going to the slaughterhouse. There was the shot of a cow with a rope tied around its horns being pulled down from the platform to its place of execution. The cow didn't want to go; it was pulling back and a man was pulling it down.

I think this may have been the first time they exposed this and the Australian people, everybody, got so upset. The livestock company stopped selling animals to Indonesia. But then I don't know what happened. Of course, everything in life is a dependent arising; one thing depends on another. So perhaps, because the big companies have all the power, the situation may have reverted again after two or three months.

At that time I thought I cannot stop this, but now, whatever teaching I do, even tantric teachings, I announce to the world to be vegetarian, so that fewer people will eat meat and fewer animals will get killed and they will suffer less. If more people refused to eat meat there would naturally be less suffering for animals.

Not eating meat *at all* in the world—that is a dream. That will not happen. But fewer people eating meat can happen. So I thought to announce this to the world. It's very simple. We ourselves don't want somebody else to use our body, to be killed for food. We don't want to suffer. In exactly the same way, why not all others? Animals, insects, they don't want to suffer. We can see that when we touch their bodies, they have such fear.

Animals can't speak. They can't demonstrate in the road or proclaim their position on TV or in newspapers. They can't parade with placards and loudspeakers. They have no power at all. Animals are powerless, totally in human hands, to be used like toilet paper. It's so pitiful. People have little

---

[98] Rinpoche is referring to his stay in hospital after manifesting a stroke in Bendigo, Australia, April 2011.

concern about their feelings. Their mind is not open at all. That is really so bad.

Learning the Buddha's teachings makes people understand. It emphasizes the need to generate compassion for all sentient beings. People have to understand the suffering of other sentient beings as the teachings explain.

I'm thinking of writing a book about Western food especially for Tibetans, for their monasteries, including Sera. Generally Tibetans from Tibet are very used to eating meat because nomads ate it and that's what we did before, with the Bön religion and with shamanism, or black Bönpo. Meat eating was common before Buddhism came. This book will explain how to make tasty, nutritious vegetarian food and will contain many photographs to make it easy for the monks and nuns to be vegetarian. If the food is not tasty they will go back to being non-vegetarians because they are so used to eating meat. And I will also explain the meditation to do while cooking, cleaning and so forth so that everything becomes Dharma.

This precious human life is more precious than a wish-granting jewel

Phagpa Pawo[99] was a very famous, learned Hindu yogi, a sadhu who became Buddhist after going to Mount Kailash and then became a great, learned Buddhist pandit. He said,

> Because of ignorance you fail to collect even a fraction of the treasury of merit and after this life enter the house of unceasing suffering. You are like a businessman who travels to the land of wish-granting jewels but comes home empty-handed.

Due to ignorance we do not collect even a tiny amount of merit and then, when we pass into the next life, we "enter the house of unceasing suffering." Because we have not met the Dharma we create nonvirtue, which brings the result of suffering, instead of experiencing happiness, which is the result of virtue. Entering the house of unceasing suffering means being reborn into the suffering of the lower realms in general and the suffering of the hell realms in particular. This is the general meaning.

---

[99] Also called (Tib:) Lobpön Pawo, (Skt:) Ashvaghosha or Aryashura, a second-century Indian master renowned for his scholarship and poetry; author of *Fifty Verses of Guru Devotion*.

He continues that this is like a businessman who goes to a land of wish-granting jewels, where he could pick up as many wish-granting jewels as he wanted, but he is not aware of this and as a result returns home empty-handed. If we are ignorant of the Dharma, if we fail to practice the Dharma, it is exactly like that. We do not know the Buddha's teachings exist in the world or we have a closed mind toward them, so we neither learn nor practice. That is just like arriving in the land of wish-granting jewels, not being aware they are there and returning home empty-handed.

In his *Letter to a Disciple*, Chandragomin said,

> With this perfect human rebirth that you have received you can be free from the oceans of samsaric suffering and furthermore you can plant the seeds of virtue for supreme enlightenment. Because of this exalted quality, this human body is much more valuable than a wish-granting jewel. Knowing this, who would dare not make use of this precious human body?

We have not only a human rebirth but a perfect human rebirth. Without this great quality we would have to suffer not just once but numberless times in each of the realms of samsara: the hell realm, the hungry ghost realm, the animal realm, the human realm and the god realm. With a perfect human rebirth we can free ourselves from the oceans of suffering rebirths and also plant the seeds of virtue of supreme enlightenment, the total purification of all obscurations and the total actualization of all realizations.

Because our human rebirth has this precious extra quality that allows us to do all that, it is like a wish-granting jewel that allows us to obtain whatever material comforts of this life we want but is unable to purify the causes of the lower realms or create the causes for a higher rebirth. Therefore this human body is so special; it is much more precious than a wish-granting jewel, and not just one wish-granting jewel but the whole sky filled with wish-granting jewels. Even if we were to have all that it would be nothing special; it could not bring us all the benefits that a perfect human rebirth can. Therefore, Chandragomin asked, knowing this to be so, who would dare use this perfect human body for meaningless things?

Having been born at a time when the Dharma has spread, we must practice the unmistaken Dharma, otherwise we will be exactly like the businessman returning from the land of wish-granting jewels empty-handed.

When I check up on one day of my life, this is what I see: I get up with ignorance and attachment to this life, dress with ignorance and attachment to this life, go to the bathroom and wash with ignorance and attachment to this life and so forth. That is my motivation—not a Dharma motivation but a worldly one.

Attachment to this life is the main motivation for everything we do; we do not have a Dharma motivation. In the same way, we eat breakfast with the nonvirtuous thought, attachment to this life. We do everything with a totally nonvirtuous motivation. Eating breakfast becomes not holy Dharma but worldly dharma. In the same way, our motivation for going to work is attachment to this life. We have no Dharma motivation, not even to benefit our future lives or to achieve liberation from samsara. However many hours of work we do, because of our motivation, they all become nonvirtuous; our work does not become Dharma.

Eating lunch with the eight worldly dharmas, with attachment to this life, cannot become Dharma. However many hours we spend over lunch, every second of eating or drinking becomes nonvirtue, the cause of the lower realms. Similarly, we eat dinner with the same motivation, attachment to this life, and so that also becomes nonvirtuous. It does not become holy Dharma.

Going to sleep is the same; again, we do it for the pleasure of this life. At the beginning there's no virtuous thought, no Dharma motivation, so however many hours of comfortable, deep sleep we get, it all becomes nonvirtue.

Even trying to do some Dharma activity like saying mantras or prayers fails to become Dharma. Our motivation is the same, the wish for the pleasure of this life, therefore our so-called Dharma activity actually becomes non-Dharma. Such motivation can make even Dharma study a worldly concern. Learning more Dharma in order to teach may not be to benefit others but for reputation and power.

If you are like me, when you check on your day you can see that because of your worldly motivation, all the activities of your body, speech and mind throughout the whole day and night have been completely nonvirtuous. And having collected no virtue in this life, only nonvirtue, the result is that in your next life, leave aside not attaining another human rebirth, you won't even hear the sound of a human voice for many eons. Once your life in the lower realms has started, because your negative karma has not been purified, because you failed to practice Dharma, you will never hear another pleasant sound.

Shantideva said,

> And if I commit no wholesome deeds (there),
> But readily amass much wrongdoing,
> Then for a hundred million eons
> I shall not even hear the words "a happy life."[100]

This time, with this human body, it should be different. We have a different body, a different life, a different way of thinking from the animals, so it should be different. But since there is no Dharma in our life, there is no real difference between the animals and us. Our mind is the same as that of animals and insects in that we are all only working for this life. The only difference is that this time we don't have horns or a tail. But besides not having a tail or horns, we are no different at all from the animals and insects.

To use the traditional examples, if we have a boat capable of crossing a river or an ocean, we should use it. Or, if a group of heroes ready to help us destroy an enemy has gathered, we should use it. That of course does not mean to harm others, which is what normal people do in the world. Here it means knowing the Dharma, using it to subdue the mind. The enemy is the inner enemy; there is no external enemy. If we have anger, delusion and so forth in our mind—the inner enemy—we will always have external enemies. If there is no inner enemy, there can be no external enemy.

Nagarjuna said,

> Killing the inner enemy of anger is like killing all external enemies.
> When you have heat, water and fertilizer you must plant your
>   crops;
> When you have a skillful horse you must take the opportunity to
>   travel to distant places.

Killing the inner enemy of anger is like killing all external enemies; if we have no anger we can have no external enemies. Therefore we must practice Dharma while we have the opportunity. This is analogous to the need to plant crops whenever the right conditions come together: heat and water and fertilizer.

There is also the analogy of the skillful horse. If we are lucky enough to have a skillful horse we should take the opportunity to travel to faraway places. Of course, these days we can go by car or plane. But anyway, this is

---

[100] *A Guide to the Bodhisattva's Way of Life*, Ch. 4, v. 19.

really the time to do our best, to make our life most beneficial for sentient beings as well as ourselves by learning Dharma, knowing Dharma and practicing Dharma.

While our cow is giving milk, we must milk her. We must not just waste the opportunity by not taking it. Whenever opportunities present themselves we should take them, otherwise they will just be wasted. These are all examples. When in the land of wish-granting jewels, take them.

Due to past merit we have received this precious human rebirth, with its five senses intact. Furthermore we have met the Buddha's teachings, we have met a guru, a virtuous friend, and we have every opportunity to practice Dharma. Now is the time. This is the time for us to make our mind free, to develop contentment and inner happiness, to overcome our confusion and problems. While at present we might be experiencing much disturbance and suffering because of our attachment, we can replace all that with peace and happiness. We must practice Dharma to achieve the happiness of all future lives all the way up to liberation and enlightenment. There is no other way.

WE MUST PREPARE FOR THE NEXT LIFE

To be able to practice Dharma we must *decide* we want to practice Dharma, and to do that we must think about death. Otherwise, we might feel that practicing Dharma is good but put it off until the "right" moment, until next year or the year after that or the year after that. We postpone it until we think we will have some free time or until we have earned our first billion dollars. I'm joking! But life becomes like that. We delay practicing Dharma until next year, and then it is the next year and then the year after that and so on. We think, "When I'm free," or "When I'm well," or something like that.

By thinking like this our fortune, our good luck to practice Dharma stops. We delay and delay and delay and then it is gone. We either have problems to deal with or else we are sick or there is some other hindrance and then...death! Then our opportunity has gone.

This sense that we have plenty of time before we need to think about death is common to all of us. We plan on living for many more years—forever, in fact. People are still thinking like that on the day they die, even five minutes before their death. For most people, death happens while they are planning on living for many more years.

Now our life is so good. However, it is like a dream. We are unbelievably fortunate that we have not died yet. We are so fortunate but, while we have yet to start practicing Dharma, our life is passing by in distraction. In order to persuade our mind to practice Dharma we need to think that we are constantly coming closer to death, all the time, day and night, morning, afternoon, evening and night, closer and closer and closer to death.

The Buddha mentioned this in the *Dhammapada*.

> Like a condemned criminal,
> With each step you come closer and closer
> To your executioner.
> A human being's life is like that.[101]

We are like a convict who is about to be executed. We are in the custody of the police, being led to the place of execution, and each step we take is a step closer to death. All human beings are like this. This is a human's life. There are only a certain number of breaths left, a certain number of seconds left until death. Life is constantly diminishing, constantly finishing; we are rushing so quickly to death.

We must not cheat ourselves. We really need to practice Dharma, to integrate the lam-rim into our life and practice the root of the path to enlightenment, correctly following the guru, and on that basis cultivate renunciation, bodhicitta and the right view of emptiness as a preparation for tantra. Then, when death happens, there will be no regrets; we will be happy.

If we can live with a good heart, living our life for other sentient beings, we will experience great joy and happiness when we die. Then, in our next life, we will be of even greater benefit to sentient beings. In that way, we go to enlightenment.

Which will come first, tomorrow or the next life?

In *A Guide to the Bodhisattva's Way of Life*, Shantideva said,

> If when I have a chance to live a wholesome life
> My actions are not wholesome,
> Then what shall I be able to do
> When confused by the misery of the lower realms?[102]

---

[101] The *Tibetan Dhammapada*, Ch. 1, v. 14.
[102] Ch. 4, v. 18.

If we don't practice Dharma now, when death suddenly comes and we have gone to the lower realms, what can we do at that time? In their previous lives, even hungry ghosts or animals such as spiders or ants might have been billionaires in a rich country. From living in a house worth many billions of dollars they become crickets. Can you imagine it? This can happen.

If we were to be born in hell with the most unbelievable suffering, what could we do at that time? Nothing. Every hope would be gone, finished. Because we did not practice when we had the chance it would be too late. Our life and death would be over and our rebirth in the lower realms already begun.

A tiny fire spark from hell is sixty times hotter than all the fire of the human world put together. That is how hot it is. Compared to that, all the fire of our world is like an air conditioner, like snowflakes dropping from the sky. It's nothing. This is also mentioned in *A Guide to the Bodhisattva's Way of Life*.

One time I was walking up from His Holiness's temple in McLeod Ganj, Dharamsala, to Tushita Retreat Centre when I saw many monkeys on the road. I thought that they have no freedom *at all*. They are totally under the control of karma and delusion; they have not the slightest freedom. For them, rebirth as a monkey has already happened and there is nothing they—or we—can do about it; nothing can be done to immediately change it. It has already happened and they have to finish their karma. They are *dro-wa*, transmigratory beings, under the control of karma and delusion.

This is true of whatever animal we look at. It has happened. Tigers are completely under the control of karma and delusion and there is no freedom at all for them. The tiger rebirth has already happened because the causes of that rebirth were not purified before, and that is because the being that is now a tiger did not meet the Dharma before. To a tiger its life is the most precious thing, but karma forces it to eat other living beings—deer, zebra and other pitiful animals—that also only want happiness and do not want any suffering whatsoever.

We have been in this situation numberless times. We have been born as a tiger in the past numberless times and have been forced to eat number-less sentient beings. In the past we have eaten every sentient being. There is no beginning to our life in samsara; our rebirths are infinite. Being reborn as a tiger and eating those pitiful animals numberless times is just one type of rebirth we have had. We have been reborn as countless different types of sentient beings and have eaten every other living being numberless times.

There is no sentient being we have not eaten. In the past, you have eaten me numberless times; I have eaten you numberless times. This might come as a big shock but that's what has happened.

This is the same rationale as when we meditate on the kindness of the mother, how the mother has been kind to us numberless times. It is very amazing. The only thing is that we cannot remember our past lives. We don't even remember coming from our mother's womb or the nine months spent in her womb.

During the one-month Kopan course we do a meditation on the continuity of the consciousness where we think about how today's consciousness comes from yesterday's and yesterday's comes from that of the day before and how this year's consciousness comes from last year's and the year before that and before that, right back to childhood, right back to when the consciousness entered the mother's womb.

After one of these meditations a nun from Israel said she remembered coming out from her mother's womb. But most people don't remember *even that*, so how can they say that past lives do not exist? Asserting that there are no past lives because they don't remember them, they would also have to assert that they had not existed in their mother's womb for nine months. How could they say that? That is completely wrong, completely stupid. Everybody knows they have come from their mother's womb.

How can we assume something has not happened just because we can't remember it? There are so many things from this life's childhood that we cannot remember, so using that way of thinking we would have to assert that we had never done them. Using an inability to remember as proof of something not happening is very funny logic, very strange logic.

A popular quote says,

> You cannot be sure which will come first,
> Tomorrow or the next life,
> Therefore, do not put effort into tomorrow's plans
> But instead it is worthwhile to attend to the next life.[103]

We just cannot be sure which will come first, tomorrow or our next life. Because of that it is unbelievably worthwhile to work for the next life, to

---

[103] Also quoted in *Liberation*, p. 311. No source given.

attend to the next life by accumulating merit to not be reborn in the lower realms. Then, if we were to die tomorrow, our work would have been done. And even if we do not die tomorrow, our work has still been done.

This is what Lama Tsongkhapa said in *Lamrim Chenmo*: by practicing Dharma with the thought that we might die today, if we do die we have made the preparation, and if we don't die then we have further opportunities to collect more merit. Therefore, thinking, "I'm going to die today," and working for future lives, practicing Dharma to benefit our future lives, is most worthwhile.

One way that the Kadampa geshes defined Dharma was that it is something that benefits future lives; something that brings happiness in future lives. If what we are practicing does not do that, it is not Dharma. Another way they defined it was that if any action of our body, speech and mind becomes an antidote to delusion, it is Dharma; if it does not become an antidote to delusion, it is not Dharma. This is how the Kadampa geshes differentiated between what is Dharma and what is not.

Renounce this life

One day Dromtönpa, Lama Atisha's translator, was walking in the forest near Reting Monastery when he saw an old man circumambulating the temple. When he asked the old man what he was doing he said, "I'm circumambulating." Gyalwa Dromtönpa replied, "It's good that you are circumambulating, but wouldn't it be better if you practiced Dharma?" After a while the old man reconsidered and thought that reading texts might be what Dromtönpa meant, so he sat down and started doing that.

Dromtönpa came upon him again and asked, "What are you doing?" to which the old man replied, "I'm reading texts." Dromtönpa said, "It's good that you are reading texts, but wouldn't it better if you practiced Dharma?" Then the old man thought that maybe meditating is what he meant by Dharma so he sat down and started meditating.

Again Dromtönpa came upon him and asked, "What are you doing?" and again the old man replied, "I'm meditating." Dromtönpa said, "It's good that you are meditating, but wouldn't it be better if you practiced Dharma?" Only then did the old man ask, "What do you mean by practicing Dharma?" Gyalwa Dromtönpa replied, "Renounce this life!"

The meaning of "renounce this life" is huge. Not renouncing this life is where all our difficulties come from—all our negative emotions, all our breakdowns, all our relationship problems and all the rest. All our problems come from attachment to this life.

All the obstacles to practicing Dharma—delaying practicing Dharma, not wanting to practice Dharma, wrong concepts, laziness, all these things—come from the attachment clinging to this life. That is the root of all the disease, mental pain and other problems in the world; all the problems that people pay psychologists for. People go to see psychologists and it is so expensive. People pay and pay and build debt on debt. It's never-ending.

The root of this is attachment; all the other problems spread out from there, like branches spreading out from the main trunk of a tree. Like this, from the root problem, all of life's problems spread out—so many problems, all kinds of problems, anger, pride and so forth.

So when Gyalwa Dromtönpa told the old man to renounce this life he meant to renounce *attachment* to this life. That means renouncing the attachment that brings with it so many expectations, which in turn cause us to work so hard to try to fulfill those expectations. From that come worry and fear and all the diseases of body and mind. So when we renounce this, we renounce *all* the other problems. Therefore, if we are able to practice Dharma, to renounce this life, there is so much inner peace and happiness in our life.

When the root has been cut, all the branches stop growing. We see in Milarepa's life story how he developed incredible peace and happiness from just this basic practice of renouncing this life, without talking about his tantric realizations.

Probably many people think that renouncing this life means throwing off your clothes and running around naked in the forest or the street. Then the police take you to prison. Of course, it's not like that. It's important to understand how renouncing this life means renouncing this life's problems. If we can think like that, it is a *huge* solution. That is what Dharma practice is. If we practice like that, we are practicing Dharma purely; if we don't, what we are doing might outwardly look like Dharma practice but in reality it won't be. We'll just be practicing attachment to this life. That is the first cause of all the confusion, all the fear, all the desire, all the problems of life.

Another thing to understand is how the fundamental suffering of this life comes from the eight worldly dharmas. There are four desirable objects—receiving comfort, receiving material things, receiving reputation and receiving praise—and four undesirable objects that are the opposites of those. The four undesirable objects are what we don't want to happen.[104]

When the four undesirable objects happen or the four desirable objects do not happen, we get angry and many problems arise. We become unhappy and our life goes down. Then when we get the four desirable objects, our life goes up—we feel happy, but in reality it is the suffering of attachment. Our mind has a very uptight quality. Just as we cannot remove oil from paper once it's soaked into it, when our mind gets attached to an object it's almost impossible to separate the attachment from it. This causes a sickness of the mind that brings much mental pain. And we have suffered from this chronic disease since beginningless rebirths.

So, whatever happens, we suffer. We feel elated when we get the four desirable objects but suffer with attachment, with so much pain. When we experience the four undesirable objects, our life goes down and again we experience great suffering.

Renouncing attachment to this life means having neither attachment to desirable objects nor aversion to undesirable ones. In our mind, both desirable and undesirable objects have been equalized and we have no expectations. At present, our life is full of the expectations that arise from the eight worldly dharmas. Working for this and working for that keeps us busy all the time. However long we live, even a hundred years, our whole life is spent like that, creating countless expectations and fears.

By renouncing this life we renounce our attachment and confusion, which are in the nature of ignorance. We see the pain that attachment for desirable objects and the wish to be separated from undesirable objects brings and, not wanting that pain, we free our mind from it. Like that, we have neither the ups nor the downs of having one of the four desirable or four undesirable objects. So, you can see how much peace we can have in our heart when we *really* practice Dharma.

Also, practicing Dharma is not only for the shrine room or the temple; it's not only reciting mantras. Practicing Dharma really means having the huge determination to give up attachment to this life, which brings incredible peace. Renunciation of this life is the basis. All other realizations naturally come from this: renunciation of samsara, realization of bodhicitta and direct perception of emptiness, followed by the realizations of the tantric

[104] See Rinpoche's *How to Practice Dharma* for extensive teachings on the eight worldly dharmas.

path. So this is just to give you an idea what Dharma practice actually
means.

Shantideva said,

> It is inappropriate to enjoy myself,
> Thinking that today alone I shall not die,
> For inevitably the time will come
> When I shall become nothing.[105]

When we think we're not going to die we become very lazy. We sit back
comfortably and do nothing. That is not practicing Dharma; that is not
worthwhile, because, as Shantideva pointed out, at some time we will be
gone, we will no longer exist. This will happen without doubt and it can
even happen today. So, it is much better to practice Dharma—to purify
negative karma and collect merit; to work to actualize the lam-rim and
make preparations for all happiness up to enlightenment; and to become
enlightened in order to free sentient beings from the oceans of samsaric suffering and bring them to full enlightenment.

[105] *Guide*, Ch. 2, v. 58.

12. Cutting the Root of Samsara

❧❦

THE DECORATION THAT PERVADES OUR LIFE

EVEN TAKING REFUGE and protecting our karma so that we will not be reborn in the lower realms and will attain a higher rebirth is not sufficient because we are still under the control of karma and delusion. That means until we can break free we will continuously circle in samsara, having to be reborn again and again. Then, not only will we suffer endlessly but we will also be unable to ever meet and practice Dharma, to actualize the path to the direct perception of emptiness. It will continue to be like that as it has been from beginningless rebirths.

How we circle in samsara is through the twelve dependent related limbs. Upon the valid base of the aggregates there is a valid labeling mind, one that merely imputes an I on those aggregates. That happens in the first moment, then in the next moment, for many of us, myself included, what happens is that what was a moment ago a valid mind merely imputing an I, now, we have no idea that was happening. We are so ignorant, so totally ignorant that we don't know that this is the reality. That merely imputed I should appear back as just that, an I merely imputed by the mind—that is the reality—but this has not happened from beginningless rebirths.

As I have mentioned, for a buddha, after the mere imputation, the I appears as merely labeled by the mind, however, this does not happen for sentient beings unless they are in meditative equipoise. Otherwise, it appears as existing from its own side. For us, in the first moment it appears as merely imputed by the mind, but in the next moment it appears as existing from its own side. That is a hallucination, a *total* hallucination. We are completely hallucinating.

I am not saying this because it is an interesting subject worthy of intellectual discussion. This is the real situation we are faced with. It is a big mistake—the *biggest* mistake—that we make, to see things as existing from their own side, existing by themselves, as truly existing. To use ordinary language, things appear real to us, real from there.

This ignorance is a hallucination; it decorates an object. I find this a very interesting way of describing it. This is how it happens. Past ignorance has left an imprint on the mind and that negative imprint decorates, projects, the hallucination, making the I appear as real.

Whatever the object of the mind is—the I, the action, the object, form, sound, smell, taste, tangible object—the whole thing appears to us as real. There is a real car, a real road, a real sky, a real shop, real ice cream, real money. On the road there is a real red light, a real yellow light, a real green light. In the real gompa there are real flowers, real thangkas, real statues. Everything is real from over there.

It is a creation, a projection, merely imputed by our mind, but we have no idea of that. We have no idea that it is only a hallucination coming from over there. We see it from there as real. This "real" thing does not exist; it has never existed. It has never come into existence and it does not exist now.

The whole thing is a hallucination. From morning to night it's like that. Since we were born until our death, our whole life—whatever we do, wherever we travel—the whole thing, the objects of our senses, including the I, appear as real from there. Everything we experience, including the real I, is a hallucination.

Nothing exists in reality. Nothing exists the way it appears to exist, as real from there. Everything is totally empty. It's like a dream, like an illusion.

Cutting the root of samsara

If we are able to meditate in this way, looking at all this as like a dream, an illusion, a mirage—all the different examples—then it becomes *very* interesting. There is nothing to become attached to because it is not real.

For example, if we recognize a dream as a dream, there is nothing to be attached to and there is nothing to be angry about. In a dream, somebody abuses us but if we can recognize the dream as a dream, the abuse does not bother us at all. Similarly, some object of desire appears in our dream, but recognizing it as just a dream, we are not agitated. Nothing disturbs us; our mind remains utterly peaceful. Anger and attachment do not arise, so we have a very, very interesting life.

Because things appear to us not as a dream but as real from their own side, which is how it has been since beginningless time, realizing emptiness is vital. It is more important than any job, than all the money in the world, than anything. To cut the root of suffering, ignorance, and be free forever from the oceans of samsaric suffering, there is nothing more important than realizing emptiness.

We need to cut the wrong belief that whatever object that appears to us is real, which is how it appears. As I have said, in the first moment the I appears as merely imputed; in the second it appears as real, as a real I; *then*, in the third moment, we believe that I to be real. *That* wrong concept is the root of samsara.

This is true of every sentient being who has not realized emptiness. Hell beings are the same; animals are the same; humans have better brains but they too are the same in this unless they have realized emptiness. No matter whether it is a king, a president, a scientist or whoever, everybody believes this I to be real, to be true.

Because we believe this I to be real, attachment to the I arises and, when somebody does something undesirable, anger erupts. That wrong concept of a real I is the root of *all* suffering—the suffering of rebirth, the suffering of old age, the suffering of sickness and the suffering of death. Having to become old comes from this; having to die without choice comes from this. Cancer and AIDS come from this. It is the root of the suffering of change, of all the temporary pleasures that never increase and never last.

Those two sufferings—the suffering of pain and the suffering of change— come from pervasive compounding suffering. Because our aggregates are under the control of karma and delusion they are pervaded by suffering and the contaminated seed of delusion. Because there is a continuity of consciousness from past lives, our mindstream carries the imprints of the karma we have created, which compounds this life's and future lives' suffering. Meeting desirable and undesirable objects, attachment, anger and ignorance arise, which motivates karma, which leaves an imprint on the mind, and then that produces future lives' suffering. So, pervasive compounding suffering, the foundation of those other two sufferings, comes from this wrong concept of a real I.

Samsaric happiness can neither increase nor give us any real satisfaction, no matter how much effort we put into it. The happiness of Dharma, on the other hand, lasts and increases, and when we achieve enlightenment it is completed. Therefore, no matter how difficult it is, Dharma practice is extremely worthwhile.

THE TWELVE LIMBS

Of the twelve dependent related limbs[106] I have described the first one, *ignorance*. The second is *compounding action*, which creates karma and leaves an imprint on the *consciousness*, the third link. Sequentially, the others are *name and form, six sense organs, contact, feeling, craving, grasping, becoming, rebirth* and *aging and death.*

Looking at the twelve dependent related limbs of this life, in a previous human life we practiced the compounding action of virtuous deeds, such as morality and so forth, and just before the end of our previous life, *craving* and *grasping*, the eighth and ninth limbs, arose, conditioning the *becoming* of another human body, the tenth limb, which lead to the eleventh, the *rebirth* of this life.

Nagarjuna said,

> Two deluded actions [links two and ten] arise from three deluded causes [links one, eight and nine]; seven uncontrolled results [links three, four, five, six, seven, eleven and twelve] arise from those two deluded actions. Again three deluded causes arise from these seven results. Such a wheel of life goes round and round.[107]

So once we are reborn the other six results occur: the consciousness of this life, name and form, the six sense organs, contact, feeling and aging and death. During this life, out of ignorance we engage in compounding actions, leaving karmic imprints on our consciousness, and at the end of our life, craving, grasping and becoming arise once more.

The wheel of life illustration seen at the door of many monasteries is symbolic. For instance, for name and form, the fourth limb, a man rowing a boat is shown: name is the mind and form is the body. After name and form come the six sense bases, depicted by an empty house, and then, after that, comes contact, symbolized by the contact of a man and a woman. From contact, feeling arises, shown as a man with an arrow in his eye.

---

[106] Also called the twelve links of dependent origination. See *Liberation in the Palm of Your Hand*, pp. 479–486 or *Steps on the Path to Enlightenment*, vol. 2, pp. 324–360.
[107] From Rinpoche's *Wish-fulfilling Golden Sun*. See that book for a clear, succinct explanation of the twelve links. Also quoted in *Steps*, vol. 2, p. 346. "The first, eighth and ninth are delusions. The second and tenth are karma. The remaining seven are sufferings."

Since our rebirth most of the other limbs have already happened and all that remains is aging and death. Normally the world defines aging by wrinkled skin and other visible signs of getting old, but aging actually starts from birth. In reality, death is the only one of those seven resultant limbs we have yet to experience.

With every action, we start another set of twelve limbs. For example, with one action we might create the potential to be born as a human being and with another the potential to be reborn in hell. Which seed will ripen when craving and grasping lead us into the becoming of our next rebirth?

It could easily be that of the hell rebirth. There are eight major hot hells, eight major cold hells, six neighboring hells and some occasional hells, ones that are anywhere rather than in a specific location. In each hell there is so much unbelievable suffering. We have experienced such rebirths countless times but cannot remember them. If we could it would be utterly terrifying.

Hungry ghosts have to suffer for tens of thousands of their years—which are much longer than human years—from not finding a drop of water or a scrap of food. They have the most unbelievable suffering but are unable to die. For tens of thousands of years they have to experience the three types of obscurations: outer obscurations, inner obscurations and obscurations of food and drink.[108] And they have to experience exhaustion, hopelessness and disappointment. Their suffering is unbelievable, horrible.

Then there are the animals, who are so foolish and ignorant. They suffer from being eaten by other animals, heat and cold, and hunger and thirst. Those that are kept by humans have to endure much torture, being used for work and food, killed for their meat, bones and other parts of their body. They have so much suffering.

For example, African elephants are killed for their tusks, which fetch a lot of money. One of our students in Singapore has a project to protect the elephants, but one of the ways they are protected is by killing the poachers. So that's thinking of the elephants but not thinking of the human beings, which seems very silly. I asked her if humans might have to die to protect elephants and she said that perhaps that was the case. Maybe later on she realized this.

I once saw a documentary on TV about a fish that hunts insects on the overhanging branches of a tree that grows by the river. The fish sees an insect from below in the water and squirts water at it to knock it off the branch.

[108] See *Liberation in the Palm of Your Hand*, pp. 340–45.

Usually it takes a few squirts to dislodge the insect, but as soon as it falls the fish shoots up and grabs it. There's also an insect that kills its prey by spitting some kind of sticky stuff at it from a distance and immobilizing it in that way.

I once saw a fight between a snake and a mongoose. Mongooses are very smart creatures—the arhat Bakula holds a wealth-producing mongoose—but this time the snake won. While in front of the mongoose the snake kept its distance, fearing the mongoose's sharp teeth, but when the mongoose got distracted by something, the snake came up from behind, grabbed it by the neck and finished it off.

This is all karma. What the Buddha said about ignorance is exactly true. Every problem is due to ignorance. Whatever suffering the animals must endure, being killed or whatever, primarily it can all be traced back to ignorance.

Humans have to experience the suffering of rebirth, old age, sickness, death, being separated from desirable objects and meeting undesirable objects. Even when we find desirable objects we are still unable to find any satisfaction at all. And then there is the suffering of having the five aggregates. These are the sufferings experienced by human beings.

Desire realm gods are completely distracted by pleasure and through their attachment to it they continuously create negative karma. Then, when they are about to die, they hear a voice telling them they will die in seven days—their days are fifty human years long—and they start to experience the very heavy sufferings of the signs of death. There are five ways they suffer. For the first time ever, dirt remains on their body. Their boyfriends and girlfriends refuse to come near them because of the signs of death but pass them flowers on the end of a stick in order to stay far away. And as they recall the blissful life they are about to leave, they can see where they are going to be reborn, which is a huge change from where they are now. Seeing this is said to be much heavier suffering than actually experiencing the hell realm. Kyabje Chöden Rinpoche said that hell beings have more physical suffering but gods have much greater mental suffering, in the same way that rich people have much more mental suffering than poor people.

Wherever we look in samsara there is so much suffering. The root of it all is this incorrect concept that believes that the I is real from its own side. It is formless, colorless and shapeless but the result of this wrong concept is the unbelievable sufferings of the six realms. The suffering we humans must endure is bad enough but that is nothing compared to the suffering of the other realms. All of this comes from something that is formless, colorless and shapeless.

Now you can see why meditating on emptiness is so important. Even though you don't have a realization of emptiness, just meditating on it is *the* most important thing to do in order to overcome karma and delusion, the cause of the oceans of samsaric suffering.

While we are circling in samsara, because of ignorance we start so many sets of twelve links. We start so many sets of twelve links each hour, so many each minute. If we create so many sets of twelve links even within a minute, think how many we must create in one day, always creating more and more samsara.

Then, even if we can free ourselves from the prison of one set of twelve links, there is another prison outside that we are caught in. And even if we can free ourselves from that, there is yet *another* one outside of that one. The prisons are numberless. Due to ignorance we have been creating samsara from beginningless rebirths and even in one hour, even in one minute we create so many sets of twelve links. It's endless and this will continue until we can actualize the direct perception of emptiness and remove the seed of delusion that causes rebirth.

ALL OUR HAPPINESS HAS COME FROM OTHER SENTIENT BEINGS

What I have been mainly talking about so far is how we must free *ourselves* from the sufferings of samsara. In exactly the same way as we are suffering, there are numberless other sentient beings who are also suffering: numberless hell beings, numberless hungry ghosts, numberless animals, numberless human beings, numberless gods, numberless demigods and numberless intermediate state beings. We are lost, but that is nothing. We are just one being. There are numberless other beings continuously suffering in samsara.

Therefore, it is not enough to achieve the blissful state of peace, nirvana, for ourselves alone while there are numberless other beings that need our help. We need to help all sentient beings.

As I have often said, we have eyes and limbs so that we can run and grab the blind person who is walking toward a precipice, mistakenly thinking there is a road there. That poor stumbling sentient being cannot see the precipice, so it is up to us. That is the first reason for helping sentient beings:

because we can—they are suffering so much and we are capable of helping them.

The next reason for helping sentient beings is that all our happiness comes from them. This is summed up in the first verse of the *Eight Verses of Thought Transformation*:

> Determined to obtain the greatest possible benefit
> From all sentient beings,
> Who are more precious than a wish-granting jewel,
> I shall hold them most dear at all times.

This is so important. All our past, present and future happiness, including nirvana and the great nirvana, enlightenment, comes from our good karma. And our good karma is the action of the buddhas.

There are two actions of the buddhas: one is the buddha's holy mind and the other is with us sentient beings, our own good karma. We create positive actions only because we understand karma—the cause of suffering and the cause of happiness—and our understanding of karma is the result of having been taught by the buddhas.

A buddha's actions come from a buddha; a buddha comes from a bodhisattva; a bodhisattva comes from bodhicitta; bodhicitta comes from great compassion; great compassion is generated by contemplating the suffering of all sentient beings. Therefore we can see that we can attain enlightenment only by depending on the kindness of sentient beings.

The mind of great compassion—the cause of bodhicitta and thus a bodhisattva and thus a buddha—can only be generated by understanding the suffering of each and every sentient being. Every sentient being must be included: every hell being, every hungry ghost, every animal, every human being, every god, every demigod, every intermediate state being. Not even one is left out. That is their great kindness.

Therefore, great compassion comes from the numberless suffering sentient beings; bodhicitta comes from the numberless suffering sentient beings; bodhisattvas come from the numberless suffering sentient beings; buddhas come from the numberless suffering sentient beings—therefore, a buddha's actions come from sentient beings. The Buddha, Dharma and Sangha, the refuge objects we always pray to, come from sentient beings. They come from every single suffering sentient being.

By their qualities, the buddhas are incredibly precious, but, by their kindness, sentient beings are even more precious. Sentient beings are really the most important.

All our past, present and future happiness, including our enlightenment, comes from every single sentient being. When we achieve the bodhisattva's path, all the unbelievable qualities we attain there come from them. And the numberless qualities of a buddha's holy body, holy speech and holy mind, all come from them, from their kindness, from every single suffering hell being, hungry ghost, animal, human being, god, demigod and intermediate state being; from *every one*.

When a person gets angry at and abuses us, whichever way we interpret the action, the fact is that every single pleasure and goodness has come from that person. Every happiness has come from every sentient being, including that person who abuses us. Because the Buddha, Dharma and Sangha come from sentient beings, sentient beings are extremely precious and the person who has abused us is the most precious one to us, the kindest, dearest one to us. He is our wish-granting jewel.

Every single sentient being is like that to us. Every one is our wish-granting jewel. This is what we have to meditate on every day. This is what we should live our life for. This is the purpose of our life, to live for them, for their happiness, to serve them. When we breathe, we should breathe in and out for them. Whatever we can do, we should try.

This second reason to benefit sentient beings is huge. Whatever we do we should do in order to benefit other sentient beings.

If you are a carer, whoever you care for, even just your own child, you should do it for all sentient beings. Whatever you do in that context—even things like saying prayers or chanting mantras—should be done without a sense of possession—my child, my wife, my husband, my, my, my—that is nothing; that is just attachment.

Caring for this precious sentient being, this child, you should think, "I'm so fortunate that I can dedicate my life, I can use my limbs to benefit even one precious sentient being—this most precious, most kind, most dear sentient being."

It's the same when taking care of an old person. It might be your father or mother or maybe you are working in an old folks' home or something and you take care of one old person. You should think the same thing, that you are so fortunate to be able to use your body, speech and mind, your limbs, to serve this one sentient being. Remembering that all your past lives' happiness, your present happiness and your future happiness all come from this person, you should see him or her as most kind, most precious, most dear.

Then you serve that person in whatever way you can. If there is something you are unable to do, what to do? We are all limited in power, but whatever you are able to do, offer that service from your heart. It's not as if you're doing it for money or some other worldly reason.

Many people who work for money, even in the care profession, come to dislike their job. They work as little as possible and at the end of the day get away as soon as they can, always longing for their day off. Many people in the West cannot appreciate how their suffering comes from the mind, from wrong concepts, from not having a good heart. That makes life so difficult. Working only for their own pleasure, they find no satisfaction.

Here, you should offer as much service as you can from your heart; offer your body, speech and mind. That is the best Dharma, the best meditation. Then you will be happy. The more you appreciate how precious serving another being is, the more you enjoy it. It doesn't have to be a guru you are serving. Your mind will be so happy to serve, whatever you can do.

This applies to even the small things in your daily life: offering your seat to somebody on the bus, helping somebody carry a heavy load or, as my guru Kyabje Serkong Tsenshab Rinpoche often mentioned, rescuing a drowning insect. Try to do whatever you can to help, according to your capacity, whether it's big or small.

By using your body, speech and mind to serve others you are repaying your parents' kindness, not making what they have done meaningless. Your mother suffered so much for you for the nine months you were in her womb. Then, during your childhood, you were constantly demanding things: "I want this, I want that." Your parents always did whatever they could to please you but still you would cry. For so many years they took care of you, giving you medicine, books, food, clothing, spending vast amounts of money on you. You must repay that kindness, giving them meaning for their great effort.

Serving others means that your parents' efforts have not been meaningless. Otherwise, they have made children simply for their own happiness. People get married, have children and then, after some time, there are many problems and finally, one day, it is finished.

Knowing how to live your life with bodhicitta, even if you are living a family life with children, means you know how to serve others, how to really appreciate others. If you must scold your child, you do it with love so that he or she will learn to be a better person.

Only by cherishing others will we attain enlightenment

The third reason to help sentient beings is that they have all been our mother and father numberless times and have all been kind in the four ways numberless times from beginningless rebirths.

If we are able to cherish one sentient being, even the enemy who gets angry at us, by cherishing that one sentient being we can achieve enlightenment. That person gives us enlightenment. Not only that, we become enlightened *for* sentient beings. And by the way, by cherishing that sentient being we also achieve the happiness of future lives and liberation from samsara.

By seeing that person as a wish-granting jewel, there is no mental suffering. By cherishing a wish-granting jewel we cannot achieve enlightenment but by cherishing that person we can. So, this person we call an enemy is more precious than a whole sky filled with wish-granting jewels. Thinking in that way, we should hold him most dear at all times, whatever state we are in, happy or unhappy, up or down. We should cherish that one person with our body, speech and mind.

Thinking like this, we ourselves become a wish-granting jewel to other sentient beings. This is not something we do only in a temple or Dharma center but not in our own home. It's not like that. We should happily dedicate our body, speech and mind to every person in our family.

The more we cherish others, the more we see their kindness, the happier we will be to serve them. The opportunity to offer service brings such great happiness. We naturally, joyfully, want to serve others as much as possible because that is where the Buddha, Dharma and Sangha come from. Even the small things we do to serve others make our life so joyful, so happy, whether they are in our family or outside it. This is how bodhisattvas feel.

For bodhisattvas, to achieve nirvana, the blissful state of peace for themselves alone, is like used toilet paper. Here the texts say "used toilet stone." I remember how in Buxa, because we used stones instead of paper, the toilets filled completely and became unusable. And it was a long time before they got fixed. When I first went to Sera in south India, the toilets were again filled with stones. So the text says "used toilet stone," but we can read that as "used toilet paper." For bodhisattvas, it is like that: achieving nirvana for themselves alone is something to immediately be thrown far away, just as we discard used toilet paper, never to use it again.

On the other hand, for bodhisattvas, the thought of being born in the hells for sentient beings—even for one sentient being—brings them unbelievable joy and happiness; much greater happiness than an arhat experiences achieving nirvana.

There is the story of one of the Buddha's previous lives, in which he was a bodhisattva and the captain of a ship carrying five hundred businesspeople. On board was a man carrying a spear with which he intended to kill those five hundred people. The bodhisattva captain saw that and, out of great compassion, was concerned that if that man killed all those people, he would be born in hell and would have to suffer there for many eons. Therefore the bodhisattva killed him and faced the consequence of his being born in hell instead. But what happened was that, in reality, killing him with such great compassion purified a hundred thousand eons of the bodhisattva captain's negative karma, which meant he was able to become free from samsara and achieve enlightenment a hundred thousand eons sooner. That is what happened, even though his wish was to be reborn in hell instead of the man with the spear.

Robin Bath

13. Practicing Tantra

HERUKA, GUHYASAMAJA AND YAMANTAKA

I HAVE ALREADY MENTIONED THE absolute guru, the unification of no more learning, the inseparability of the two kayas, the two bodies of a buddha. This is the goal of tantric practice, the unified state of Vajradhara that is achieved as the final result, with its seven qualities such as embracing, great bliss, completely full, unceasing and so forth; the union of clear light and illusory body, the inseparability of the holy body—the rupakaya—and the holy mind—the dharmakaya. Then the dharmakaya manifests as the sambhogakaya and the nirmanakaya to benefit the numberless sentient beings until they achieve enlightenment.

Before the unification of the clear light and illusory body, we first have to achieve the clear light and illusory body separately. Although both the isolation of clear light and the isolation of illusory body are stages in any Highest Yoga Tantra practice, some tantras emphasize clear light more and some illusory body. The tantras that emphasize clear light are called mother tantras whereas those that emphasize the illusory body are called father tantras.

Even though both father and mother tantras show how to achieve the clear light and illusory body, the Guhyasamaja tantra explains how to achieve the cause of the rupakaya, the illusory body, more extensively and in more detail than any other tantra. I have heard that before Lama Tsong-khapa's time there was no really clear, extensive explanation of this, so that is one of the benefits of Lama Tsongkhapa coming to teach. When he began studying, the Nyingma, Kagyü and Sakya traditions were already established. He and his main disciples, Gyältsab Rinpoche and Khedrub Rinpoche, were originally Sakya.

Lama Tsongkhapa had received teachings directly from Manjushri well before the time that Gyältsab Rinpoche came to meet him. At first he was not a disciple and sat on the same throne as Lama Tsongkhapa, but later, seeing the profundity of Lama Tsongkhapa's teachings and their great benefit, he sat below him as a disciple.

Khedrub Rinpoche was also Sakya before he became Lama Tsongkhapa's disciple. After that, he would debate with anybody who criticized Lama Tsongkhapa's teachings, especially his right view, which was the most subtle one—the Prasangika view actualized by the Buddha, Nagarjuna and Padmasambhava. Later on, Khedrub Rinpoche even debated with famous meditators who contradicted Lama Tsongkhapa's view in order to dispel their wrong concepts.

Having received teachings directly from Manjushri, Lama Tsongkhapa was able to explain the Buddha's teachings on sutra and tantra in the clearest possible way, even the most difficult points, clarifying the past mistakes of the many famous meditators. We are unbelievably lucky to have met his teachings.

As Pabongka Rinpoche said in *Calling the Guru from Afar*,

> Thinking of how the actual form of all buddhas arises in the aspect of the lama
> And mercifully guides me—reminds me of you, Lama.
> Thinking of how you show the excellent unmistaken path to me,
> An unfortunate wretched being, abandoned by all the buddhas—
> reminds me of you, Lama.

Pabongka calls himself an "unfortunate wretched being." Likewise, we too are unfortunate because we have been abandoned by all the buddhas of the past. That means *all* the buddhas—Guru Shakyamuni Buddha, Buddha Kashyapa[109] before him and the buddhas before that. Even though during the Buddha's time there were so many enlightened beings, we were not able to be their disciple and directly receive teachings from them either.

Thinking about this shows us the kindness of the guru, how he has revealed the unmistaken teachings, and particularly the teachings of Lama Tsongkhapa, his teachings on the Prasangika right view of emptiness as well

---

[109] Of the thousand buddhas of this fortunate age, Buddha Kashyapa is the third and Buddha Shakyamuni the fourth, the first two being Krakucchanda and Kanakamuni. Maitreya will be the next.

as tantra, the details of how to achieve the illusory body. With study we can recognize how precious the teachings of Lama Tsongkhapa are; how they are the correct, unmistaken teachings.

As Pabongka Rinpoche said, thinking about this reminds us of the very special kindness of the guru. So we are unbelievably fortunate. However, if we don't study Dharma, if we don't study the teachings of Lama Tsongkhapa, if we don't meditate, we are wasting this precious life, this unbelievably precious opportunity we have.

We need to practice both father and mother tantra, therefore we need to practice both Guhyasamaja and Heruka. But there can be many obstacles, both outer and inner, to successfully actualizing these two paths of the illusory body and the clear light, therefore we also need to practice Yamantaka. Yamantaka is not just a wrathful deity but the most wrathful aspect of Manjushri, the embodiment of all the buddhas' wisdom. By practicing that, there is no more powerful way to pacify obstacles to the two practices and achieve enlightenment. That is what Manjushri advised Lama Tsongkhapa. We need to practice these three deities without separation. This is regarded as very important.

In the past, yogis first did a Yamantaka retreat to pacify obstacles to the success to their Dharma practice and then they did their other retreats. His Holiness Zong Rinpoche also mentioned that.

Why practicing Heruka is important

There are four reasons why it is important to practice Heruka.[110] One is that when Vajrapani requested Heruka teachings, Buddha Vajradhara manifested the mandala on the top of the Mount Meru and it was never absorbed, so it is still there. Because of that, if we practice Heruka we can achieve enlightenment more quickly.[111]

Another reason is that there are twenty-four holy places associated with Heruka. Because they are the embodiment of Heruka, we first visualize them on our body and then do our practice. Immediately we do that, we invoke the numberless dakas and dakinis of those holy places. When we

---

[110] See *The Ecstatic Dance of Chakrasamvara*, pp. 41–42, for all four reasons.

[111] H.H. Trijang Rinpoche elaborates, "Having been requested by Vajrayogini, the Buddha manifested as Heruka and taught the root tantra of Heruka on the summit of Mt. Meru, and when requested by Vajrapani, taught the explanatory tantra." See *Various Aspects of Tantra* at LamaYeshe.com.

invoke them, just like stretching out our arms, the dakas and dakinis come, absorb into our body and bless our drops, chakras and winds. This makes them functional so we can use them for meditations like those in the *Six Yogas of Naropa*, allowing the winds to enter, abide and absorb, helping to absorb the gross and subtle minds and then the extremely subtle mind so we experience the clear light, simultaneous-born bliss. From that we can achieve the dharmakaya. If we get the experience of the clear light, the great bliss non-dual with emptiness, we can achieve enlightenment in this life.

One of my gurus, Gomo Rinpoche, wrote to me from Mussoorie that he had had these experiences after he had finished a Vajrayogini or Tara Cittamani retreat. I took a *chöd* initiation and six-session yoga teachings from him, but I was not able to receive all the teachings, just half. I also requested many initiations from him, but when he gave them at Istituto Lama Tzong Khapa I was somehow unable to get there, possibly because there was also some problem with Dolgyal at that time.

Khejok Rinpoche, a friend from Sera Me, wrote to me that he had had a similar experience. He didn't announce it publicly; it was his personal story. He just told close friends. I think many other meditators have such experiences of the clear light and illusory body. We can see from the way they look externally. Those who have that experience look very special.

This is an incredible opportunity because the dakas and dakinis of the holy places in this world bless us through the body mandala practice. That is one reason why this is a quick way to achieve enlightenment. The other reasons were mentioned in the *Heruka Body Mandala* transmitted by Pabongka Dechen Nyingpo, which I received from Kyabje Trijang Rinpoche and Kyabje Zong Rinpoche.

There is a story that Heruka promised Pabongka Rinpoche that whoever practices Heruka for seven lifetimes can be born in the Dakpa Khachö pure land. Similarly, Vajrayogini promised this to Kyabje Lhatsun Rinpoche. Kyabje Denma Lochö Rinpoche received the Vajrayogini initiation from him and I took it from Denma Lochö Rinpoche several times. So, if we practice Vajrayogini for seven lifetimes, we will be guided in the pure land for up to seven lifetimes.

If we're born in that pure land we can definitely achieve enlightenment there. That is the special benefit it has. It is very easy for common people to be born in the Amitabha pure land but, although that frees you from the lower realms forever, you don't have this special opportunity.

Taking initiation: the samayas of the five Buddha families

His Holiness the Dalai Lama does Yamantaka self-initiation every day. He has said that when he does, he keeps Geshe Kelsang[112] in his heart. Geshe Kelsang is totally against His Holiness; he demonstrates and criticizes so much, but His Holiness says he keeps him in his heart. He told us this.

Sera Je Geshe Dawa was the first resident teacher at Tara House, Melbourne, and also taught at Buddha House in Adelaide and later at Vajrayana Institute in Sydney. Then he started to rebuild his old monastery in Tibet. He is now extremely old. When he heard His Holiness say that about Geshe Kelsang he said, "Oh, I wish I was that!" Geshe Dawa said he wished he were like Geshe Kelsang so that His Holiness would hold him in his heart!

That is a very good practice. When His Holiness takes the bodhisattva vows he keeps Geshe Kelsang—who complains about and criticizes him so much—in his heart. If there is somebody who criticizes you, who abuses you, who blames you, it is good to remember that and, following His Holiness's practice, keep that person in your heart.

When you take a Highest Yoga Tantra initiation you must also take the bodhisattva and tantric vows. Taking the bodhisattva vows is like your contribution to world peace. With these vows, you dedicate your life to helping all sentient beings.

Keeping the tantric vows is the fundamental practice of a tantric practice. Even if you don't meditate on the path, if you keep the vows purely you can become enlightened, if not in this life then within three, seven or *definitely* sixteen lifetimes.

There are five samayas that go with the tantric vows, the samayas of Vairochana, Akshobhya, Ratnasambhava, Amitabha and Amoghasiddhi. The first one, *the samaya of Vairochana*, represents the three types of morality: the moralities of abstaining from nonvirtue, ripening your own mind and ripening others' minds.

The first morality is the morality of abstaining from the ten nonvirtues and so forth. That is self-explanatory. Then there is the morality of ripening your own mind, which in this context means bringing the practice of the six perfections into whatever you do. When you make charity, within that

---

[112] Kelsang Gyatso is the head of the New Kadampa Tradition, which promotes the practice of Dolgyal.

there is the practice of the six perfections. When you do a mandala offering, within that there is the practice of the six perfections. Within any activity you do, within any practice you do, there is the practice of the six perfections. The third morality is the morality of ripening others' minds. There are about eleven different methods to help sentient beings mentioned in the lam-rim, for example, guiding, showing the path to somebody who is lost. That is one of the practices of morality you should keep.

Sentient beings are numberless; you are one. No matter how much you suffer in samsara, you are one. But sentient beings have been suffering from beginningless rebirths up to now. There are numberless hell beings, numberless hungry ghosts, numberless animals, numberless human beings, numberless gods, numberless demigods and numberless intermediate state beings. Just like you, they have been suffering from beginningless rebirths, but they are numberless and they have the most unbelievable suffering. This is utterly unbearable. It's as if your mother had fallen into a red-hot fire. You could not stand seeing her there for even one second. Therefore you need to become enlightened quickly in order to free sentient beings from samsaric suffering and lead them to enlightenment as soon as possible. This is your motivation for taking the tantric vows.

The samaya of Vairochana also includes taking refuge in the Three Rare Sublime Ones, the Buddha, Dharma and Sangha. Relying on them so that you (and because of that, all others) can be saved from samsara is causal refuge. Resultant refuge is the belief that you will achieve the state of Buddha, Dharma and Sangha in your mental continuum in the future and taking refuge in that. Going for refuge to the resultant refuge is the samaya of the Buddha Vairochana.

Next is *the samaya of Akshobhya*, which has four types: vajra, bell, mudra and guru. The samaya of the vajra is in order to remember the holy mind of transcendental wisdom of great bliss. Holding the vajra and remembering that wisdom is keeping the vajra samaya. There is the interpretive vajra—remembering emptiness only, *tong-pa-nyi*—and the definitive vajra, remembering the meaning of the wisdom of great bliss.

The samaya of the bell is to remember the wisdom of emptiness, which is the interpretive meaning of the bell. Holding the bell is keeping the samaya of the bell. This is why, when you are trying to practice tantra, you must always have a vajra and bell, even very small ones, like on the counter of a mala. You have to secretly keep them in order to remember and practice the definitive meaning of vajra and bell. Even a drawing of the six mudras of the father and the five of the mother that has a vajra and bell helps keep this samaya. For this reason, like statues, the vajra and the bell are holy objects.

If possible, the actual vajra and bell you use in practice should also be kept secret. Although the Kadampa geshes practiced tantra, they didn't show it externally. When they died people would find a small vajra and bell sewed secretly into the collar of their coat or somewhere like that.

The third samaya of Akshobhya is the samaya of the mudra, where you visualize your body transforming into the Buddha Vajradhara father-mother, the desire deity. It is very important to understand the reason for this. In Highest Yoga Tantra the meaning of vajra and bell together is the transcendental wisdom of great bliss non-dual with emptiness. Like an atomic bomb, that is the quickest way to cease even the subtle obscurations, the obscurations to knowledge. That allows you to achieve enlightenment in a brief lifetime of the degenerate age without needing to prolong your life for hundreds or thousands of years, as you do with the lower tantras.

There is a method where you visualize your body in pure form as, for example, Heruka father-mother or Vajradhara father-mother. Visualizing the father-mother embracing while holding your vajra and bell helps you to develop this experience. It's like an atomic bomb to speed you quickly to achieve enlightenment. That is why you see many statues and thangkas of male and female deities embracing.

This practice is only for those who have very high intelligence, who have the highest merit, who need such a practice in order to cease the dualistic mind and dualistic views and attain enlightenment as quickly as possible. It doesn't suit everybody, so you are very fortunate to have met tantra at this time.

The last samaya of Akshobhya is the samaya of the guru, which means correctly following the virtuous friend, the guru, the vajra master, who is the root of all realizations, the root of the path to enlightenment.[113]

Next is *the samaya of Ratnasambhava*, which involves practicing the four kinds of charity six times a day: miscellaneous charity, the giving of Dharma, the giving of fearlessness and the charity of giving loving kindness.

An example of miscellaneous charity is when, in Mahayana practice, you eat food and make charity of it to all the sentient beings—the worms and so forth—that are living in your body. Nagarjuna explained this in the

---

[113] Rinpoche's book *The Heart of the Path* explains every last detail of how to do this.

Mahayana eating yoga practice.[114] Whenever you eat food and think like that, it becomes miscellaneous charity.

You can also relate this to what you do in your daily life, such as feeding your pets. Eating meat is very common in Tibet. There are some lamas who don't eat meat but the majority do. Kyabje Serkong Tsenshab Rinpoche told me that when eating he would throw some meat from his plate to the small dogs that were in his room, and this became the practice of miscellaneous charity from the six-session guru yoga. If you are feeding birds or other animals, even ants, or giving food or other things to people, you can also make this the practice of miscellaneous charity. There are many different ways you can do it.

Next is the charity of giving Dharma. If you recite mantras or texts such as the *Vajra-Cutter Sutra*, the *Golden Light Sutra* or the *Heart Sutra*, either by heart or by reading, aloud you can think that you are giving Dharma to all the numberless hell beings, hungry ghosts, animals, human beings, gods and demigods. Think that you have received the recitation from the Buddha, have realized the meaning and are now reciting it for all sentient beings and they are realizing it too.

In Aptos, when we go round the stupa, partly for exercise but also for purification and to collect merit, I explain to the other monks and nuns that whenever we recite prayers by reading from texts or an iPad, we should visualize that we are giving teachings like this. Reciting prayers and mantras aloud for animals or any people around, even if they have no serious interest in Dharma, is also making charity of Dharma. And again, when doing this we should think that we are giving Dharma to the numberless other sentient beings as well.

Then, there is the charity of giving fearlessness. Reciting mantras such as the mantras of Maitreya, Medicine Buddha or OM MANI PADME HUM to animals or people as they are dying stops them from being born in the lower realms. Giving advice to people who are suicidal, talking them out of killing themselves, is also the charity of fearlessness. You can think of many things like this.

The charity of giving loving kindness means causing sentient beings to have happiness. There are many actions you can do, from playing music to reciting prayers such as the four immeasurables, but when your motivation

---

[114] See Rinpoche's *Yoga of Offering Food* at LamaYeshe.com.

is to benefit others and bring them happiness, that is the charity of loving kindness.

When you do the practice of taking and giving, *tong-len*, even if you have no specific sentient being you are doing it for, it encompasses all four charities. Giving your body, possessions, materials and merit to the sentient beings of the six realms is not only miscellaneous charity but the charity of fearlessness, loving kindness and many other things as well.

Next is *the samaya of Amitabha*. This means following the two types of Dharma and the three yanas, or vehicles, individually. The two types of Dharma are outer Dharma and secret Dharma, which mean respectively the lower tantras—Kriya Tantra and Charya Tantra—and the higher tantras—Yoga Tantra and Highest Yoga Tantra.

The three yanas refer to the Hearer Listener Vehicle, the Solitary Realizer Vehicle, and the Mahayana Paramita Vehicle.[115] These are the three yanas and you pledge to practice them without missing, which means that you actually practice the ones you are capable of following and just wish to practice those you are as yet incapable of following.

The last samaya is *the samaya of Amoghasiddhi*, which is to protect all the samayas that I have just explained and to do the four types of offerings—outer, inner, secret and absolute—as well.

You set up and offer the outer offerings: the two waters, *argham* and *padyam*, and the six desire objects, *pushpe, dhupe, aloke, gandhe, naividya* and *shapta*.[116]

Then you bless and offer the inner offering, the red bodhicitta from the female and the white bodhicitta from the male[117] as well as the elements. Since we have no high tantric realizations and our mind is full of superstitions, we don't actually take those substances but visualize doing so instead.

The third offering is the secret offering. Through meditation you generate

---

[115] Shravakayana, Pratyekabuddhayana and Paramitayana. The first two are regarded as Hinayana; the latter, one of the two Mahayana vehicles, the other being the Vajrayana. The three yanas can also refer to the two Hinayana ones and the Mahayana in general.

[116] Traditional offerings to the Three Rare Sublime Ones, they are: water for drinking (Skt: *argham*), water for cleaning the feet (*padyam*), flowers (*pushpe*), incense (*dhupe*), light (*aloke*), perfume (*gandhe*), food (*naivedya*) and music (*shabda*).

[117] "Bodhicitta" here refers to the bodhicitta drops or subtle substances that permeate the body. The white drop, which originated from the father, is said to reside in the crown chakra and the red drop, which originated from the mother, is said to reside in the navel chakra. This is according to Guhyasamaja tantra; other tantras may describe them slightly differently.

the four blisses, the last of which is the simultaneously-born great bliss, the clear light. Having generated that, you make the offering, which is the secret offering. Again, you can only do this when your mind is at that level of realization, so now we just visualize making the offering.

Finally there is the absolute offering. The great bliss you generated in the secret offering understands emptiness and you offer that. That is the absolute offering.

Then you make a promise to generate both wishing and entering bodhicitta and to protect the nineteen samayas, the samayas of the five types of buddhas.

The hearer listener and solitary realizer arhats and the bodhisattvas who have attained the pure bhumis—the eighth, ninth and tenth—are free from the disturbing-thought obscurations but not the subtle ones. You want to free these arhats and bodhisattvas from even these subtle obscurations. And you want to liberate ordinary sentient beings, those who are neither arhats nor higher bodhisattvas living in the last three bhumis and are therefore not free from either disturbing-thought obscurations or subtle obscurations. You want to liberate them from both kinds of obscuration.

You want to "give breath" to all lower realm beings, such as those in hell, who are "unable to breathe" because of the unbelievably heavy suffering they have to experience, which means you want to free them from the suffering of the lower realms. In that way, you promise to lead all sentient beings to enlightenment, the non-abiding sorrowless state. That is the purpose of taking the tantric vows with these commitments.

Sentient beings are most kind, most precious, most dear. All your past, present and future happiness, including enlightenment, every collection of goodness, comes from every sentient being. You need to understand this deeply and also see how much they are suffering. They want happiness but they always destroy the cause of happiness. They dislike suffering but day and night they are always busy creating the cause of suffering. They are always running toward suffering. They destroy their merits because they don't know Dharma.

Think, "I must free the numberless mother sentient beings from the oceans of samsaric suffering and bring them to full enlightenment, the state of the omniscient mind, by myself alone. Therefore, I must achieve the state of the omniscient mind as quickly as possible." This is the kind of motivation you need to bring with you when you take an initiation.

Using the damaru, vajra and bell

When you use the damaru, you have to hold it in your right hand together with the vajra while holding the bell in your left hand. Then, as Kyabje Zong Rinpoche explained, you think, "In order to achieve enlightenment for the benefit of all the mother sentient beings I am going to practice the two bodhicittas." The vajra symbolizes the method of great bliss and the bell symbolizes the wisdom of emptiness, which means you are going to practice method and wisdom respectively, or, in terms of the two bodhicittas, conventional and absolute bodhicitta.

Because holding the vajra and bell symbolizes the inseparability of method, great bliss, and wisdom, emptiness, you never put either of them down in order to use the damaru. You hold them both at the same time to show the essence of tantric practice: the inseparability of method and wisdom.

Whether you can remember that every time or not, at least when you're doing a puja try to remember this meaning at least once! (Kyabje Zong Rinpoche didn't say that; I'm saying it!) Anyway, you need to remember to always hold the two together. People also commonly play the damaru incorrectly. You should hold the bell at your heart to actualize clear light and play the damaru at your navel.

Once when I was at a long life puja for His Holiness the Dalai Lama in Dharamsala, I was watching to see who did all this as His Holiness Zong Rinpoche explained. Only Samdhong Rinpoche, the previous Tibetan prime minister, was doing it correctly.

The current prime minister is Lobsang Sangay, who seems to have much more recognition and respect from the Indian government, which is very good. I think it's important that people in the Tibetan government know Dharma well, and as a former principal of the Central Institute of Higher Tibetan Studies in Sarnath, Samdhong Rinpoche was an expert in sutra and tantra. But of course, Lobsang Sangay is an expert in politics and other things, having a law degree from Harvard University. One of the FPMT's major benefactors was asked by His Holiness's Private Office to help fund his studies there and it seems that the Private Office might have planned for him to run for office for a long time, so it seems very good, excellent.

So I was watching all these lamas using the damaru at the puja and only Samdhong Rinpoche was doing it correctly, holding it at his navel. Of course he knows; the rest were holding theirs up like you do in *chöd* practice.

So you should not do that, but play it at the navel in order to persuade, or hook or attract, the dakinis into your navel chakra to bless it.

To succeed in the *tum-mo* practice of the *Six Yogas of Naropa* in order to attain clear light and great bliss and achieve the state of Vajradhara as quickly as possible in this life for the sake of sentient beings you need to persuade the dakinis to pay attention to you, to hook them to abide in and bless your navel chakra. So this is not like playing the big chöd damaru. If you're doing chöd, that's different, but even then, there are various ways of playing it. I learned to do it one way; His Holiness Khalkha Rinpoche,[118] who is kind of like the Dalai Lama of Mongolia, does it another. But holding the small damaru like a chöd damaru has no meaning. The bell, too, has many explanations.

My suggestion is that generally, always dedicate any practice or puja you do for sentient beings, not just yourself. I'm sorry to say this but even my Mickey Mouse *gek-tor* practice is done for all sentient beings. In the world there are so many sick people, so many people facing difficulties, number-less people experiencing great suffering, and they all need gek-tor done for them. So we do it here not just for those of us taking the initiation but for all sentient beings.

For example, if you are doing a *Four Mandala Offerings to Tara* puja, dedicate it for all sentient beings. Generate bodhicitta not only at the begin-ning but also, during the puja, remind yourself that you are doing it for all the sentient beings who need that Tara puja. There is so much suffering in the world. There are numberless sentient beings who are sick or who have difficulties in business or other things, so while you can dedicate the puja for whatever problems you have personally, you should also dedicate it to all the numberless sentient beings who also need it.

Whatever puja you do, dedicate it to all sentient beings. If you do a Medi-cine Buddha puja, dedicate it for them. Of course you can think of yourself, but there are numberless sentient beings who also need the Medicine Bud-dha puja. Even if you have to do a puja for a specific sick or dying person, dedicate it for all the people, all the sentient beings who need a Medicine Buddha puja, not just the one you're doing it for. Dedicating any puja or practice you do for the numberless sentient beings who need it in this way is fantastic.

---

[118] The Ninth Khalkha Jetsun Dhampa. See jetsundhampa.com.

The interpretation of dreams

In major initiations that span two days, the disciples are asked to remember and interpret whatever dreams they have after the first day.

Positive dreams are ones in which you are listening to Dharma from, for example, a lama or a statue of the deity radiating light and then your own body becomes the deity's holy body; or there are children or women who are well-dressed and adorned with ornaments; or you are able to climb without difficulty to the tops of mountains or trees; or you go into beautiful houses, put up prayer flags, blow conch shells or fly in the sky. Actually, dreaming of flying in the sky is not necessarily a good sign. It could mean you will be reborn as a bird.

I once asked Lama Yeshe how a certain monk would be reborn. At first it looked good, that he would be reborn in a pure land, but then in the monastery he was given the responsibility of running a khangtsen and at some point he dreamed he was flying in the sky. It seems that his mind had degenerated while he was running the khangtsen, because Lama said that he now had the karma to be reborn as a bird. So Lama gave him the Dorje Khadro fire puja to do to purify the pollution.

So dreaming of flying at other times is not necessarily auspicious but, in the preparation for an initiation, dreaming of flying in the sky is a good sign; it means you will succeed in your practice. Dreaming of drinking milk and eating good food are also good signs.

Bad dreams include your body being burned by fire or taken by water, falling down precipices, or riding on a donkey or a camel going toward the south. Also, walking on a sandy or dusty road or entering a dark room or a cave—where there is darkness instead of light—or having difficulty climbing something are also all inauspicious.

If you have a bad dream, there is a method to dispel the obstacles and that is to see that no phenomenon, including the bad dream, exists from its own side. Nothing is real—or whatever word you use in normal language—from its own side. The texts use terms such as existing from its own side, existing by itself or being truly existent. Phenomena do not exist from their own side. They are all empty, including your dream. When you meditate like that, meditating on Manjushri, you will see that all phenomena are empty. Then as well as meditating on emptiness you can recite OM KANDHAROHI HUM HUM PHAT and offer a burning puja. This will dispel the obstacles.

In particular, do gek-tor—offer a torma to the interferers. Then the obstacles, the interferers who interfere with your being granted the initiation, are dispelled.

VAJRAYANA AND EMPTINESS

Vajrayana, the Secret Mantra vehicle, the resultant vehicle, is based on the Mahayana sutra vehicle, the causal vehicle, and that is based on the Hinayana. This is very important to understand. You should not see the Hinayana, Mahayana and Vajrayana as three separate vehicles; that there is the Mahayana and then there is the Vajrayana separate from it. Tantra is an aspect of the Mahayana. There are many people who think that tantra is a separate vehicle from the Mahayana. That is a very common belief in places like Singapore and Taiwan, but it is a big mistake. The Mahayana has two aspects, Mahayana sutra and Mahayana tantra.

If you try to practice tantra without the renunciation of samsara of the Hinayana, it fails to become the cause for the renunciation of the whole of samsara—you have to see that the entire desire realm, form realm and formless realm are in the nature of suffering. You have to understand that that is the base. Then, if you try to practice tantra without bodhicitta you cannot achieve enlightenment. Even if you were able to reach the completion stage of Highest Yoga Tantra, still you would be unable to attain enlightenment.

Of course, practicing tantra without even the renunciation of this life doesn't become Dharma—it becomes nonvirtue, the cause of the lower realms. You have to understand that.

The other traditions—Kagyü, Nyingma and Sakya—separate renunciation into the renunciation of this life and the renunciation of future lives' samsara, but in Lama Tsongkhapa's tradition, renunciation means renunciation of samsara, which includes renunciation of this life.

Practicing tantra without understanding emptiness does not become the remedy that cuts the root of samsara, that eliminates ignorance. It only develops more ignorance. That is unbelievably important to understand.

Therefore, without the three principal aspects of the path—renunciation, bodhicitta and wisdom—there is no correct way to practice tantra. So, while it is correct to differentiate between Paramitayana and Tantrayana within Mahayana, to think that tantra is not part of Mahayana means you practice tantra without renunciation, bodhicitta or emptiness.

Vajrayana combines method and wisdom in one mind

It is impossible to practice tantra properly without emptiness. In Highest Yoga Tantra there is the transcendental wisdom that realizes emptiness *as it is* empty and that experiences great bliss. That great bliss that is non-dual with emptiness generates into the deity, if possible, the result-time dharmakaya, the pure form, Heruka.

But, when you become Heruka, if you again become truly existent, the *real* Heruka, that is incorrect. Your understanding of emptiness must be continuous. As you focus with wisdom on the holy body of Heruka, your wisdom understands that the deity Heruka that appears to us sentient beings as a real one is not true. That real Heruka does not exist. It's like when you recognize a dream as a dream. Even though it appears, you know it is not true. You understand that despite appearances it does not exist from its own side. As you understand that, focus simultaneously on the deity Heruka's holy body. Meditating on emptiness is the wisdom side and focusing on the deity's holy body is the method side. Therefore, method and wisdom are inseparably combined here in one non-dual mind.

Focus on the deity's holy body that appears as real while at the same time understanding that what appears as real is not real, that it is nonexistent from its own side, like recognizing a dream as a dream or recognizing a mirage as being the false appearance of water. While at the same time you are focusing on the deity's holy mind you can think that it is merely labeled by the mind, or empty. It comes to the same point: merely labeled means empty.

In the Mahayana Paramitayana, method and wisdom are practiced together but not by one mind. Each is practiced by a separate mind. What makes tantra the quick path to enlightenment in one life is practicing method and wisdom together, in one mind.

That becomes "vajra." That is the diamond or the vajra, the thing that can cut all other things. Just as a diamond can cut glass or many other things but nothing else can cut the diamond itself, *this* vajra alone can cut the dualistic mind, the dualistic view, the impure appearance, the impure mind.

Practicing method and wisdom simultaneously, focusing on the deity's holy body becomes the cause to achieve the rupakaya, a buddha's holy body, and the awareness that it does not exist from its own side become the cause to achieve the dharmakaya, a buddha's holy mind. If you can actualize that vajra, it takes you to enlightenment. That is why it is called a yana, or vehicle.

Just as a car takes you to the place you want to go, this vehicle takes you to enlightenment. Therefore it is called the Vajrayana. This is why, in order to practice method and wisdom in one mind, inseparably, it is so important to really understand emptiness.

Tantra is the resultant vehicle

Not only does tantra become the quick path to enlightenment in one lifetime because it allows one mind to practice method and wisdom simultaneously, it also allows you to meditate on the path similar to the result, hence its other name, the resultant vehicle.

That is the reason why there is usually a commitment to recite the long, medium or short sadhana daily and to visualize the deity and the mandala. It's not because you have nothing better to do. Like in the West, when people get old, when they are retired, they have nothing to do. They don't recite OM MANI PADME HUM or anything worthwhile. They just garden, put flowers around their house and so forth to distract their mind but no matter whatever else they do, their life is so boring. Doing your sadhana is not like that. You don't do it just to stop your mind from getting bored.

By doing the meditations of the resultant vehicle you achieve the four complete purities, the purities of body, place, deeds and offerings.

The final result of the path is that you become a buddha; your body becomes the deity's pure, holy body. What you are going to attain in the future, the deity's holy body, you visualize *now*. That is the practice—you visualize that you have *already* achieved the deity's holy body. That is the purity of body. Because this practice purifies the mind of all obscurations, of all dualistic views and concepts, it becomes the quick path to enlightenment. You collect the most unbelievable merit and purify so much.

And in the same way, just as you become the deity, the environment appears to you in the form of the mandala—*that* is what you visualize now. That is the purity of place. Visualizing the mandala of the deity purifies ten million eons of negative karma. On top of that, when you enter the mandala visualized in the sadhana—this perfect environment you will achieve in the future—that also becomes the most unbelievable purification.

In the future, when you become a buddha, you will be able to do unbelievably extensive deeds. Sending even one beam of light to sentient beings will liberate them from suffering. That is what you will be able to do and so, in your sadhana, you visualize that as happening now. That is the purity of deeds.

When you become a buddha, due to your mind developing into a totally pure, holy mind, without even subtle obscurations, you are able to enjoy numberless completely pure offerings. This is what will happen when you become a buddha and this is what you visualize now. And again you collect unbelievable merit. That is the purity of offerings.

In the Paramitayana, completing the collections of the merit of transcendental wisdom and the merit of virtue, the causes of the dharmakaya and rupakaya, takes three countless great eons. But here, in tantra, especially in Highest Yoga Tantra, because of great skill, meditating on the path similar to the four complete purified results becomes a path to achieve enlightenment in one lifetime.

That is why we need to practice tantra, and especially Highest Yoga Tantra, right now, without delaying even a second. Only when we achieve full enlightenment, the state of the omniscient mind, can we free the numberless sentient beings from the oceans of samsaric suffering and bring them to full enlightenment. If we achieve the omniscient mind, we can do that perfectly, without the slightest mistake. Even an arhat or a bodhisattva on the tenth bhumi cannot do that.

Robin Bath

Chronology

Where and when these teachings were given.

Bibliography[119]

Aryadeva. *Four Hundred Verses (Catuhsataka-shastra-karika).* Published as *The Yogic Deeds of Bodhisattvas: Gyeltsap on Aryadeva's Four Hundred,* with commentary by Geshe Sonam Rinchen, translated by Ruth Sonam. Ithaca: Snow Lion Publications, 1994.

Ashvaghosha. *The Fifty Verses of Guru Devotion.* Online at LamaYeshe.com

Atisha. *A Lamp for the Path to Enlightenment.* Translated by Ruth Sonam. See appendix 2 of *Teachings from Tibet.* Boston: Lama Yeshe Wisdom Archive, 2015.

———— & Dromtönpa. *The Book of the Kadam.* Translated by Thupten Jinpa. Boston: Wisdom Publications, 2008.

The Buddha. *Lankavatara Sutra.* Translated by Red Pine. Berkeley: Counterpoint, 2012.

————. Heart Sutra (*Prajnahridaya/Bhagavatiprajnaparamitahridayasutra, She rab nying po/Chom dän de ma she rab kyi pha röl tu jin pa'i do*). Available at fpmt.org.

————. *Sutra of the Fortunate Eon (Bhadrakalpikasutra, Kel-pa zang-po'i do).* Published as *The Fortunate Aeon: How the Thousand Buddhas Became Enlightened.* Cazadero: Dharma Publishing, 1986.

————. *Sutra of Golden Light (The King of Glorious Sutras Called the Exalted Sublime Golden Light: A Mahayana Sutra.)* (*Suvarnaprabhasottamasutrendrarajahmahayanasutra, Phag pa ser ö dam pa do de'i wang po'i gyäl po she ja wa theg pa chen po'i do*). Available at fpmt.org.

————. *Vajra Cutter Sutra (aka Diamond Cutter Sutra)* (*Aryavajra-cchedika-nama-prajnaparamita-mahayana-sutra; phag pa she rab kyi pha röl tu chin pa dor je*

---

[119] Since this is not an academic work, in the interests of simplicity we have decided not to use diacritical marks and to use pronounceable Tibetan phonetics rather than transliteration.

chö pa she ja theg pa chen po'i do). Available in several languages at fpmt.org as *Vajra Cutter Sutra*.

Chandragomin. *Letter to a Disciple*. Published as *Letter to a Great King by Matrceta and Letter to a Disciple by Chandragomin*. Translated by Michael Hahn. Berkeley: Dharma Publishing, 1999.

FPMT. *Essential Buddhist Prayers: An FPMT Prayer Book, Volume 1, Basic Prayers and Practices*. Portland: FPMT, 2011.

———. *Liberation Box, Tools for a Fortunate Rebirth*. Available at fpmt.org.

Gyaltsen, Khunu Lama Tenzin. *The Jewel Lamp: A Praise of Bodhicitta* (published in English as *Vast as the Heavens, Deep as the Sea*). Translated by Gareth Sparham. Boston: Wisdom Publications, 1999.

Gyaltsen, Panchen Lobsang Chökyi. *Lama Chöpa (Guru Puja)*. Portland: FPMT, 2013.

Gyatso, Tenzin, the Fourteenth Dalai Lama. *The End of Suffering and the Discovery of Happiness: The Path of Tibetan Buddhism*. Carlsbad: Hay House, Inc., 2012.

———. *Path to Bliss: A Practical Guide to the Stages of Meditation*. (Based on Panchen Chökyi Gyaltsen's *Path to Bliss Leading to Omniscience*.) Translated by Thupten Jinpa. Ithaca: Snow Lion Publications, 1991.

——— and Alexander Berzin. *The Gelug/Kagyü Tradition of Mahamudra*. Ithaca: Snow Lion Publications, 1997.

Khenchen Konchog Gyaltshen. *Opening the Treasure of the Profound: Teachings on the Songs of Jigten Sumgön and Milarepa*. Boston: Snow Lion Publications, 2013.

Lati Rinbochay. *Mind in Tibetan Buddhism*. Translated by Elizabeth Napper. Ithaca: Snow Lion Publications, 1980.

——— and Denma Lochö Rinbochay. *Meditative States in Tibetan Buddhism*. Translated by Leah Zahler and Jeffrey Hopkins. Boston, Wisdom Publications, 1983, 1997.

Norbu, Thinley. *A Cascading Waterfall of Nectar*. Boston: Shambhala Publications, 2006.

Pabongka Rinpoche. *Liberation in the Palm of Your Hand*. Translated by Michael Richards. Boston: Wisdom Publications, 1991, 2006. (Page numbers in footnotes refer to the latter edition.)

———. *Liberation in Our Hands* (three parts). Translated by Geshe Lobsang Tharchin and Artemus B. Engle. Howell: Mahayana Sutra and Tantra Press, 1990, 1994, 2001.

Rabten Geshe. *The Essential Nectar: Meditations on the Buddhist Path*. Edited with verse translation by Martin Willson. Boston: Wisdom Publications, 1984, 2014.

———. *The Mind and its Functions*. Le Mont-Pèlerin: Editions Rabten Choeling, 1978, 1992.

Ribush, Nicholas (ed). *Teachings from Tibet: Guidance from Great Lamas.* Boston: Lama Yeshe Wisdom Archive, 2005, 2015.

Rinchen, Geshe Sonam. *How Karma Works: The Twelve Links of Dependent Arising.* Translated and edited by Ruth Sonam. Ithaca: Snow Lion Publications, 2006.

————. *The Thirty-seven Practices of Bodhisattvas: An Oral Teaching.* Translated and edited by Ruth Sonam. Ithaca: Snow Lion Publications, 1997.

Shabkar Tsogdruk Rangdrol, *The Life of Shabkar: The Autobiography of a Tibetan Yogin.* Translated by Matthieu Ricard. Ithaca: Snow Lion Publications, 2001.

Shantideva. *A Guide to the Bodhisattva's Way of Life (Bodhisattvacaryavatara, Jangchub sem-pa'i chö-pa la jug-pa).* Translated by Stephen Batchelor. Dharamsala: Library of Tibetan Works and Archive, 1979, 2010.

Sopa, Geshe Lhundub. *Steps on the Path to Enlightenment* (three volumes). Boston: Wisdom Publications, 2004, 2005, 2008.

Sparham, Gareth (trans). *The Tibetan Dhammapada: Sayings of the Buddha.* Boston: Wisdom Publications, 1986.

Tangpa, Langri. *The Eight Verses of Thought Transformation.* In, for example, *Teachings from Tibet* and *Everflowing Nectar of Bodhicitta* (see below).

Thurman, Robert. *The Central Philosophy of Tibet: A Study and Translation of Jey Tsong Khapa's* Essence of True Eloquence. (Previously published as *Tsong Khapa's Speech of Gold in the* Essence of True Eloquence: *Reason and Enlightenment in the Central Philosophy of Tibet.*) Princeton: Princeton University Press, 1984.

Trijang Rinpoche Losang Yeshe, Kyabje. *The Ecstatic Dance of Chakrasamvara: Heruka Body Mandala Practice & Commentary.* Seattle: Dechen Ling Press, 2013.

Tsongkhapa. *The Foundation of All Good Qualities (Yön-ten shir-gyur ma),* in *Essential Buddhist Prayers: An FPMT Prayer Book, Volume 1.* Portland: FPMT, 2009.

————. *The Fulfillment of All Hopes: Guru Devotion in Tibetan Buddhism: A Commentary on Ashvaghosha's* Fifty Verses of Guru Devotion. Translated and introduced by Gareth Sparham. Boston: Wisdom Publications, 1999.

————. *The Great Treatise on the Path to Enlightenment (Lamrim Chenmo)* (three volumes). Translated by the Lamrim Chenmo Translation Committee. Ithaca: Snow Lion Publications, 2000, 2002, 2004.

————. *Middle Length Lam-rim (Lam-rim Dring-po).* Additional outline by Trijang Rinpoche, translated by Philip Quarcoo. Portland: FPMT, 2008 (available at fpmt.org).

————. *Songs of Spiritual Experience: Condensed Points of the Stages of the Path.* Translated by Thupten Jinpa. Available at tibetanclassics.org.

————. *The Three Principal Aspects of the Path (Lam-tso nam-sum),* in *Essential Buddhist Prayers: An FPMT Prayer Book, Volume 1.* Portland: FPMT, 2009.

Zopa Rinpoche, Lama. *Advice on Benefiting Animals.* Available at LamaYeshe.com.

———. *Bodhisattva Attitude: How to Dedicate Your Life to Others.* Edited by Sarah Thresher. Boston: Lama Yeshe Wisdom Archive, 2012.

———. *Everflowing Nectar of Bodhicitta.* Portland: FPMT, 2008.

———. *Heart of the Path: How to See the Guru as Buddha.* Edited by Ailsa Cameron. Boston: Lama Yeshe Wisdom Archive, 2009.

———. *How to Enjoy Death: Preparing to Meet Life's Final Challenge without Fear.* Edited by Robina Courtin. Boston: Wisdom Publications, 2016.

———. *How to Practice Dharma: Teachings on the Eight Worldly Dharmas.* Edited by Gordon McDougall. Boston: Lama Yeshe Wisdom Archive, 2012.

———. *Liberating Animals from the Danger of Death.* Portland: FPMT, 2009.

———. *The Method to Transform a Suffering Life into Happiness (Including Enlightenment).* Portland: FPMT, 2015.

———. *The Perfect Human Rebirth: Freedom and Richness on the Path to Enlightenment.* Edited by Gordon McDougall. Lama Yeshe Wisdom Archive, 2013.

———. *Practicing the Five Powers Near the Time of Death.* Portland: FPMT, 2012.

———. *Teachings from the Vajrasattva Retreat.* Edited by Ailsa Cameron and Nicholas Ribush. Boston: Lama Yeshe Wisdom Archive, 2000.

———. *The Wish-fulfilling Golden Sun of the Mahayana Thought Training: Directing in the Short Cut Path to Enlightenment.* Edited by Nicholas Ribush. Kathmandu: Kopan Monastery Publications, 1975. Available at LamaYeshe.com.

LAMA YESHE WISDOM ARCHIVE

The LAMA YESHE WISDOM ARCHIVE (LYWA) is the collected works of Lama Thubten Yeshe and Lama Thubten Zopa Rinpoche. Lama Zopa Rinpoche, its spiritual director, founded the ARCHIVE in 1996.

Lama Yeshe and Lama Zopa Rinpoche began teaching at Kopan Monastery, Nepal, in 1970. Since then, their teachings have been recorded and transcribed. At present we have well over 12,000 hours of digital audio and some 90,000 pages of raw transcript. Many recordings, mostly teachings by Lama Zopa Rinpoche, remain to be transcribed, and as Rinpoche continues to teach, the number of recordings in the ARCHIVE increases accordingly. Most of our transcripts have been neither checked nor edited.

Here at the LYWA we are making every effort to organize the transcription of that which has not yet been transcribed, edit that which has not yet been edited, and generally do the many other tasks detailed below.

The work of the LAMA YESHE WISDOM ARCHIVE falls into two categories: *archiving* and *dissemination*.

Archiving requires managing the recordings of teachings by Lama Yeshe and Lama Zopa Rinpoche that have already been collected, collecting recordings of teachings given but not yet sent to the ARCHIVE, and collecting recordings of Lama Zopa's on-going teachings, talks, advice and so forth as he travels the world for the benefit of all. Incoming media are then catalogued and stored safely while being kept accessible for further work.

We organize the transcription of audio, add the transcripts to the already existent database of teachings, manage this database, have transcripts checked, and make transcripts available to editors or others doing research on or practicing these teachings.

Other archiving activities include working with video and photographs of the Lamas and digitizing ARCHIVE materials.

Dissemination involves keeping up with evolving technology and making the Lamas' teachings available through various avenues including books for free distribution and sale, ebooks on a wide range of readers, lightly edited transcripts, a monthly e-letter (see below), social media, DVDs and online video, articles in *Mandala* and other magazines and on our website. Irrespective of the medium we choose, the teachings require a significant amount of work to prepare them for distribution.

This is just a summary of what we do. The ARCHIVE was established with virtually no seed funding and has developed solely through the kindness of the many people all over the world who partner with us in this amazing and beneficial work. We are indebted to you all.

Our further development similarly depends upon the generosity of those who see the benefit and necessity of this work, and we would be extremely grateful for your help. Thus we hereby appeal to you for your kind support. If you would like to make a contribution to help us with any of the above tasks or to sponsor books for free distribution, please contact us:

LAMA YESHE WISDOM ARCHIVE
PO Box 636, Lincoln, MA 01773, USA
Telephone (781) 259-4466
info@LamaYeshe.com
www.LamaYeshe.com

The LAMA YESHE WISDOM ARCHIVE is a 501(c)(3) tax-deductible, non-profit corporation dedicated to the welfare of all sentient beings and totally dependent upon your donations for its continued existence. Thank you so much for your support. You may contribute by mailing a check, bank draft or money order to our Lincoln address; by making a donation on our secure website; by mailing us your credit card number or phoning it in; or by transferring funds directly to our bank—ask us for details.

LAMA YESHE WISDOM ARCHIVE MEMBERSHIP

In order to raise the money we need to employ editors to make available the thousands of hours of teachings mentioned above, we have established a membership plan. Membership costs US$1,000 and its main benefit is that you will be helping make the Lamas' incredible teachings available to a worldwide audience. More direct and tangible benefits to you personally include free Lama Yeshe and Lama Zopa Rinpoche books from the ARCHIVE and Wisdom Publications, a year's subscription to *Mandala*, a year of monthly pujas by the monks and nuns at Kopan Monastery with your personal dedication, and access to an exclusive members-only section of our website containing the entire library of publications in electronic format. Please see LamaYeshe.com for more information.

SOCIAL MEDIA AND MONTHLY E-LETTER

Follow us on Facebook, Twitter, Instagram and Google Plus and every day read gems from our online teachings, view amazing images and keep up to date with our latest offerings. Also, each month we send out a free e-letter containing our latest news and a previously unpublished teaching by Lama Yeshe or Lama Zopa Rinpoche. See our website for links.

LYWA eBooks and Audio books

All Lama Yeshe Wisdom Archive titles are available as ebooks from all major online bookstore vendors such as Amazon, Apple, and more. Our free titles are also available to read online, or download in pdf format, on our website.

We also offer titles in ebook format only, such as Lama Zopa Rinpoche's "Lamrim Teachings from Kopan 1991" series.

In addition to the hundreds of hours of audio that can be listened to on our website, LYWA also offers a selection of our titles as audio books on Audible.com. Listen anytime to Dharma teachings from the LYWA collection.

LYWA Multimedia Titles

Published November 17, 2015

Freedom - Courage - Realization
The Three Principal Aspects of the Path
LAMA YESHE

We also invite you to explore our growing collection of free multimedia titles presenting teachings by Lama Yeshe and Lama Zopa Rinpoche on a wide range of Dharma topics. These titles offer the teachings in all their multimedia aspects: edited original transcripts enhanced by images, audio and video from that teaching and supplemented by related informal teaching clips, advice and other relevant teaching materials from the Archive.

Explore the LYWA online store at www.LamaYeshe.com where you can find links to our print, ebook, audiobook and multimedia editions.

The Foundation for the Preservation of the Mahayana Tradition

The Foundation for the Preservation of the Mahayana Tradition (FPMT) is an international organization of Buddhist meditation study and retreat centers—both urban and rural—monasteries, publishing houses, healing centers and other related activities founded in 1975 by Lama Thubten Yeshe and Lama Thubten Zopa Rinpoche. At present, there are more than 160 FPMT centers, projects and services in over forty countries worldwide.

The FPMT has been established to facilitate the study and practice of Mahayana Buddhism in general and the Tibetan Gelug tradition, founded in the fifteenth century by the great scholar, yogi and saint, Lama Je Tsongkhapa, in particular.

Twice a year, the Foundation publishes a wonderful news journal, *Mandala*, from its International Office in the United States of America. To subscribe or view back-issues, please go to the *Mandala* website, mandalamagazine.org, or contact:

FPMT
1632 SE 11th Avenue, Portland, OR 97214
Telephone (503) 808-1588; Fax (503) 808-1589
info@fpmt.org
www.fpmt.org

The FPMT website also offers teachings by His Holiness the Dalai Lama, Lama Yeshe, Lama Zopa Rinpoche and many other highly respected teachers in the tradition, details about the FPMT's educational programs, an online learning center, a complete listing of FPMT centers all over the world and, especially, those in your area, a link to the excellent FPMT Store, and links to FPMT centers—where you will find details of their programs—and other interesting Buddhist and Tibetan pages.

What to do with Dharma Teachings

The Buddhadharma is the true source of happiness for all sentient beings. Books like this show you how to put the teachings into practice and integrate them into your life, whereby you get the happiness you seek. Therefore, anything containing Dharma teachings, the names of your teachers or holy images is more precious than other material objects and should be treated with respect. To avoid creating the karma of not meeting the Dharma again in future lives, please do not put books (or other holy objects) on the floor or underneath other stuff, step over or sit upon them, or use them for mundane purposes such as propping up wobbly chairs or tables. They should be kept in a clean, high place, separate from worldly writings, and wrapped in cloth when being carried around. These are but a few considerations.

Should you need to get rid of Dharma materials, they should not be thrown in the rubbish but burned in a special way. Briefly: do not incinerate such materials with other trash, but alone, and as they burn, recite the mantra OM AH HUM. As the smoke rises, visualize that it pervades all of space, carrying the essence of the Dharma to all sentient beings in the six samsaric realms, purifying their minds, alleviating their suffering, and bringing them all happiness, up to and including enlightenment. Some people might find this practice a bit unusual, but it is given according to tradition. Thank you very much.

Dedication

Through the merit created by preparing, reading, thinking about and sharing this book with others, may all teachers of the Dharma live long and healthy lives, may the Dharma spread throughout the infinite reaches of space, and may all sentient beings quickly attain enlightenment.

In whichever realm, country, area or place this book may be, may there be no war, drought, famine, disease, injury, disharmony or unhappiness, may there be only great prosperity, may everything needed be easily obtained, and may all be guided by only perfectly qualified Dharma teachers, enjoy the happiness of Dharma, have love and compassion for all sentient beings, and only benefit and never harm each other.

LAMA THUBTEN ZOPA RINPOCHE was born in Thangme, Nepal, in 1945. At the age of three he was recognized as the reincarnation of the Lawudo Lama, who had lived nearby at Lawudo, within sight of Rinpoche's Thangme home. Rinpoche's own description of his early years may be found in his book, *The Door to Satisfaction*. At the age of ten, Rinpoche went to Tibet and studied and meditated at Domo Geshe Rinpoche's monastery near Pagri, until the Chinese occupation of Tibet in 1959 forced him to forsake Tibet for the safety of Bhutan. Rinpoche then went to the Tibetan refugee camp at Buxa Duar, West Bengal, India, where he met Lama Yeshe, who became his closest teacher. The Lamas went to Nepal in 1967, and over the next few years built Kopan and Lawudo Monasteries. In 1971 Lama Zopa Rinpoche gave the first of his famous annual lam-rim retreat courses, which continue at Kopan to this day. In 1974, with Lama Yeshe, Rinpoche began traveling the world to teach and establish centers of Dharma. When Lama Yeshe passed away in 1984, Rinpoche took over as spiritual head of the FPMT, which has continued to flourish under his peerless leadership. More details of Rinpoche's life and work may be found in *The Lawudo Lama* and on the LYWA and FPMT websites. In addition to many LYWA and FPMT books, Rinpoche's other published teachings include *Wisdom Energy* (with Lama Yeshe), *Transforming Problems, The Door to Satisfaction, Ultimate Healing, Dear Lama Zopa, How to Be Happy, Wholesome Fear* and many transcripts and practice booklets.

GORDON MCDOUGALL first met Tibetan Buddhism in Hong Kong in 1986 and was the director of Cham-Tse Ling, the FPMT center there, for two years. Since then he has been involved with various FPMT centers and projects. In 2001 he became the spiritual program coordinator of Jamyang Buddhist Centre, London, where he worked with the resident teacher, Geshe Tashi Tsering, to develop the Foundation of Buddhist Thought, the two-year campus and correspondence course that is part of the FPMT core education program. He administered the course and worked at Jamyang for seven years, editing the six FBT books, first as study books for the course and then as "stand-alone" books for Wisdom Publications. He has also led lam-rim courses in Europe and India and was involved with the creation of the Discovering Buddhist program. After moving to Bath, England, he became a full time editor with the LAMA YESHE WISDOM ARCHIVE in 2008, managing the Publishing the FPMT Lineage project and editing the books published in the series.